The Korean War and American Politics: The Republican Party as a Case Study

The Korean War and American Politics:
The Republican Party as a Case Study

by Ronald J. Caridi

University of Pennsylvania Press
Philadelphia, 19104

SBN 8122–7581–0
Manufactured in the United States of America

FOR
ROBERT LONG

ACKNOWLEDGMENTS

I would like to express my gratitude to Professor Henry Bamford Parkes of New York University, who guided me through a considerable portion of this study while I was a doctoral candidate. Professor Parkes has transmitted to me his deep interest, enthusiasm and respect for the American experience.

I am also indebted to the staffs of the New York Public Library, New York University Library, Columbia University Library, Brooklyn Public Library and the Boston Public Library. Alexander P. Clark of the Princeton University Library was very kind to me while I was examining the papers of Senator H. Alexander Smith.

John Bernheim of the University of Pennsylvania Press was most generous with his time and valuable assistance.

Finally, I would like to dedicate this volume to my colleague, mentor and friend, Dean Robert Long of Roger Williams College. He is of the Eighth Day.

R.J.C.

New York City
June, 1968

TABLE OF CONTENTS

Chapter 1

Introduction: The Republican Party
Before Korea

The Republican party's attitude toward the Far East in the late 1940's and early 1950's was heavily influenced by the events surrounding the United States' involvement in World War II. Generally speaking, the party was divided into two camps—the noninterventionists and the internationalists. The more orthodox, conservative wing of the party was strongly inclined toward the America First movement; this group, largely Midwestern and headed by Robert E. Wood of Sears, Roebuck and Company, believed that the United States in 1940 could still choose whether to enter the war, and they urged the nation to decide against intervention. At the same time the party's more liberal wing (which included many Eastern Republicans and was typified by President Roosevelt's Secretary of War, Henry L. Stimson, and his Secretary of the Navy, Frank Knox) favored an internationalist stance toward the events in Europe.

The conservative wing of the party was largely anti-British and fervently believed that if the United States' entry into the war became absolutely necessary, America should not fight in concert with other nations, but rather along national lines.

When Japan launched its attack on Pearl Harbor, the question of the United States' involvement in the conflict disappeared. But a new issue was raised by those orthodox Republicans who insisted that we concentrate our efforts in Asia, rather than in Europe. They argued that the immediate threat existed in the Far East and so this nation should not become involved in Europe. President Roosevelt, however, decided to give first priority to Europe, thus throwing the full force of the

United States behind Winston Churchill's efforts to defeat Germany.

This decision to let Asia wait while the European menace was brought under control naturally eclipsed the influence of those Republicans who were pro-Asian, and brought to the fore those who supported the President's Europe-first strategy. Additionally, there was a good deal of feeling that Roosevelt had become more militant after his 1940 victory and had thereby "pushed" the nation into war. (Many of these charges were later repeated by a number of revisionist accounts of the war that appeared in the late 1940's and early 1950's.[1])

William S. White, in his book *The Taft Story*, sums up the position of the orthodox faction of the GOP as follows:

> The Taft Republicans felt that their counsel had been rejected out of hand and that we had got into a war we need not have fought. They felt that once in we had, again by the rejection of their counsel, gone about it the wrong way and had been taken in by the British. And finally they felt that uncharacteristic and therefore unworthy Republicans had reached undue place and power.[2]

It is therefore not surprising to discover that when the war was over those Republicans who found themselves beyond the seat of power were anxious to regain prominence within the party. They were aided in this drive back to dominance by three factors: the defeat of the GOP in the election of 1948; the removal of Arthur H. Vandenberg from the Senate because of illness; and the series of diplomatic disasters that occurred at the end of the decade—particularly the "fall" of China.

In the congressional elections of 1946 the GOP won a decisive victory, but this was primarily the result of domestic

---

[1] See, for example, Charles A. Beard, *President Roosevelt and the Coming of War, 1941* (New Haven, 1948); William H. Chamberlain, *America's Second Crusade* (Chicago, 1950); George E. Morgenstern, *Pearl Harbor: The Story of the Secret War* (New York, 1947); and Charles C. Tansill, *Back Door to War* (Chicago, 1952).

[2] William S. White, *The Taft Story* (New York, 1954), pp. 158–59.

issues, particularly the rash of strikes and the alarming inflation that followed the termination of the war. The Republicans asked the voters if they had "had enough?" and the
answer was an emphatic "Yes." In the Senate the GOP took
the lead over the Democrats 51 to 47, and in the House the
tally was 246 Republicans to 188 Democrats.

These impressive congressional victories gave the Republicans extravagant hopes for success in 1948. The party's three
main contenders for the Presidential nomination were Governor Thomas Dewey, Senator Robert Taft, and Governor Harold
Stassen. Stassen's "liberalism" and Taft's weak showing in a
primary race in his home state of Ohio undermined the positions of both these men, leaving the convention with Vandenberg as a possible "stop-Dewey" candidate. Yet many of the
party's conservatives, particularly Colonel McCormick of the
Chicago Tribune, considered Dewey's internationalist leanings
less dangerous than Vandenberg's, and so the New Yorker
not only won the nomination but was able to choose Governor
Earl Warren of California, another internationalist, as his
Vice-Presidential choice.

Dewey's surprise defeat at the hands of the underrated
Truman precipitated a movement within the party to reject
bipartisanship, both in domestic and foreign affairs. It was
assumed by those in revolt that the party in power would reap
the credit for successful legislation despite the aid rendered
by the minority party. Leaders of the GOP's orthodox wing—
particularly Senators Taft, Wherry, and Bridges—were now of
the opinion that the most politically expedient policy to follow
was to oppose Administrative proposals and in the process
develop an alternative program. If the Eightieth Congress,
under the guidance of the internationalist Senator Vandenberg, cooperated with the Truman Administration in such
programs as the Truman Doctrine and the Marshall Plan, the
newly elected Republican members of the Eighty-first Congress had no intention of continuing such cooperation. Dewey's "me-tooism" had been formulated as a result of the nominee's own internationalist leanings, his confidence in winning

the election, his desire to have the cooperation of the Democrats once he was in the White House, and his concern over the Berlin crisis, which erupted during the campaign. With his defeat the very term "bipartisanship" became anathema to the more conservative members of his party. In the opinion of one student of the election, Dewey had clearly gone too far in his attempt to associate his party's goals with those of the Democrats. H. B. Westerfield writes that "Dewey overextended the scope of his bipartisanship on foreign affairs to areas where he had no 'duty' to do so. Thereby he weakened his own campaign, and hence the future political attractiveness of *any* form of 'bipartisanship.'" [3]

A second major factor contributing to the ascendency of the Taft wing of the party was the illness of Vandenberg in 1949. In the fall of that year the Michigan Senator underwent a major operation, and although he returned to the Senate after a protracted absence, the operation was only partially successful and he was forced to leave his post in 1950. Hard on the heels of Vandenberg's illness and eventual death came John Foster Dulles' defeat in a special New York election for the Senate seat of the late Robert F. Wagner. Like the Michigan Senator, Dulles had been an active supporter of cooperation in foreign affairs. Unfortunately Dulles, in his race against Lehman, chose to strike a conservative pose on *domestic* matters, thus challenging the Fair Deal. Truman vigorously supported Lehman's candidacy despite Dulles' past friendliness to the President's foreign policy objectives. Although the race was a close one, Lehman's victory gave those Republicans who would no longer cooperate with the Democrats more proof that their party could not win by associating itself with the program of the opposition.

With the loss of Vandenberg and Dulles, orthodox leaders such as Taft and Wherry were clearly directing the party's foreign policy objectives. Once in that position events proved

---

[3] H. Bradford Westerfield, *Foreign Policy and Party Politics* (New Haven, 1955), p. 323. Emphasis his.

to be such that they were provided with massive amounts of ammunition to use against the Democratic Administration, and thus further their partisan gains. One of the most important factors aiding the Republicans in their attack on Democratic foreign policy was the widespread disillusionment and suspicion among the public over the general policy of containment. Developed by the State Department's Policy Planning Staff under the direction of the diplomat-scholar George Kennan, containment was essentially defensive in design. It called for neither the overthrow of the Russian government nor the reclamation of areas lost through Russian aggression. It was, instead, a plan whose limited objective was to hold the line against further Communist expansion. Kennan has written that "it is clear that the main element of any United States policy toward the Soviet Union must be that of a long-term, patient but firm and vigilant containment of Russian expansive tendencies." [4] To a nation which had conquered the Germans and the Japanese so resoundingly, this defensive posture was disquieting in its underlying assumption that the United States would have to accept a partially hostile world as status quo.

To make the policy even more unappealing to conservative thinkers, President Truman and Secretary of State Marshall envisioned as part of the containment program a plan to prevent the Communists from taking advantage of the social and political turmoil occurring in various parts of the world. Massive economic and military aid to the free nations was the proposed solution. The Truman Doctrine was the first step in this new program, initiated in March of 1947 when the President requested $400 million in emergency funds to aid the governments of Greece and Turkey, which were on the verge of collapse.

Less than two months after the passage of Truman's aid bill Marshall declared in the course of a Harvard commencement

---

[4] George F. Kennan, *American Diplomacy, 1900–1950* (Chicago, 1951), p. 119.

address that this nation had decided to make impressive amounts of economic aid available to a Europe that was on the verge of economic disaster.

> Our policy [is] directed not against any country or doctrine, but against hunger, poverty, desperation, and chaos. Its purpose should be the revival of a working economy . . . so as to permit the emergence of political and social conditions in which free institutions can exist.[5]

The Taft wing opposed the bill on the grounds that the plan ignored Asia and would bankrupt America in its attempt to aid Europe. But under the guidance of Senate Majority Leader Vandenberg the measure passed on April 2, 1948 and Taft voted in the affirmative. The fears of more "global New Dealism" were undercut by the course of events: the Communist takeover of Czechoslovakia in February 1948; fears that Finland would become the next victim of aggression; and the threat posed by the Communists in the Italian elections of April.[6]

Despite some resistance to these new aid programs designed to bolster the economies of Europe, the Republicans could not fail to see that the Administration was successful in Europe. From this it followed that both by their own predisposition toward Asia and by the demands of partisan politics, members of the right wing of the Republican party began to concentrate more and more on the Far East. Yet in doing so they revealed a basic inconsistency in their position, for foreign involvement went against the grain of a number of the party's beliefs. That is, this branch of the GOP was characterized by a philosophy which favored a government dominated by the legislature rather than the executive, a relatively laissez-faire economy, a balanced budget, and limited governmental expenditures. An active foreign policy would strengthen the

---

[5] Quoted in Harry S. Truman, *Memoirs, Vol. II: Years of Trial and Hope* (Garden City, 1956), p. 317.

[6] Eric Goldman, *The Crucial Decade—and After* (New York, 1960), pp. 77–78.

executive branch, it would be costly, and it might very well involve greater controls on the entire economy. Hence it could be argued that internationalism brought with it threats to the entire conservative philosophy of government.

Conservatism in international affairs in the late 1940's was influenced to a considerable extent by domestic economic conservatism. The demands of reconversion, a serious housing shortage, and an acute demand for consumer goods tended to turn the attention of the business community inward. Furthermore, it was apparent that United States involvement in world affairs would preclude any meaningful reduction in the national budget while, at the same time, it would extend the sway of a federal government which was considered by many to be overly powerful. Finally, what guarantee did these businessmen have that foreign aid funds would not be used to socialize overseas economies? [7]

In his study of neoisolationism, Norman Graebner has written that "it has been said that a neo-isolationist was one who wanted to fight in China." [8] This aspect of the thought of Taft and those of his kind cannot be avoided. Unwilling to fight in Europe, and agreeing only reluctantly to such commitments as the Marshall Plan and the United Nations, this group advocated a rigidly militant position toward Communism in the Far East. There is a good deal of truth in the generally held notion that to orthodox Republicans the island of Formosa was more important than the island of England. [9]

In good part the reason for this emphasis on Asia is historic. America's dynamic energies in the nineteenth century were directed toward the west, and it can be argued that American interest in China, Japan, and the Far East was a continuation into the twentieth century of that flow west. More specifically, the United States became involved in Asia through the "opening" of Japan and a series of trading agreements with China.

---

[7] Selig Adler, *The Isolationist Impulse* (New York, 1957), p. 349.

[8] Norman A. Graebner, *The New Isolationism* (New York, 1956), p. 27.

[9] Truman, *Memoirs*, II, p. 466.

The culmination of this movement was the Open Door policy at the turn of the century, a policy whose object was to include American commerce in the China trade and investment markets. At the same time, we committed ourselves to preserving the political and territorial integrity of China, although events proved that we were not willing to fight for this objective—at least not until World War II. Yet the myth existed that we had a special responsibility toward China— that Western civilization, Christinity, and democratic ideals had been brought to the Far East and that therefore we had a major commitment to the entire area. The notion of America as China's friend and protector persisted.

There is another, more subjective, element to this interest in the Far East on the part of the Republican party. White, unable to define the attitude precisely, best explains it as a "cult."

> The Asian cult was, in fact, almost mystically based, and one gets onto a sticky terrain in attempting to describe how it could come to dominate the whole Taft wing of the Republican party, to a greater extent than it dominated Taft himself. It rested most of all, one thinks, on a strong concept of American nationalism; on long inherited suspicion of the British; on a wish, conscious or not, to have this country go it alone; on an attitude of rejection toward Europe.[10]

Whatever one accepts as the basis of this Asian "cult" it is clear that the events surrounding the "fall" of China in 1949 gave the Republicans their most powerful weapon with which to attack their Democratic opponents. Militarily, Nationalist China began to collapse in September of 1948, and Chiang's downfall became readily apparent by the end of January of 1949 when Manchuria and most of North China (including Peking) fell to the Communists. In very general terms it might be said that the Truman Administration in the early months of 1949 adopted the position that enormous social and political changes within the Chinese nation had made the defeat of

---

[10] White, *The Taft Story*, pp. 167–68.

Chiang inevitable, and that the Generalissimo's failure to curb corruption, to democratize his government, and to halt the offensive actions taken by the secret police all led to the political crisis. Underlying these factors was his failure to undertake long-needed social reforms such as land distribution and tax revision.

As Chiang was pushed south, the Republicans repeatedly charged that the Chinese leader had been defeated because of the stupidity or by the design of the Democratic Administration. Since the Administration had not consulted the Republicans in the formulation of a policy on China, it was even more vulnerable to assault. Thus Republicans continually referred to their pre-1949 warnings of the Communist danger in China.

On the China issue, as on most other issues of foreign policy, the Republican party remained divided. Once again it was Vandenberg who emerged as the spokesman for the more "liberal," pro-Administration view. In February of 1949 Truman met with Secretary of State Dean Acheson, Vandenberg, and Vice-President Barkley in an attempt to establish an official attitude toward the imminent collapse of China that would mollify congressional critics. Vandenberg urged the Administration not to abandon the Nationalist government outright, for he feared that the United States would "never be able to shake off the charge that we [were] the ones who gave poor China the final push into disaster." [11] The Michigan Senator was not sanguine about Chiang's chances against the Communists; he simply believed that the Administration should forestall positive action in China until Chiang's fate was "settled *by China* and *in China* and not by *the American government in Washington.*" [12]

While the Administration hoped to sustain a wait-and-see posture toward the China tangle, the press of events in China forced it to make a definite statement of policy. On August 5th

---

[11] Arthur H. Vandenberg, Jr., ed., *The Private Papers of Senator Vandenberg* (Boston, 1952), p. 531.
[12] *Ibid.* Emphasis Vandenberg's.

the thousand-page China White Paper was issued; in a summary cover letter Acheson concluded that

> The unfortunate but inescapable fact is that the ominous result of the civil war in China was beyond the control of the government of the United States. Nothing that this country did or could have done within the reasonable limits of its capabilities could have changed that result; nothing that was left undone by this country contributed to it. It was the product of internal Chinese forces, forces which this country tried to influence but could not. A decision was arrived at within China, if only a decision by default.[13]

The China bloc of orthodox Republicans was absolutely outraged, and said so. On August 21st Bridges, Knowland, Wherry, and McCarran (a Democrat who sided with the Republicans on this issue) made public a statement labeling the White Paper

> a 1,054-page whitewash of a wishful, do-nothing policy which has succeeded only in placing Asia in danger of Soviet conquest with its ultimate threat to the peace of the world and our own national security. . . .
>
> What the Chinese army lacks more than anything else are the weapons which the State Department dangerously advises be withheld from its armies. Against the Communist troops, deprived of arms and equipment by this short-sighted State Department policy, the Communists fight with a wealth of weapons.[14]

While contesting the validity of the Administration's explanation of the fall of Nationalist China, the Republicans demanded that Chiang's sanctuary on Formosa be preserved. This demand ran directly counter to Administration policy, for early in August of 1950 Acheson sent members of the State Department a memorandum predicting the fall of Formosa, and on August 16th the Joint Chiefs of Staff met and "reaf-

---

[13] *The New York Times,* August 6, 1949, p. 4.
[14] *The New York Times,* January 4, 1950, pp. 1 and 6.

firmed their previous views that overt United States military action to deny Communist domination of Formosa would not be justified."[15] When the Chinese Nationalist government abandoned mainland China in the second week of December, the State Department once again voiced its intention of steering clear of Chiang. Acheson, in secret guidance papers to United States Missions abroad, indicated that the importance of Formosa was to be minimized since "Formosa has no special military significance. . . . Loss of the island is widely anticipated and the manner in which civil and military conditions there have deteriorated under the Nationalists adds weight to this expectation."[16] When the contents of this directive became known, the China bloc was again furious with the Administration. Knowland characterized the directive as "amazing" and demanded that its contents be examined at a public congressional hearing.[17] Predictably, the more liberal faction of the GOP disagreed with the China bloc on the question of our commitment to Formosa.

It is important to note that the demands of the Korean War led the Administration to change its position toward Formosa considerably. The positioning of the Seventh Fleet in the Formosa Straits shortly after the outbreak of the war provided military protection to Formosa—protection that the Republicans ironically resented because they believed that Truman's action had prevented Chiang from attacking the mainland!

At the same time the GOP was also fighting a fierce battle to prevent the Administration from granting recognition to Red China. Ignoring the principle of *de facto* recognition and voicing great expectations that Chiang could be returned to the mainland, the Republicans of the China bloc viewed the recognition of Red China as the height of perfidy.

While these Republicans were insisting that the Administration give active support to Chiang and withhold recognition

---

[15] Quoted in Westerfield, p. 362.
[16] *The New York Times,* January 4, 1950, p. 14.
[17] *Ibid.,* p. 1.

of Mao's regime, they were also formulating a theory concerning the reason for the fall of China and the entire disaster in the Far East. Rejecting the thesis contained in the China White Paper that monumental social and political upheavals *within* China explained the victory of the Communists, the Republicans charged that a conspiracy existed among pro-Communist elements in the Roosevelt and Truman Administrations to "push" the Chinese over to the Communists. Soon a purge was demanded to rid the federal government (and especially the State Department) of traitorous figures.

It was this demand that led to the uneasy alliance of Taft and McCarthy—Taft because of his interest in Asia and McCarthy because of his interest in Red baiting. In Wheeling, West Virginia on February 9, 1950, McCarthy delivered the speech which resulted in his lending his name to an era.

> The reason why we find ourselves in a position of impotency [in international affairs] is not because our only powerful potential enemy has sent men to invade our shores, but rather because of the traitorous action of those who have been treated so well by this Nation. . . . The bright young men who are born with silver spoons in their mouths are the ones who have been worst. . . . In my opinion the State Department, which is one of the most important government departments, is thoroughly infested with Communists.[18]

Throughout the work that follows the reader will note that in almost every phase of the Korean War debate the Republican conservatives made use of this charge.

Adding force and appeal to the McCarthy charges were two events that contributed greatly to the growing hysteria over the "Red menace." The first of these was Truman's announcement on September 23, 1949 that within recent weeks the Soviet Union had exploded an atomic device. Another prop to the security of America as a nation had been withdrawn, and it was relatively easy for those who were declaring that the United States was being undermined from within to

---

[18] Quoted in Goldman, p. 142.

point to the existence of the Russian atomic bomb as a further
example of treasonable activities within the government.

Another occurrence shattering the confidence of the American public and giving credence to McCarthy's charges was the
conviction of Alger Hiss of perjury growing out of his declaration under oath that he had never been a member of the

Reprinted from *The Herblock Book* (Beacon Press, 1952)

Communist Party and had never known his accuser, Whittaker Chambers. Hiss, who had been a high-ranking member of the State Department and was at the time of his trial the director of the Carnegie Endowment for International Peace, was accused by Chambers of passing government secrets to Communist agents. More important than the actual facts that emerged in the two trials (Hiss was eventually convicted of perjury on January 21, 1950) was the emergence of Hiss as a symbol of everything detested by the conservative wing of the Republican party. He personified the New Deal, intellectualism, and internationalism. Throughout the early years of the 1950's members of the GOP repeatedly charged that men like Hiss had maneuvered the United States into a position where its very existence was threatened.

Hiss, the "fall" of China, and the explosion of the Russian atomic bomb were used by the Republican party in the late 1940's and early 1950's to prove to the American people that the Democratic party was utterly unable to cope with the dangers confronting the nation. All of this helps explain the radical decline of the spirit of bipartisanship, symbolized by Vandenberg's leadership in the passage of the Marshall Plan and the Truman Doctrine. To the end of his stay in the Senate the Michigan Senator sought to convince his party that a bipartisan foreign policy need not work to its disadvantage. In January of 1950 he wrote:

> To me "bipartisan foreign policy" means a mutual effort, under our indispensable two-Party system, to unite our official voice at the water's edge so that America speaks with maximum authority against those who would divide and conquer us and the free world. It does not involve the remotest surrender of free debate in determining our position. On the contrary, frank cooperation and free debate are indispensable to ultimate unity. In a word, it simply seeks national security ahead of partisan advantage. Every foreign policy must be *totally* debated . . . and the "loyal opposition" is under special obligation to see that it occurs.[19]

---

[19] Vandenberg, pp. 552–53.

Yet Vandenberg's appeal was hardly heard above the clamor for a change in the party's strategy. There was an election to be won in November of 1950 and the Republicans had become convinced that victory could be achieved only by opposition, and not by cooperation. The direction that this opposition took from June of 1950 to July of 1953 is the subject of this study. Graebner has suggested in his book *The New Isolationism* that "The real test of wisdom that confronts any party which attempts to expand its influence through the successful use of foreign policy symbols is whether its assumptions will form the basis of responsible alternatives that recognize national limitations." [20] Perhaps the major underlying conclusion of this book is that the Republicans failed in this test, even though the party was obviously successful in November of 1952 in transforming popular discontent into political victory.

Supporting Truman's June 1950 decision to use force in the face of Communist aggression against South Korea, the party hierarchy quickly seized the opportunity to use the frustrations of the war to further their partisan gains. The alternatives offered the country by the spokesmen for the party (before the emergence of Eisenhower in July of 1952) were unsatisfactory. Alternately advocating complete withdrawal from the peninsula or the waging of an all-out war against China, the leadership of the GOP offered a confused nation a policy which, if adopted, would have seriously threatened global warfare. It was not until the election of Eisenhower that the party majority recognized it would have to settle for limited goals in the Korean conflict. This is not to say, however, that this new policy met with the approval of the entire party—the conservative wing, particularly Taft, Knowland, and McCarthy, continued to denounce the settlement agreed to by their own party. Deeply divided to the end of the war, the party remained unable to reach a consensus on the most

---

[20] Graebner, p. 4.

effective method of meeting the challenges of the postwar world.

*   *   *

It would be appropriate to make some mention of the internal structure of the GOP before beginning this study of the party's response to the Korean War. A major—if not the fundamental—difficulty in dealing with such a subject is determining who speaks for the Republican party. Had the GOP been the majority party in 1950 (in the sense of at least occupying the White House if not dominating both houses of the Congress) then one could point to the statements of the President as having considerable party sanction. But this of course was not the case in June of 1950, and was not to be the case until the election of General Eisenhower nearly thirty months later. And too, the Republicans did not control either the Senate or the House, for the Eighty-first Congress, elected in November of 1948, contained 42 Republican senators and 171 Republican congressmen; while the Democratic majorities were reduced in the Eighty-second Congress, the Republicans were still in a minority in both houses. It was only with the Eisenhower sweep in 1952 that the Republicans managed to muster a majority in the Congress, but even here their hold over both branches was precariously slim—a margin of 48 to 47 in the Senate, and 221 to 213 in the House.

For most of the Korean War, then, the Democrats controlled the Presidency, the Senate, and the House. Stephen K. Bailey, in a publication sponsored by The Fund for the Republic, outlines the obvious difficulties in such a situation:

> If the in-party has problems in creating a clear party image, the task is many times more difficult for the out-party. No real answer has yet been found to the question of who speaks for the party when it does not control the White House, or when no presidential campaign is in progress. Over the years, some of the major contenders for the job of out-party spokesmen have been congressional leaders, national committee chairman, national executive committees, ex-Presidents, defeated presidential candi-

dates, *ad hoc* groups established by the national committees, congressional policy committees, congressional campaign committees, and most recently, a permanent advisory council to the national committee. . . .

Obvious problems arise in having the congressional leaders speak for the out-party. Congress itself is bifurcated, and its power . . . tends to gravitate into the hands of men who are not necessarily responsible to the party majorities. On occasion, the minority or majority leader in the Senate, or the Speaker or minority leader of the House, may claim to speak for his own party. But whether anybody inside or outside the Congress believes that the voice of the party has been heard in the land depends either upon coincidence with already accepted party formulations or upon the personal prestige and political virtuosity of these congressional spokesmen.[21]

This difficulty was all the more pronounced by 1950 because the Grand Old Party had been without White House leadership for twenty years—the longest period that the Republicans had been denied the Presidency in all of their history. And of the four Republicans sent to do battle with F.D.R., only Hoover had considerable political standing with the congressional leadership. The ideas of the other three—Landon, Willkie, and Dewey—were seen as too liberal or too international-minded by much of the congressional leadership. Despite Hoover's popularity with some segments of the GOP, it would be a serious error to see the former President as the major spokesman of the party in 1950! Furthermore, this congressional hierarchy, which had rejected many of the policies of the former titular leadership, tended to be comprised of conservatives from safe Republican strongholds; how responsive they were to national, as opposed to local, interests is of serious question.[22]

The lineup of the congressional leadership in both 1950 and

---

[21] Stephen K. Bailey, *The Condition of Our National Political Parties* (The Fund for the Republic, 1959), p. 9. Reprinted by permission.

[22] Wilfred E. Binkley, *American Political Parties: Their Natural History* (New York, 1962), p. 422.

1953 is indicative of this general conservative orientation. In 1950 the congressional hierarchy was comprised largely of Martin, House Minority Leader; Wherry, Senate Floor Leader; Taft, chairman of the Senate Republican Policy Committee; Millikin, chairman of the Senate Republican Conference; and Saltonstall, Republican Whip. Of these five, only Saltonstall was representative of the so-called Eastern liberal wing of the party. Nor had the Republican congressional leadership profile changed by early 1953, for after the Eisenhower victory the GOP was represented by Martin, Speaker of the House; Halleck, House Floor Leader; Taft, Senate Majority Leader; Bridges, President Pro Tempore of the Senate; and Saltonstall, Majority Whip. Only Saltonstall and Bridges could be seen as representative of the moderate or liberal wing of the party, and these two, noncoincidentally, occupied positions of secondary importance within the hierarchy. During Taft's illness and after his death in July of 1953, Knowland (who had been chairman of the Republican Policy Committee) became Senate Majority Leader, thus ensuring the continued conservative domination. Of related, if not direct interest is the fact that of the eight new Republican senators elected in November of 1950, six (Nixon, Dirksen, Case, Bennett, Butler of Maryland, and Welker) were conservatives; only Carlson and Duff (both ex-governors) were of the liberal persuasion.[23]

Thus the Republican party throughout the Korean War period was beset by a kind of bipolarization that has been defined so astutely by James MacGregor Burns in *The Deadlock of Democracy*. On the one hand was the Presidential or executive wing of the party represented by the ideals of such former titular heads as Landon, Willkie, and Dewey. To this group must of course be added the names of Eisenhower and Dulles, both of whom were soon to do considerable battle for more moderate internationalist goals. Confronting this group,

---

[23] See Stephen Hess and David S. Broder, *The Republican Establishment* (New York, 1967), p. 23.

and making it impossible for the party to speak with one clear voice, were the conservatively oriented congressional leaders mentioned above. Writing in *The Atlantic* in 1960, Burns characterized the split as follows:

> We can understand our party system best if we see each major party divided into presidential and congressional wings that are virtually separate parties in themselves. They are separate parties in that each has its own ideology, organization, and leadership. In political outlook, the congressional Republican Party slants sharply to the right, and the congressional Democrats lean almost as far in that direction. The congressional Republican . . . party operates through the congressional Republican chieftans, the Republican campaign committees in both chambers, and through the congressional committee system, with its rule of seniority. Across the aisle, the congressional Democrats . . . operate ideologically somewhat closer to the center. They too have their apparatus of committees and procedures bolstering their power on Capitol Hill.

> The two presidential parties operate through very different institutions: the Democratic and Republican national committees, the national conventions, and the political organizations under them. Whichever party wins the presidency wins also the vast political power and machinery of the White House. Both parties have their heroes of old and leaders of today: Willkie, Eisenhower, and Nixon; and Wilson, Roosevelt, and Truman. But the main difference between the presidential and congressional parties is over policy, both presidential parties are more liberal and internationalist than both congressional parties.[24]

Further qualification must be made, for even to speak of congressional Republicans as if they were in some sort of basic agreement in the area of foreign (or for that matter, domestic) policy would be most misleading. Any student of partisanship in recent American foreign policy is in considerable

---

[24] James MacGregor Burns, "White House vs. Congress," *The Atlantic*, Vol. 205 (March 1960), p. 65. Reprinted by permission. For a more complete treatment of this concept, see James MacGregor Burns, *The Deadlock of Democracy: Four-Party Politics in America*, rev. ed. (Englewood Cliffs, 1963).

debt to H. Bradford Westerfield's *Foreign Policy and Party Politics*. For the purposes of the present work this study is important because it concentrates on the eight-year period immediately preceding the outbreak of the Korean War. Identifying the five major regions of the United States for the purposes of his analysis as the Northeast, Midwest, South, Mountain, and Pacific areas, Westerfield arrives at the following conclusion concerning the Republican voting pattern:

> Midwestern Republicans always shrank from two-party majorities; Eastern Republicans recoiled from the party line. The party was consistently divided.

> Session by session over the eight-year span the Republican regional pattern showed little change in the relative willingness of different sections to support the party line. In the Eightieth Congress, to be sure, Republicans from the Coasts were even less willing than usual to join their colleagues in a partisan front —and for once the Midwest Senators seemed to feel the same way; Vandenberg's leadership was certainly important in holding the latter's party-line average down to 59 percent in 1947 and 1948. But with that single exception, in not one Congress, House or Senate, was the average of Midwest party-line support ever *less* than 75 percent. And in no Congress, House or Senate, was the average of East or Pacific "party-lining" ever higher than 75 percent. Only once did it reach as high as 75; usually it stood in the sixties.

The reader will find at the conclusion of this study an Appendix (pp. 282–301) dealing with the voting pattern of Republican senators in critical roll-call votes taken during the Korean War. This Appendix contains both a breakdown of the vote in terms of the five sections utilized by Westerfield, along with specific information on how each Republican senator voted, in an attempt to highlight this aspect of the sectional cleavage within the party. (The Senate Republicans are emphasized both in the Appendix and in the study as a whole because of the special place this branch occupies in the formulation of foreign policy. As Senator J. William Fulbright has insisted in his recent call for a restoration of the traditional role of the Senate in the area of foreign relations, the Constitution entrusts to the Senate "the responsibility to review the conduct of foreign policy by the President and his advisers, to render advice whether it is solicited or not, and to grant or withhold its consent to major acts of foreign policy.") [25]

There were a number of instances during the Korean War when these sectional divisions caused painful struggles within the Republican party. In Chapter 5 the so-called Great Debate involving an increase in American troop commitment to Europe is discussed, and one finds that of the various possible philosophies regarding American participation in world affairs, Republicans ranged over a broad area which was bounded by former President Hoover's concept of the creation of a Gibraltar of the Western Hemisphere, to the desire of a small group of Eastern Republicans (particularly Governor Dewey) for wide participation in world affairs. Throughout the 1950–53 period the party was seriously divided over the question of transforming the unification of Korea from a political to a military goal. The same can be said of the party's attitude toward the participation of our allies in the Korean War, the question of permitting Chiang Kai-shek's troops to join the United Nations Command, and the MacArthur formula for victory on the peninsula. Even after the peace terms had been signed in July of 1953, the party was racked by an internal division concerning the nature and implications of the Eisenhower peace.

---

[25] J. William Fulbright, *The Arrogance of Power* (New York, 1966), p. 44.

Chapter 2

The Commitment

At the opening of World War II Korea was in the hands of Japan, largely because of two wars in Northeast Asia at the turn of the century, wars that involved China, Japan, and Russia. Both Japan and Russia had been seeking supremacy in Asia through domination of China, and toward this end they saw Korea as both a gateway to Manchuria and a source of year-round harbors. China's interest in Korea, on the other hand, centered about her search for a barrier against the ambitions of Japan and Russia.

The Sino-Japanese War was thus rooted in this centuries-old conflict for control of Korea. In April of 1885 a conference between China and Japan was held in Tientsin, and it was decided that the two nations would remove their troops from Korea and refrain from sending any troops in the future unless the other side was notified. This settlement was short lived, however, for when a domestic revolt occurred in southern Korea under the direction of the Tonghas Society, the Korean ruler appealed to China for help. The Chinese government sent 5,500 troops and notified Japan, according to the Tientsin agreement; Japan, in turn, sent in 8,000 men. As the two powers massed men and material on the peninsula the Tonghas revolt subsided and China and Japan were left facing each other in Korea. Old hostilities led to an eight-month war, a sweeping victory for Japan, and the signing of the Treaty of Shimonoseki, by which China recognized the independence of Korea and Japan obtained Formosa.

Ten years later, in 1904–05, Japan was at war with Russia, the result of the desire of both parties to dominate the Far East, and Manchuria and Korea in particular. The Japanese executed a stunning victory over the Russians, and through the mediation efforts of Theodore Roosevelt the Treaty of Portsmouth was signed whereby Russia recognized Japan's predominant interests in Korea and agreed not to oppose any steps Japan might take in Korea. After the Portsmouth Conference, Japan assumed full control of Korea's economic, political, and social life. Japan formally annexed Korea on August 22, 1910, renaming her colony Chosen. Japan lost control of the peninsula after her defeat in World War II.

The fact that Korea was controlled by Japan forced the Allies during World War II to make some arrangement for the eventual disposition of the territory upon Japan's defeat. It was decided by the United States, England, and China at the Cairo Conference of 1943 that once the Japanese had capitulated, Korea was again to become a free and independent nation. At the Potsdam Conference of 1945 these same powers reaffirmed this pledge.

\ When the Soviet Union declared war against Japan in August of 1945, it formally agreed to stand by these pledges. The section of the Cairo pledge that Russia agreed to uphold reads as follows: "The aforesaid three great powers, mindful of the enslavement of the people of Korea, are determined that in due course Korea shall become free and independent." [1]

While it is true that in this same month a line was drawn across Korea at the thirty-eighth parallel, this was done to facilitate the arrangements made for the surrender of Japanese troops in the area: Russia would accept the surrender of Japanese forces north of this line, while the United States would handle those troops surrendering south of the line.[2] It should be remembered that this line had no justification outside the immediate necessity of dealing with Japanese soldiers. The thirty-eighth parallel was thus the result of a temporary expediency, having nothing to do with natural boundaries, politics, or the history of the country.

---

[1] Ruhl J. Bartlett, ed., *The Record of American Diplomacy* (New York, 1964), p. 661.
[2] Harry S. Truman, *Memoirs*, II, p. 317.

Problems arose when it became apparent that the Soviets were regarding the line as a permanent political division. Interestingly, *The New York Times'* correspondent Richard J. H. Johnson wrote on September 30, 1945, "The Koreans' great fear is what will be inherited by them when the day comes for the removal of Allied controls. Will the country be torn by political strife resulting from the establishment of two opposing ideologies?" [3] From 1945–47, the United States attempted to fulfill the Cairo and Potsdam agreements by seeking to induce the Soviet Union to remove the boundary it had imposed. The failure of such efforts led the Americans to seek the aid of the United Nations, and that body established in 1947 a United Nations Temporary Commission on Korea. This commission was to officiate over a free, nationwide election in Korea for the purpose of establishing an independent government. Russia, however, would not agree to supervised elections in her "zone," and so the United Nations was forced to limit the scope of its activities to what had emerged as South Korea. Elections were held in May of 1948. At the end of the month the Korean Assembly met, and elected Syngman Rhee the first president two months later. (The new president of Korea had had a good deal of educational training in the United States—he received a master's degree from Harvard and a doctorate in international relations from Princeton.) The Republic of Korea was officially called into being by the United Nations on August 15, 1948.

While the United States and the United Nations were seeking a political solution to the Korean problem, Russia was insisting that the action which the United Nations had taken was illegal. In September 1948, the Democratic People's Republic of Korea, a Russian-dominated state in North Korea, was established with Kim Il Sung at its head. (Sung had been a member of the Communist underground in Korea which had fought the Japanese from 1935. He fled to Russia in 1938, and

---

[3] *The New York Times,* September 30, 1945, Section IV, p. 4.

returned to Korea in 1945 as a major in the Russian occupational army.)

Meanwhile, both the United States and the Soviet Union were withdrawing troops from Korea, although about 500 American advisors remained in South Korea in June 1949, for the purpose of building and training an army for the Republic of Korea. And too, while the U.S.S.R. claimed that she had completely withdrawn her military from North Korea, she also retained some men to build and train an army for that portion of the country which she then controlled.

The period between the withdrawal of the majority of American and Soviet troops in 1948–49, and the invasion of South Korea in June 1950, was an uneasy time on the peninsula. North Korea was harassing the republic to the south with a series of raids, border disturbances, and propaganda campaigns. So hostile was the northern regime toward the government to the south that on September 9, 1949, *The New York Times* printed the text of a letter sent by North Korea to the United Nations announcing her intention to unite Korea by force.[4]

These aggressive, though limited, acts foreshadowed the invasion of the Republic of Korea.

❊   ❊   ❊

At four o'clock in the morning of June 25, 1950 (Far Eastern time) the Communists of North Korea attacked the Republic of Korea. The telephone circuits to Korea were closed on Sunday morning, and so the Department of State did not get word of the attack until 9:26 p.m. It was at this time that a telegram was received from our Ambassador in Seoul, John Muccio, stating that ". . . It would appear from the nature of the attack and the manner in which it was launched that it constitutes an all-out offensive against the Republic of

---

[4] *The New York Times,* September 9, 1949, p. 1.

Korea." [5] Dean Rusk received the telegram at the State Department, and he in turn forwarded the message to Secretary of State Dean Acheson. The news of the invasion was relayed by Acheson to Truman, who was spending the weekend with his family in Independence, Missouri. It was decided that Truman would return to Washington for a meeting with his top advisors, and that United Nations Secretary-General Trygve Lie would be requested to hold an emergency Security Council meeting on Sunday, June 25 (United States time).

Truman's *Memoirs* contain two revealing statements of his thoughts upon hearing of the invasion. While flying back to Washington, he writes, he

> . . . felt certain that if South Korea was allowed to fall Communist leaders would be emboldened to override nations closer to our own shores. If the Communists were permitted to force their way into the Republic of Korea without opposition from the free world, no small nation would have the courage to resist threats and aggression by stronger Communist neighbors. If this was allowed to go unchallenged it would mean a third world war, just as similar incidents had brought on the second world war. It was also clear to me that the foundations and the principles of the United Nations were at stake unless this unprovoked attack on Korea could be stopped.[6]

And too, in reference to his actions those first days, Truman has written.

> Every decision I made in connection with the Korean conflict had this one aim in mind: to prevent a third world war and the terrible destruction it would bring to the civilized world. . . . Every one of these steps had to be taken without losing sight of the many other places where trouble might break out or of the danger that might befall us if we hazarded too much in any one place.[7]

---

[5] Quoted in Truman, *Memoirs*, II, p. 381. The most complete discussion of the decision-making process that led to American intervention in the Korean War is to be found in Glenn D. Paige, *The Korean Decision* (New York, 1968).

[6] Truman, *Memoirs*, II, p. 333.

[7] *Ibid.*, p. 346.

The Security Council met on Sunday afternoon, Jun
at the request of the United States. It passed a formal resolution calling for: (1) immediate cessation of hostilities; (2) the
withdrawal of the North Korean army to the thirty-eighth
parallel; (3) the cooperation of all United Nations members
in carrying out these demands. (The Russian delegate, Jacob
Malik, was absent from this session because of a protest
against the Security Council's refusal to seat Red China instead of Nationalist China.) This was the first of the three
significant resolutions passed by the Security Council in the
fifteen days under discussion here.

On June 26th, news from Korea continued to be ominous.
As a result there was a second Blair House meeting, at which
it was decided that the United States would provide air and
sea cover for South Korean forces and would, in addition,
send the Seventh Fleet into the Formosa Straits to prevent an
attack on Formosa. While the announcement of official U.S.
policy was made at 12:30 p.m., June 27th, it was not until later
that same day that the Security Council passed the second of
its resolutions concerning Korea, once again at the insistence
of the U.S. By a 7–1–2 vote, the Council moved that United
Nations members "furnish such assistance to the Republic of
Korea as may be necessary to repel the armed attack and to
restore the international peace and security in the area." [8]

It is important to note here that the United States took its
action before this resolution was passed by the United Nations. We were at this point acting unilaterally in Korea.

Since the whole question of United States' motivation in the
Korean situation will be of great importance in the subsequent
discussion of the changing attitude of the Republican party,
some fundamental distinctions should be established. The
very fact that we acted unilaterally on the 27th should make
clear that at best our action in Korea was a combination of
idealism and practical power politics. There is, of course, a
good deal to be said for the thesis offered in a very recent and

---

[8] Bartlett, p. 769.

excellent work on the Korean War, in which the author states that "the Korean decision was primarily a political decision in the Jeffersonian tradition of American idealism." [9] That is, it can be argued that America's reaction to the North Korean action was based upon its outrage over the invasion by the Communists of a nearly defenseless country—a country, incidentally, that we had helped call into existence.

However, as Rees recognizes, United States' action in South Korea was motivated to a large extent by self-interest. As Truman states in his *Memoirs*, one of his great fears was that if action were not taken a third world war might ensue, involving the United States and the rest of the world.[10] Before discussing this further, two terms—containment and limited war—should be mentioned because of their importance in later discussions of GOP policy. The concept of containment was defined in Chapter 1; its major tenet was the halting of Communist aggression through a series of political-economic-military alliances. Rather than stand by and wait for Soviet encroachments to stimulate a world holocaust, Kennan's policy was to halt (contain) Communism.

The point to be made here is that this policy was much in evidence in the Truman Administration's strategy at the outset of the Korean crisis. Truman's *Memoirs* makes this clear, as do the debates in the Congress that will be discussed below.

A recognition of the *Realpolitik* of the situation leads to a second large concept that must be defined—that of limited war. Henry A. Kissinger has written the following concerning the characteristics of limited war:

A limited war . . . is fought for specific political objectives which, by their very existence, tend to establish a relationship between the force employed and the goal to be attained. It reflects and attempts to *affect* the opponent's will, not to *crush* it, to make the conditions to be imposed seem more attractive

---

[9] David Rees, *Korea: The Limited War* (New York, 1964), p. 11.
[10] Truman, *Memoirs*, II, pp. 333–46.

than continued resistance, to strive for specific goals and not for complete annihilation.[11]

A limited war tends to be a political war (a fact which General MacArthur never really understood) and it is a particularly frustrating war to wage. In a full-scale conflict one's aims are relatively simple: to use maximum force to destroy the enemy. In a less extensive conflict the military is restrained by the political demands of the home government—a fact of life that disturbed the Republican party nearly as much as it did the commander in the field.

All of this leads to two final issues: Why did the U.S. decide to intervene in Korea, and why did we do so on a limited basis? While these questions might seem, at first, to be far afield of the central topic, they are important because a good deal of the debate in Congress—and much Republican attention—was centered around these two issues. On the question of why we intervened, there are the twin motivations of idealism and of national security discussed above. Some, unfortunately, lost sight of the fact that a great part of our decision to intervene was based on *Realpolitik*, and therefore they became bitter when what they *thought* our objectives to be turned out to be unrealistic and unrealized. The debates in Congress show that the example of World War II and of the Munich-Chamberlain appeasement fiasco hardened the resolve of many not to repeat past mistakes.

The problem can be seen in terms of two polar tugs: the determination not to repeat past mistakes and the practical necessity of avoiding all-out war with the Communists. This was the central core of the frustration. How, in other words, does a powerful nation decide on the one hand that it must put a stop to aggression and on the other that it must not greatly handicap itself in so doing. In the main, it would seem fair to say that the United States decided to conduct a limited operation because of three reasons: (1) we did not want to

---

[11] Henry A. Kissinger, *Nuclear Weapons and Foreign Policy* (New York, 1957), pp. 140–41.

provoke Russia into beginning a third world war; (2) we were afraid that if we extended ourselves in Korea the free world would be vulnerable to attack elsewhere; (3) our allies were extremely hesitant to expand the war elsewhere.

Somewhat related to the nature of America's response to the Korean invasion is the question of the degree of responsibility the U.S. must bear for the attack on South Korea. Often mentioned is the fact that the United States withdrew its troops too quickly from South Korea, thereby failing to provide a military establishment which could match the one that Russia had set up in the northern sector of the peninsula. In September of 1947 the Joint Chiefs of Staff made the decision to withdraw American troops from South Korea on the basis of two military considerations: that the area was not of sufficient military importance to warrant our continuance there, and that in the light of America's general manpower shortage, the troops of the U.S. stationed in Korea might be more useful elsewhere. These opinions of the Joint Chiefs of Staff, taken together with the fact that Russia announced that she was withdrawing her troops from North Korea, led Truman to decide in the spring of 1949 that our men should leave Korea.[12]

Many Republicans strongly condemned this withdrawal, and in July 1949, a House Minority Report was issued stating "Our forces . . . have been withdrawn from South Korea at the very instant when logic and common sense both demanded no retreat from the realities of the situation. . . . Our position is untenable and indefensible." [13] Republican Representative Walter Judd of Minnesota went even further when he charged that the Administration's Korean aid program was no more than "an attempt to make the Koreans and the world think that we are carrying out a commitment which we are not prepared to carry out." He then predicted that once we

---

[12] Robert E. Osgood, *Limited War: The Challenge to American Strategy* (Chicago, 1957), pp. 167–68.
[13] Quoted in Trumbull Higgins, *Korea and the Fall of MacArthur* (New York, 1960), pp. 11–12.

removed our troops, the Communists would capture the entire country within a year.[14]

Often quoted in this connection is a statement made by Senator Tom Connally, Democratic Chairman of the Senate Foreign Relations Committee, who said publicly in May of 1950 that the U.S. would "probably" not intervene if Russia seized South Korea.[15] Statements and policies such as these have led Eisenhower in his *Mandate for Change* to declare that our lack of military preparedness in June of 1950, along with Acheson's "defense perimeter" speech, were two factors encouraging the Communists to attack South Korea.[16]

If it can be argued that we left South Korea open for attack because of our military withdrawal from that area, surely a second reason for our lack of preparedness is to be found in the economy drive of the Republican-dominated Eightieth Congress, which cut back on defense spending. The army was a chief victim of the drive to cut expenses, for at the time of the invasion there were only one and one-third divisions in the continental United States. Truman is quite bitter about these military slashes, for he has written that Congress took four months to approve a request he sent for $150 million in economic aid to Korea for fiscal 1949. When he requested another $60 million for the same purpose in the 1950–51 budget, "the request was actually defeated in the House of Representatives," he writes, "with most of the negative votes coming from the Republican members. While it was later passed as part of a combined Korea-China aid bill, it can be said that, generally, Congress was in no hurry to provide the aid which had been requested for Korea by the President." [17]

Eisenhower mentioned Acheson's "defense perimeter" speech as a prime factor in encouraging the North Koreans to attack. This by now infamous speech was delivered by the

---

[14] Quoted in *ibid.*, p. 12.

[15] "Connally," *U.S. News & World Report*, May 5, 1950, p. 30.

[16] Dwight D. Eisenhower, *The White House Years, Vol. I: Mandate for Change* (Garden City, 1963), pp. 172–74.

[17] Truman, *Memoirs*, II, p. 329.

Secretary of State to the National Press Club in January of 1950, and in it he stated that in the Pacific, the United States' protective arm extended from the Aleutians to Japan, through Okinawa to the Philippines. He went on to say that areas not included in this perimeter, such as Korea and Formosa, would have to depend upon the United Nations and their own provisions for defense. There has been a good deal of attention paid to this speech, but it should be remembered that Acheson did not necessarily rule out U.S. intervention on the behalf of countries outside the perimeter, particularly under the aegis of the United Nations. Furthermore, it is naive to assume either that the Russians were unaware of our military weakness in the Korean area or that the West would under all circumstances accept a Communist offensive against an Asian nation.

Finally, we have perhaps for too long viewed MacArthur's position concerning the defense of the Far East as being absolutely antithetical to that of Acheson and the Administration. He, too, can be cited as affording the Communists some hope that their aggression would not be opposed. In the March 2, 1949 issue of *The New York Times* MacArthur outlined what he termed an American "line of defense" in the Far East that did not include the Korean peninsula. In this interview MacArthur said "Now the Pacific has become an Anglo-Saxon lake and our line of defense runs through the chain of islands fringing the coast of Asia. It starts from the Philippines and continues through the Ryukyu Archipelago, which includes its main bastion, Okinawa. Then it bends back through Japan and the Aleutian Island chain to Alaska." [18]

Returning to our course of events in these early days of the Korean War, we find that on Friday, June 30th, Truman issued the following statement, in which he authorized the use of ground troops and the bombing of military targets north of the thirty-eighth parallel. Part of this document reads: "In keeping with the United Nations Security Council's request for support to the Republic of Korea in repelling the North

---

[18] *The New York Times*, March 2, 1949, p. 22.

Korean invaders and restoring peace in Korea, the President announced that he had authorized the United States Air Force to conduct missions on specific military targets in *northern* Korea wherever militarily necessary, and he had ordered a naval blockade of the entire Korean coast. General MacArthur has been authorized to use certain supporting ground units." [19] The long-range import of this, naturally, was considerable.

The third important resolution passed by the Council in the first fifteen days of conflict was approved on July 7, 1950. It was at this time that the U.N. stated that all forces fighting Communism in Korea would be placed under a unified command; that the United States would name a commander (Truman immediately nominated MacArthur); and that the U.N. flag would be flown beside the various national flags.[20]

❃ ❃ ❃

When we turn to a close examination of the attitude of the Republican party in the early days of the Korean War, we find that the members of the party unanimously approved of the actions that the Administration had taken. Nevertheless, the party had serious reservations about a good deal of our past (and some of our present) foreign policy. What will be attempted here is a delineation of the Republican party's position in the early days of the war, with particular emphasis upon the ways in which members of the GOP qualified their approval of the Administration's decisive action in Korea.

Between June 26th and July 10th twenty-two Republican Senators (out of a total of forty-two) spoke on the Korean War, and without exception they favored the action that the United States had taken, although the tone of these views varied from the genuinely warm and seemingly total approval of, let us say, Lodge, to the hostility that accompanied the speeches of Taft, Malone, and McCarthy.

Despite the variations of tone, the Republicans were clearly

---

[19] Reprinted in *The Congressional Record,* June 30, 1950, p. 9534.
[20] *The New York Times,* July 8, 1950, p. 1.

By The Horns

Reprinted from *The Herblock Book* (Beacon Press, 1952)

pleased that the United States was determined to halt this latest evidence of aggression. Speaking on the first day of debate, Senator Knowland issued a strong statement in which he warned against a Munich-like appeasement that would be heard many times in the future. He indicated that we must stand up strongly to the Communist threat in Asia because if South Korea falls, all of Asia is in danger. Referring to Munich, Knowland ended his remarks by stating that "Appeasement then, as now, is but surrender on the installment plan." [21]

Five Republican Senators spoke on the Korean situation on the 26th. Styles Bridges of New Hampshire stressed the concept that the line against Communism must be drawn here and now.[22] Alexander Wiley, ranking minority member of the Committee on Foreign Relations because of Vandenberg's illness, warmly approved of the action that had been taken.[23] Toward the end of the session, Malone of Nevada delivered a lengthy speech on America's lack of a foreign policy up to this time, and insisted, nevertheless, that his remarks were not to be construed as meaning that he did not approve of the present course of action.[24] Last to speak was Jenner of Indiana, who was extremely hostile toward the State Department, but approved of the steps Truman had taken.[25]

One of Truman's warmest Republican supporters in this early phase of the debate was Alexander Smith of New Jersey. Long an advocate of a stronger policy toward the Far East, Smith saw the President's actions as a complete reversal of past trends, and he heartily approved. Speaking on the day that the President decided to send air and sea support to the South Koreans (June 27th) Smith declared that "The President's statement is in line with our responsibility under the United Nations' Charter to meet this crisis." He then called for support of Truman: "I feel that all of us should back up the action of the President in what I believe to be a real stand in the Far East, comparable to the stand we have taken in the Atlantic area." [26]

---

[21] *Congressional Record,* June 26, 1950, p. 9158.
[22] *Ibid.,* p. 9154.
[23] *Ibid.,* pp. 9160–61.
[24] *Ibid.,* p. 9188.
[25] *Ibid.*
[26] *Ibid.,* p. 9230.

On July 5th Smith asked to have placed in *The Congressional Record* an interview in which he had been asked if the Republican party planned to use its repeated call for stronger action in the Far East for political purposes in November. Smith replied: "Of course it will . . . but I want to emphasize this point. We Republicans to a man—while we have been critical of the Far Eastern policy of the past—are united now with the administration. All of us as loyal Americans want to see the matter through to a successful conclusion." [27] Wayne Morse of Oregon, on the second day of debate, backed up the position of Smith, Knowland, Lodge, and others by saying of Truman: "By his action the President has given renewed hope of freedom for peoples of the world who are still willing to stand up for freedom in spite of growing Russian threats." [28]

Easily the most significant speech to be given during these first days of discussion was delivered by Robert Taft on Wednesday, June 28th. It was at the conclusion of this speech that William S. White (who was later to write a biography of Taft) commented that "While Taft was sharp . . . [his] speech was welcomed by the internationalists; they felt that, for him, it was remarkably soft toward the President and toward the whole enterprise." [29] Truman's press secretary, Charles Ross, is reported to have been thunderstruck: "My God! Bob Taft has joined the United Nations and the United States." [30] These statements, clearly, are exaggerations; as we shall see when we discuss the ramifications of the Republi-

---

[27] *Congressional Record*, July 5, 1950, p. 9666. Also see "Statement of Senator H. Alexander Smith on Far Eastern Policy," June 28, 1950, Section IV, Box 100, Smith Papers (Princeton University Library).

[28] *Congressional Record*, June 26, 1950, p. 9232. It should be noted here that when Morse entered the Senate in 1945 he did so as a Republican. Increasingly he moved away from the position of his party, and in 1952 backed Stevenson for the Presidency while calling himself an Independent. In 1954 he became affiliated with the Democratic party, and is a Democrat today. See William S. White, *Citadel: The Story of the United States Senate* (New York, 1956), pp. 186–89.

[29] Quoted in Goldman, p. 165.

[30] *Ibid.*

cans' hostility toward past policy in Asia, Taft was hardly an admirer of Truman. However, there is an important kernel of truth in these comments by White and Ross, because Taft did say toward the end of his address:

> I welcome the indication of a more definite policy, and I strongly hope that having adopted it the President may maintain it intact . . . since I approve of the changes now made in our foreign policy, I approve of the general policies outlined in the President's statement. . . . Whether the President chose the right time for his new policy, or the right place, can be discussed in the future.[31]

On the fourth day of debate—Thursday, June 29th—the Democratic chairman of the Senate Foreign Relations Committee, Tom Connally, referred to a statement made by General Eisenhower to the effect that ". . . the President's course was correct, and that the President could not do anything else." [32]

Minority Leader Kenneth S. Wherry of Nebraska was one of the harsher critics of Administration policy during the Korean discussions in the Senate. Yet even Wherry, when discussing a military-assistance bill, declared: "The President must have our unanimous support. Refusal to give it to him would be interpreted in the eyes of our enemy as reflecting lack of unity in this country. And there must be no disunity in the face of a threat so imminent as that of today." [33]

Senator McCarthy did not speak on the Korean War until the 6th of July. Predictably, he centered a substantial portion of his remarks on the failure of United States foreign policy because of Communists in the State Department. McCarthy, nevertheless, voiced grudging approval of what Truman was doing. In what must be regarded as a classic in the art of the left-handed compliment, the Senator declared "Mr. Truman has at a dangerously late date decided to follow the advice

---

[31] *Congressional Record,* June 28, 1950, p. 9322.
[32] *Congressional Record,* June 29, 1950, p. 9460.
[33] *Congressional Record,* June 30, 1950, p. 9539.

those men [various Republican senators] have been urging upon him for years. We welcome him even at what may be a disastrously late date." [34]

Finally, on June 28th, former President Herbert Hoover issued the following statement in reference to the Korean conflict: "When the United States draws the sword, there is only one course for our people. Like others, I have opposed many of our foreign policies, but now is not the time to argue origins, mistakes, responsibilities, or consequences. There is only one way out of such situations as this: That is to win. To win, we must have unity of purpose and action." [35]

✻   ✻   ✻

Hoover's call for a kind of unthinking unity of purpose went unheeded by much of the Republican party. In the relatively few days that are under study in this chapter the party did indeed argue "origins, mistakes, responsibilities and consequences." The nature and extent of the party's endorsement of Truman's stand is our immediate problem.

Hoover's plea for unity and bipartisanship was supported by many Republicans at the outset of the war. After a lengthy telephone conversation with Dean Acheson, the titular head of the party, Governor Dewey, sent Truman the following telegram: "I wholeheartedly agree with and support the difficult decision you have made today to extend American assistance to the Republic of Korea in combatting armed Communist aggression. Your action there, in Formosa, the Philippines and Indo China was necessary to the security of our country and the free world. It should be supported by a united America." [36] Harold Stassen, then president of the University of Pennsylvania, concurred with Dewey's view, as did the future standard-bearer of the party, General Dwight D. Eisen-

---

[34] *Congressional Record,* July 6, 1950, p. 9715.
[35] *The New York Times,* June 29, 1950, p. 18.
[36] *The New York Times,* June 28, 1950, p. 4.

hower, who stated that "there was no recourse but to do what President Truman did." [37]

Among congressional Republicans, Minority Leader Wherry was quite critical of Administration policy, yet even he stated that "Certainly there is no partisanship in this situation." [38]

❉ ❉ ❉

When these Republicans stated that it was gratifying that Truman at this late date saw fit to draw the line against Communist expansion in Asia, China was most clearly on everyone's mind. The "fall" of China to the Communists had occurred just a year earlier, and the Republicans had considerable experience in berating the lack of firmness on the part of the Administration toward the Soviet threat. In his initial speech to the Senate, Bridges begged his fellow senators not to repeat past fiascos. He charged that the people of the free world ". . . know we gave away Manchuria and found excuses not to intervene in China. They know we allowed Poland to fall. They know what has happened to Czechoslovakia, Rumania, and Bulgaria." [39]

Of all Republican critics in the Senate of Administration policy toward Asia in the past, Malone was perhaps the most vehement.

. . . we have made every mistake possible, starting with Yalta in 1945 in Asia and in Europe, and if we do not bring on a war it certainly will not be our fault.

. . . it is fairly clear that what happened in China and what is now happening in Korea were brought about deliberately by the advisers of the President at Yalta and by the advisers of the State Department since then.[40]

---

[37] *The New York Times,* June 29, 1950, p. 18. For Stassen statement see *The New York Times,* June 28, 1950, p. 4.
[38] *Congressional Record,* June 30, 1950, p. 9539.
[39] *Congressional Record,* June 26, 1950, p. 9155.
[40] *Ibid.,* p. 9184.

Taking his cue from Malone, Jenner (who would shortly become a warm supporter of McCarthy) contended that "The Korean debacle also reminds us that the same sell-out-to-Stalin statesmen who turned Russia loose are still in the saddle, riding hard on the American people [who] can no longer entrust [their] future to those who have betrayed the past." [41]

Taft's grudging approval of Truman's actions did not mean that he was in any way sanctioning the past actions of the Administration. "From the past philosophy and declarations of our leaders, it was not unreasonable for the North Koreans to suppose that they could get away with it [the invasion] and that we would do nothing about it . . . this entirely unfortunate crisis has been produced first, by the outrageous aggressive attitude of Soviet Russia, and second, by the bungling and inconsistent foreign policy of the administration." [42] Taft backed up these charges by pointing out a number of past decisions which he regarded as grievous mistakes: our decision not to support the Nationalist Chinese with sufficient force during the civil war; Acheson's defense-perimeter speech; the Acheson-Truman decision not to send troops and arms into Formosa; the failure to make sure that money appropriated under the Mutual Defense Assistance Act of 1949 actually got into South Korea; and Connally's statement in *U.S. News & World Report* of May 5, 1950, that the Administration was going to seriously consider the abandoning of South Korea because of her proximity to Russia and because she was not an essential part of our defense strategy. [43]

In his first major speech before the Senate on the Korean War, McCarthy bitterly attacked the whole call for unity: "Anyone who criticizes the murderous incompetence of those who are responsible for this disaster, anyone who places the finger upon dupes and traitors in Washington, because of

---

[41] *Ibid.,* p. 9188. Also see *Congressional Record,* June 27, 1950, p. 9228.

[42] *Congressional Record,* June 28, 1950, p. 9320.

[43] *Ibid.,* pp. 9320–21. Also see "Connally," *U.S. News & World Report,* May 5, 1950, p. 30.

whose acts young men are already dying, will be guilty of creating disunity." Past policy, he declared, has been made under the advice of ". . . that group of Communists, fellow travelers, and dupes in our State Department—a group who make Benedict Arnold look like a piker. . . . I think the Communists within our borders have been more responsible for the success of Communism abroad than Soviet Russia has been responsible for that success." [44]

These Senate Republicans, therefore, were clearly not going to let Truman wash away past sins by his one act of courage. Both Bridges and Knowland declared at the outset that Administration moves represented "another case of too little too late." [45]

Another aspect of this attack on past policies involved the question of our relative aid to Europe as compared to what we had been offering Asia. As in so many other issues, Knowland was the first to put his finger on this GOP complaint.

> We have with wide publicity hurried shipments of such planes to Europe where the immediate danger was not as pressing [as in Asia]. It but underscores the fact that the whole Far East has been given a much lower priority than many of us have thought wise. Far East funds in the pending arms implementation bill [Mutual Defense Assistance] are less than 10 percent of those allotted to Europe and the Middle East.[46]

More specifically, the Republicans were indicting the Administration not only for ignoring the whole Far East, but for failing to build up the South Korean army. They continually complained that under the Mutual Defense Assistance Act of 1949 and the second supplemental appropriation act passed on October 28, 1949, South Korea should have received $10,500,000 in military aid. This money was set aside to enable the country to build up forces to resist external attack. The

---

[44] *Congressional Record,* July 6, 1950, pp. 9715–16.
[45] *Congressional Record,* June 26, 1950, p. 9158.
[46] *Ibid.*

point here was that although the money had been allocated it never reached its destination.[47]

It was perhaps inevitable that all this criticism of the State Department would find Secretary of State Dean Acheson bearing a good deal of the punishment. Immediately following his approval of what he interpreted to be changes Truman had made in our foreign policy, Taft called for the removal of the Secretary of State. "I suggest . . . that any Secretary of State who has been so reversed by his superiors and whose policies have precipitated the danger of war, had better resign and let someone else administer the program to which he was, and perhaps still is, so violently opposed."[48] The *Congressional Record* reports that upon completion of this statement there was applause on the floor and in the galleries of the Senate—the only time, it is interesting to note, in the fifteen days under discussion here, that such an outburst was reported (it is against Senate rules to make demonstrations of approval or disapproval of this nature).

Easily the most vehement in his denunciation of Acheson was Senator McCarthy, who included him into that ". . . group who make Benedict Arnold look like a piker." McCarthy, as we have seen, approved of Truman's position, but warned the President that "we do not welcome the motley crowd that he is bringing with him to put into effect this program, the type of program against which they have dedicated themselves throughout their careers in the State Department." Acheson, then, should leave government service because his views are not those of either the President or the people.[49]

The State Department was not the only branch of the government that was under sharp attack as a result of the North Korean invasion—our entire intelligence system bore

---

[47] *Congressional Record,* June 28, 1950, p. 9321. Also see *Congressional Record,* June 30, 1950, p. 9528 and *Congressional Record,* June 26, 1950, p. 9158.

[48] *Congressional Record,* June 28, 1950, p. 9322.

[49] *Congressional Record,* July 6, 1950, p. 9716.

the brunt of much criticism, for Republicans were particularly shocked that a Pearl Harbor-like surprise attack should have once again occurred. It was often pointed out that Admiral Hillenkoetter, Director of Central Intelligence, had told the *New York Daily News* on the Tuesday following the attack that "a Korean invasion had been expected for a year, but we were not able to predict the time." [50]

Another target of Republican hostility was the attitude of our allies during the crisis—this was a complaint that began in these early days and grew stronger as the war waxed in intensity. This aspect of the debate began rather mildly on June 27th when John W. Bricker of Ohio asked Majority Leader Lucas if the other nations of the United Nations were following the lead of the United States in supporting the Security Council resolution. Lucas' answer was that he did not know at the time, but was confident that they would. [51]

This answer did not satisfy the GOP, and the next day Wherry quoted a news release whose content, he believed, showed that England's participation in the conflict left much to be desired. The release read:

> The informant said Britain for the moment is trying to confine her participation in the Korean situation to a noncombatant role. The use of British warships for humanitarian work around Korea, it was explained, would release American naval units for other operations. . . . The source said the British feel direct involvement in the Korean fighting might lead to a break with Communist China, whose government they offered to recognize early this year. [52]

Wherry was clearly unhappy over this state of affairs, for he asked: "We are tied to certain countries, but are they tied to us? Is what I have just read going to be the position of Great Britain? Is she going to fight or is she simply going to go along

---

[50] See, for example, *Congressional Record,* June 27, 1950, p. 9239.
[51] *Congressional Record,* June 27, 1950, p. 9230.
[52] *Congressional Record,* June 28, 1950, p. 9312.

and appease the Red Communists in China, finally recognizing them, and not resisting the expansion of communism?" [53]

While Truman's course of action in Korea was often called by Republicans an act of courage, he too did not lack critics of his handling of the crisis. In large part this criticism stemmed from the conviction that the actions Truman had taken constituted acts of war, and as such required the official sanction of the Congress. Senate Republicans did not disapprove of what he had done, but they insisted that he had not used legal channels. In part, too, it was legislative jealousy—the fear that the President was usurping a power which rightfully belonged to them. The key to this whole question was the statement that Truman made on Tuesday, June 27, concerning future United States policy in the Far East. Because this document will be referred to many times in this work, it will be outlined below:

    1. In answer to the Security Council's request that members render assistance to implement the Security Council's call on North Korea to cease hostilities and withdraw to the 38th parallel, Truman ordered air and sea support to the South Korean government.

    2. Because "the occupation of Formosa by Communist forces would be a direct threat to the security of the Pacific area and to United States forces performing their lawful and necessary functions in that area," Truman ordered the Seventh Fleet into the Formosa Straits and called on Formosa to stop its operations against the mainland.

    3. "The determination of the future status of Formosa must await the restoration of security in the Pacific, a peace settlement with Japan, or consideration by the United Nations."

    4. Increased assistance to France in Indochina.

    5. A pledge that the United States would uphold the "rule of law" rather than the "rule of force" in international affairs. [54]

Many Republicans objected to this directive on the grounds that by ordering the Seventh Fleet into the Formosa area

---

[53] *Ibid.*, p. 9313.

[54] Harry S. Truman, *Public Papers of the Presidents of the United States, 1950* (Washington, 1965), p. 492.

Truman had taken it upon himself to declare war with utter disregard of Congress. While the Democrats were later to present a detailed defense of the constitutionality of the President's action, they at first limited their defense to the assertion that as Commander-in-Chief the President had broad emergency powers. Majority Leader Lucas explained:

> I undertake to say that with world conditions as they exist at this very moment, with Communism creeping into every nook and corner which it can possibly go, with the unusual situation as it exists today, if the President of the United States believes, as I do, and as I think every other Senator believes, that the safety, the security, and the honor of this country are involved as a result of what is going on in the Orient, he had the right to move as he did with the powers he had under the Constitution as Commander-in-Chief of the military forces.[55]

This, however, did not stem the tide of Republican criticism. Taft bluntly declared that "there is no legal authority for what he [Truman] has done,"[56] although in the next breath he declared that if the President asked for a joint resolution for the purpose of registering approval of his actions, he would vote in the affirmative.

Not all Republicans questioned the legality of Truman's policy. Knowland labeled our intervention in Korea "police action" (apparently Truman was not the first to use this soon-to-be infamous phrase) and went on to declare that since the President's recent moves did *not* constitute an act of war, he had full power as Commander-in-Chief for the steps he had taken. Furthermore, the Californian justified Truman's actions on the basis of the time element involved—Truman had to move very quickly or else risk great losses by attempting to fight an entrenched enemy.[57]

Despite Knowland's position, the Democrats were alarmed over the charges that Truman's acts were unconstitutional,

---

[55] *Congressional Record,* June 28, 1950, p. 9328.
[56] *Ibid.,* p. 9320.
[57] *Congressional Record,* June 30, 1950, p. 9540.

and so Senator Paul Douglas of Illinois quickly presented an elaborate defense of the action taken by the leader of his party. Douglas first addressed himself to the war powers of the Congress. The original wording of the Constitutional Convention, he pointed out, was to the effect that Congress shall have the power to "make" war. But, Madison's notes tell us, this was changed to "declare" war for the purpose of " 'leaving to the Executive the power to repel sudden attacks.' "

Not content to stand behind the authority of James Madison, Douglas argued that the speed of the Korean attack necessitated a quick response, and that submitting the question to Congress might have entailed a dangerous delay because of possible stalling tactics of a small minority in opposition. Also, the fact that the Congress by unanimous vote had passed an extension to the draft (in addition to the military aid bill) showed that it was in favor of the action taken by the President.

Finally, Douglas cited the numerous times in American history that executive action alone was responsible for the use of the armed forces: Jefferson's expedition against the Barbary pirates, 1804; Polk's occupation of disputed Texas-Mexican border territory, 1846; Intervention in Samoa, 1840–41, 1888, 1899; Boxer Rebellion in China, 1900; Theodore Roosevelt's intervention in Panama, 1903; Wilson's intervention in Vera Cruz, 1914; and the pursuit of Pancho Villa, 1916.[58]

A good deal of Truman's justification for his use of armed forces in Korea stemmed from his contention that he was carrying out the mandate of the United Nations. Some Republicans, though by no means a majority, were discontented by our following directives of the U.N. instead of permitting Congress to retain exclusive control over the committing of American troops to combat.

Despite Republican criticism, there seems to be little doubt that Truman's actions were legal. The pertinent articles of the United Nations Charter dealing with this action are:

---

[58] *Congressional Record,* July 5, 1950, pp. 9647–48.

Article 39: The Security Council shall determine the existence of any threat to the peace, breach of the peace, or act of aggression and shall make recommendations, or decide what measures shall be taken in accordance with Articles 41 and 42, to maintain or restore international peace and security.

Article 40: In order to prevent an aggravation of the situation, the Security Council may, before making the recommendations or deciding upon the measures provided for in Article 39, call upon the parties concerned to comply with such provisional measures as it deems necessary or desirable. Such provisional measures shall be without prejudice to the rights, claims or position of the parties concerned. The Security Council shall duly take account of failure to comply with such provisional measures.

Article 41: The Security Council may decide what measures not involving the use of armed force are to be employed to give effect to its decisions, and it may call upon the Members of the United Nations to apply such measures. These may include complete or partial interruption of economic relations and of rail, sea, air, postal, telegraphic, radio, and other means of communication, and the severance of diplomatic relations.

Article 42: Should the Security Council consider that measures provided for in Article 41 would be inadequate or have proved inadequate, it may take such action by air, sea, or land forces as may be necessary to maintain or restore international peace and security. Such action may include demonstrations, blockade, and other operations by air, sea, or land forces of Members of the United Nations.

Article 43: 1. All Members of the United Nations, in order to contribute to the maintenance of internal peace and security, undertake to make available to the Security Council, on its call and in accordance with a special agreement or agreements, armed forces, assistance and facilities, including rights of passage, necessary for the purpose of maintaining international peace and security.

2. Such agreement or agreements shall govern the numbers and types of forces, their degree of readiness and general location, and the nature of the facilities and assistance to be provided.

3. The agreement or agreements shall be negoti-

ated as soon as possible on the initiative of the Security Council. They shall be concluded between the Security Council and Members or between the Security Council and groups of Members and shall be subject to ratification by the signatory states in accordance with their respective constitutional processes.[59]

In addition, under a bill passed to implement the United Nations Charter, Section 6 deals with the question of when armed force may be used to support the United Nations:

> The President is authorized to negotiate a special agreement or agreements with the Security Council which shall be subject to the approval of the Congress by appropriate act or joint resolution, providing for the numbers and types of armed forces, their degree of readiness and general location, and the nature of facilities and assistance, including rights of passage, to be made available to the Security Council on its call for the purpose of maintaining international peace and security in accordance with Article 43 of said Charter. The President shall *not* be deemed to require the authorization of the Congress to make available to the Security Council on its call in order to take action under Article 42 of said Charter and pursuant to such special agreement or agreements the armed forces, facilities, or assistance provided for therein: *Provided,* that nothing herein contained shall be construed as an authorization to the President by the Congress to make available to the Security Council for such purpose armed forces, facilities, or assistance in addition to the forces, facilities, and assistance provided for in such special agreement or agreements.[60]

In interpreting this bill, one must, it seems, refer back to Article 42 of the Charter. The conclusion would thus be that if the military action is justified under Article 42, the President is not required to seek authorization from Congress so long as he does not go beyond the specific United Nations agreement. While many Republicans apparently had acquiesced to this idea, Taft and Malone—to mention two—did not.

The degree to which the United States should commit itself

---

[59] Bartlett, pp. 683–84.
[60] *Congressional Record,* June 28, 1950, p. 9323.

in backing Security Council desires to halt the Korean aggression is an issue that reached its climax in the famous Truman-MacArthur controversy, which is a subject for later discussion. The United Nations, like the United States, was committed to a limited war. But the question remains, what constitutes limited participation? One of the earliest evidences of what was to come along these lines is contained in the early congressional discussions over whether or not the United States should use ground troops in Korea (in addition to the air and sea support that was pledged on July 27th). After the announcement of the 27th, Lodge said that not only was he in favor of the Presidential message, but that he believed that if necessary the army should be used: "I applaud the firm leadership of the President of the United States. I wish merely to add the hope that he will not shrink from using the Army, if the best military judgment indicates that that is the effective course to take." [61] Malone, certainly less friendly toward the Administration than Lodge, said on this same day that if the integrity of Korea is important for our ultimate safety, then we should ". . . send jet planes, fighter planes, bombs, munitions, *and men* to protect Korea and fight back the aggressor." [62]

On Friday, June 30th, the Senate learned—in a rather dramatic fashion—that Truman had decided to commit land forces to Korea. Senator Harry P. Cain was addressing the chamber on the necessity of greater aid to that war-torn country when a note was passed to him citing White House authorization for the use of troops. Quite clearly the majority of Republican senators (at the time) were very much in favor of the introduction of more force in Korea through the use of ground troops. It was often said that the only thing that the Russians understand is force, and so only a display of force on our side could deter them from entering into the conflict.

The Republicans, then, qualified their endorsement of Truman's stance in Korea. They attacked past foreign policy

---

[61] *Congressional Record,* June 27, 1950, p. 9230.
[62] *Ibid.,* p. 9243. Emphasis mine.

mistakes; took the Administration to task for virtually ignoring South Korea's military defenses; launched a personal attack against Secretary of State Acheson; ridiculed the Allies for not aiding America sufficiently; questioned the validity of our obeying Security Council directives; debated the constitutionality of Truman's actions; and, finally, voiced the opinion that even though we were committed in Asia we were not giving sufficient aid to that part of the world.

Despite the harshness of some critics like Jenner, McCarthy, and Malone, the tenor of the debates could not be said to be decisively hostile to either Truman or the Administration, so long as one concentrated on the Republican assessment of the steps taken after June 25th. In sum, the Republican hierarchy in the early days of the Korean War were in overall agreement with what had been done to halt Communist aggression in South Korea between June 25th and July 10th.

Chapter 3

Anticipations

Wars and politics are inseparable, and the Korean conflict was no exception. The previous chapter sought to demonstrate both the extent and limitation of the Republican party's initial acceptance of the role Truman had chosen for the United States in this crucial post-World War II struggle with Communism. We have seen that in the main the principal spokesmen of the GOP regarded the Administration's quick intervention as an indication of a firmer policy toward the spread of Communism, and applauded its decision. We now turn to an examination of the second phase of the party's response to the crisis in the Far East, this time dealing with the period bounded by July 10th and September 15th (the date of the daringly brilliant amphibious landing of MacArthur's troops at Inchon).

Militarily, the period resembled the torment of a man sliding down the slippery side of a hill, desperately searching for some place to grasp and break his slide. The first big foothold that the United Nations forces found was at Taejon, a city to the south of the Kum River, and one that was particularly important because of its domination over the main road leading south to the Naktong River and the city of Pusan. The North Korean army, however, attacked the city of Taejon on July 19th while it was being held by a 4,000 man force under Major-General William F. Dean of the 24th Division. So intense was the battle that by the next day Dean's division had to abandon the city.

Still sliding down the "hill," the Eighth Army decided early in August that it would withdraw behind the Naktong River and set up a defensive perimeter around Pusan, an area in the form of a rectangle, eighty miles from north to south and fifty miles from west to east. North Korea's main offensive against the Pusan perimeter occurred between August 31st and September 1st, with the Communists breaking through the perimeter at several points, but unable to take advantage of these gains because of the defensive ability of the U.N. forces. This, then, was the military situation as of mid-September—the United Nations forces were in the humiliating position of being huddled at the southern tip of the Korean peninsula, knowing full well that one more effective thrust by the enemy would push them into the sea. It was not until MacArthur's amphibious landing of September 15th that the tide (at least temporarily) turned.

Politically, Republicans on Capitol Hill could not help but be affected by this military setback, although on the whole these two months saw the continued support by the GOP of major Administration bills related to Korea. In fact, most members of the party continued to applaud our participation in Korea (if not the results we were achieving), although the enthusiasm of the early days of the war was clearly gone and a more pronounced tone of bitterness permeated the congressional debates on the war.

John Foster Dulles, a Republican in the service of the Truman Administration, perhaps represented the extent to which his party was willing to cooperate with Truman's policy of handling the crisis through the United Nations. In a speech heralded by many members of his party, Dulles told the Commonwealth Club of San Francisco that "The Korean crisis has opened our eyes to the great possibilities of good inherent in the United Nations. There has developed a momentum of action, a lift of spirit, which should be used to realize the high hopes which the whole world felt when, five years ago, the United Nations was born here in San Francisco." [1]

When the Republican members of the Foreign Relations Committee issued their formal statement on American foreign

---

[1] *The New York Times,* August 1, 1950, p. 10. Also see *Congressional Record,* August 1, 1950, p. 11491.

policy, they specifically singled out Truman's action in Korea for special commendation. "We . . . pledge our full support to the national effort to build strength for victory. . . . The President's decision to sustain, by military action, the stand of the United Nations against aggression in Korea must receive united support." [2]

Yet changes were apparent. The party's Senate representation did not praise Truman nearly as often as it had in the first days of the war, and more importantly, some members began to express doubts about the meaning of intervention for America. Senator Wiley attempted to verbalize this change of mood:

> I speak now about the world situation as it confronts us today. The newspapers say there is a feeling of relief in Washington now that the bickering and indecision has disappeared and that we are rallying to the President's support. *I am not so sure that that feeling now exists to the extent it did immediately after the President sent American forces to Korea.* I am sure that in the hinterland people are thinking, and thinking, and thinking about where we are going.[3]

Republicans were doing a good deal of thinking too, for if the party's members of the Foreign Relations Committee praised Truman's June 25th decision, by August they had serious misgivings about the way in which the war was being run. The minority report (often called the Republican White Paper on Foreign Policy) was signed by Wiley, Smith (N.J.), Hickenlooper, and Lodge and included a note to the effect that while Vandenberg's illness prevented him from contributing to the report, he endorsed its contents. In this report the senators declared that they "shall not sleep peacefully at night until our Government's policy is based on the full realization that world domination by communism is still the goal of the Kremlin. It will continue to be the goal until the free nations of the world, each contributing its fair share, realistically join

---

[2] *Congressional Record*, August 14, 1950, p. 12436.
[3] *Congressional Record*, July 12, 1950, p. 9994. Emphasis mine.

together through the United Nations to establish peace in the free world." More specifically, the United States was called upon to:

> regain the initiative and the power for the organization and preservation of lasting peace, which it threw away in 1945. This means that the present intolerable military weakness of the free world must be remedied by us and our friends at top speed. Never again must we allow ourselves to be caught, as we were when Korea was invaded, in a position where our failure to foresee the possible implications of our basic foreign policy will result in our being inadequately prepared to carry out that policy in time of crisis.[4]

In a very revealing working draft of the broad outlines of this 56-page report, Senator Smith indicated that his party must support, in every possible way, the President's running of the war so that the same degree of national unity that was in evidence during World War I and World War II might once again be displayed to the world. This document acknowledges the responsibility of an opposition party to discuss both the causes and the conduct of the war, but stresses the idea that the actual winning of the Korean War must be given first priority. Nevertheless, the Senator concludes with the idea that any degree of cooperation extended to the Administration must be offered with the understanding that the Truman government is to be held strictly accountable for past, present, and future actions.[5]

Thus the reassuring consensus which Truman had achieved in the early weeks of the crisis was slowly crumbling, and if the GOP was not ready to launch an all-out campaign against the Administration, it was only because of the party's awareness of the gravity of the situation and because the GOP had

---

[4] *Congressional Record*, August 14, 1950, pp. 12436–37. A copy of this extensive report is to be found in Section IV, Box 101 of the H. Alexander Smith Papers (Princeton University Library).

[5] "Suggested Republican Statement on Foreign Policy," Section IV, Box 100 of the H. Alexander Smith Papers. Document is dated July 24, 1950.

not worked out an alternative program of its own. It is, of course, both the right and the duty of a minority party to act as critic of the policies of the party in office and to offer the voters of the country a choice of policies. But such a party's ethics are seriously in question if it preys upon the fears of an electorate in time of crisis for the sake of political gains.

Long before the party even attempted to develop a formula for success in Korea it slowly undermined the all but united front that had been built in June. The so-called conspiracy theory, the idea that Korea was but one link in a chain of events that stretched backward at least to Yalta, was one that gained wide credulity before the Inchon invasion. The "conspiracy group" within the party, led by Malone and Jenner (and soon to be joined by McCarthy, Wherry, Martin, and others) was very much inclined to argue, as Malone did, that "It all fits into a pattern—we deliberately lose Manchuria, China, Korea and Berlin. We follow the pattern of sometimes apparently unrelated events—but it all adds up to losing strategic areas throughout the world." [6]

Related to this charge was of course the contention that both South Korea and the United States were not prepared to meet this latest case of Communist aggression. Beween 1947 and 1950 $53 billion had been appropriated for defense, and many Republicans found our military setbacks on the peninsula during July and August incomprehensible in the light of these expenditures. To make matters worse, the GOP continued to complain that we had left South Korea defenseless while Russia built a strong army in the north.

The military reverses in Korea were also undermining the willingness of some party members to follow Dulles' enthusiasm for the role of the United Nations in the confrontation. Those of the conspiracy school displayed an unfortunate penchant for stressing Trygve Lie's so-called Communist leanings, but even those who eschewed personal attacks against the Secretary General were greatly irritated by the fact that the

---

[6] *Congressional Record*, September 5, 1950, p. 14214.

chairmanship of the Security Council would be held by Russia as of August 1. To chair these sessions Russia would have to end her boycott of the United Nations, and she did. In response to this Knowland called upon the Administration to demand that "no person may assume the chairmanship of the Security Council without first taking an oath to support the action of the Security Council. To invite or permit Mr. Malik to gain the chairmanship by rotation is like permitting a member of the Capone crime syndicate to head the F.B.I." [7] Welcoming United Nations intervention on behalf of goals sponsored by the United States, most Republicans at this time seemed unable to accept the fact that this nation's freedom of action had to be limited once we joined the international organization.

But the U.N. did not suffer nearly so much at the hands of the GOP as did our allies, who from the very first had been denounced for their reluctance to participate in the Security Council's sanctions against North Korea. Those allies who were actually trading with Communist countries were harshly criticized, and England in particular was singled out for her continued oil shipments to Red China. By the 18th of July England had announced that she would no longer ship oil to Red China, but the Republicans declared that the decision had come too late. England was not the only object of vilification. Fulbright told the Senate on August 9th that Turkey had offered to send 4,300 fully equipped combat troops to serve in the Korean War, but a month later these troops had not arrived and Republicans demanded to know why, seventy days after the outbreak of hostilities, the only troops in Korea besides those sent by this country was a 1,500-man contingent that England had transferred from Hong Kong. Other Republicans scored the Administration for not insisting that all members of the U.N. contribute to the force being deployed on the peninsula.

An understandable result of this bitterness toward the allies was an increased animosity toward the foreign aid program.

---

[7] *Congressional Record,* July 31, 1950, p. 11346.

Many of the critics of this program had long-standing objections, and they used the growing frustration over the events in northeast Asia as a sounding board for past grievances. Jenner was only one of a group of Republicans who saw the Korean affair as proof that the "dole" had been a dismal failure because it represented "the squandering of American resources and manpower down the rat holes of Europe and Asia." [8] Many of the more internationalist-minded Republicans, such as Dulles and Smith (N.J.) believed that we must both continue the struggle in Korea and recognize our duty toward the rest of the world, especially Japan, Europe, and the United Nations.

Another characteristic of this period was the increased interest in China, especially as it was related to the possibility of Chinese intervention in the war. (It should be remembered, however, that greater concern was expressed in this period over the possibility of Russian intervention. This was to be expected, since there was almost unanimous agreement that it was Russia, and not China, who had inspired the North Koreans to attack on June 25th.) As early as June 27th Morse acknowledged the "tremendous international risks which I am sure we all recognize we are running," while Wherry declared the next day that "There is no turning back. We are gambling; we are taking a calculated risk. But appeasement and retreat is a far worse gamble. Appeasement has failed every time. Strength may and I believe will succeed this time." [9]

Nevertheless, Wiley, ranking GOP member of the Senate Foreign Relations Committee, also warned that "Apparently the manpower available to the [Chinese] is inexhaustible. It may be that we shall be pushed out of Korea . . . the most menacing element in the whole world situation is the possibility that hundreds of thousands of crack Chinese Communists will move into the Korea area." [10]

---

[8] *Congressional Record,* July 21, 1950, p. 10789.
[9] *Congressional Record,* June 27, 1950, p. 9231 and June 28, 1950, p. 9336.
[10] *Congressional Record,* July 12, 1950, p. 9995 and August 17, 1950, p. 12733.

Another reason for the increased interest in China was a plan, reportedly set forth by India, whereby in return for a seat in the United Nations for Red China, Russia would agree to terminate her aid to North Korea and thus bring the war to a close. India was hardly a favorite among Republicans anyway, and this plan stimulated much anger among party members. Many Republicans were already predisposed to see a Red skeleton in every State Department closet, and were sure that State officials were cooperating with the Indian plan so as to get China into the U.N. by the back door. The "Senator from Formosa," Knowland, ridiculed the idea of Mao Tse-tung becoming an Asiatic Tito, although the world has seen some variation of this concept come to fruition.

> Coming after five years of attempting to paint the Chinese Communists as agrarian liberals, and later to force the Communists into a coalition with the Government of the Republic of China, the State Department now comes up with the novel theory that Mao-Tse-tung may become an Asiatic Tito. Though this slightly dead fish or red herring has been peddled far and wide by the appeasers at Lake Success and Washington, it has not had widespread acceptance in Congress or throughout the Nation.[11]

Formosa as an issue in the Korean War rose to prominence in the July 10th to September 15th period. It will be remembered that in his directive of June 27th Truman declared that he was ordering the Seventh Fleet into the Formosa Straits and was also calling upon Nationalist China to halt its operations against the mainland. At the same time the President stated that "The determination of the future status of Formosa must await the restoration of security in the Pacific, a peace settlement with Japan, or consideration by the United Nations."[12] While some Republicans (such as Morse) believed that the President was absolutely correct in his position because he showed a recognition of the special responsibility

---

[11] *Congressional Record,* September 5, 1950, p. 14202.
[12] Truman, *Public Papers,* p. 492.

the United States had toward the island, others charged that the positioning of the Seventh Fleet in the Formosa straits both prevented Chiang from fighting Communism and left the Chinese Communists free to join the North Koreans—if they wished to do so. Hence when it was announced that the Chinese Communists had bombarded the island of Quemoy (also known as Kinman Island) on July 24th, the Asialationists called for the "unleashing of Chiang."

Truman apparently hoped to smooth the ruffled feathers of his congressional critics by announcing at an end-of-August press conference that as soon as the Korean War was over it would not be necessary to keep the Seventh Fleet in the Straits of Formosa, since the Fleet had been placed there to offer protection to our troops in Korea.[13] Even this move failed to satisfy Administration critics, for on September 6th H. Alexander Smith wrote to Dulles to ask if the projected withdrawal of the fleet was part of a yet-undisclosed agreement made with the Russians. More specifically, the Senator wanted to know if in exchange for withdrawal of the fleet Russia had agreed to end the Korean War. The advantage to Russia was obvious: once a military vacuum was created in the Formosa area, Russia would take over the island.[14] Dulles replied to his friend that no agreement had been made to give up Formosa in exchange for peace in Korea.[15]

The somewhat confused status of Formosa in the "defense perimeter" of the United States related directly to the beginning of the Truman-MacArthur controversy, the first skirmish of which was played out during the two-month period here under discussion. One of the most stubborn beliefs of the "conspiracy" school was that Chiang Kai-shek must be supported and eventually returned to the mainland. The Formosa issue was complicated too by the resentment felt by many

---

[13] A portion of the transcript of this press conference reprinted in *Congressional Record*, September 1, 1950, p. 14049.

[14] H. Alexander Smith to John Foster Dulles, September 6, 1950, Section IV, Box 107, Smith Papers.

[15] John Foster Dulles to H. Alexander Smith, September 9, 1950, Section IV, Box 107, Smith Papers.

Republicans over the placing of the Seventh Fleet in the Formosa Straits and the restrictions placed upon Chiang. Truman further shocked "Asialationist" sensibilities by declining Chiang's offer to send approximately 33,000 men to Korea. The Administration felt that these troops should be deployed on the island fortress for the purpose of its own defense; it was also believed that the introduction of Nationalist Chinese troops to Korea would trigger the use of Communist Chinese forces on the peninsula.

MacArthur, sharing the displeasure of those Republicans who objected to the Administration's handling of the Nationalists, requested permission to visit Chiang at the end of July; a reluctant Truman gave his consent. According to the President's *Memoirs,* there was widespread fear among Administration officials that the General had used the visit to ensure long-range American support to Chiang. Anxious to dispel this impression, Truman sent W. Averell Harriman to Tokyo to explain the official line to the Commander. Actually, the government had no intention of abandoning Formosa, for the President relates that on July 27th the National Security Council recommended (and he approved) three concrete proposals concerning Nationalist China. These proposals included "the granting of extensive military aid . . . ; a military survey by MacArthur's headquarters of the requirements of Chiang Kai-shek's forces; and [a] plan to carry out reconnaissance flights along the China coast to determine the imminence of attacks against Formosa." [16]

Politically, MacArthur's trip of the 31st of July was important because the Generalissimo's aides went to considerable pains to publicize the fact that Chiang and MacArthur were in full accord as to future action regarding the island. Truman tells us that "The implication was—and quite a few of our newspapers said so—that MacArthur rejected my policy of neutralizing Formosa and that he favored a more aggressive method." [17]

---

[16] Truman, *Memoirs,* II, p. 349.
[17] *Ibid.,* p. 354.

Chiang's aides, however, were not the only ones stirring up these troubled political waters. On August 10th the General himself issued a statement concerning his trip and his resentment over his private restrictions vis-a-vis Formosa. The final sentence of this statement is most revealing of MacArthur's disagreement with these restrictions, for he declared that his visit to Chiang had been "maliciously misrepresented to the public by those who invariably in the past have propagandized a policy of defeatism and appeasement in the Pacific." [18] Republican critics of Administration policy in the Far East, already decidedly hostile, were to take full advantage of this and subsequent statements by the Far Eastern Commander, for they had come to regard him as the spokesman of decisive and successful action in the Pacific area.

Truman became even more apprehensive when Harriman returned from his Tokyo meeting with MacArthur and reported a disturbing lack of rapport between himself and the General.

In my first talk with MacArthur, I told him the President wanted me to tell him he must not permit Chiang to be the cause of starting a war with the Chinese communists on the mainland, the effect of which might drag us into a world war. He answered that he would, as a soldier, obey any orders that he received from the President . . .

For reasons which are rather difficult to explain, I did not feel that we came to a full agreement on the way we believed things should be handled on Formosa and with the Generalissimo. He accepted the President's position and will act accordingly, but without full conviction. He has a strange idea that we should back anybody who will fight communism, even though he could not give an argument why the Generalissimo's fighting communists would be a contribution towards the effective dealing with the communists in China . . . MacArthur feels that we have not improved our position by kicking Chiang around, and hoped that

---

[18] Quoted in Courtney Whitney, *MacArthur: His Rendezvous with History* (New York, 1956), p. 375.

the President would do something to relieve the strain that existed between the State Department and the Generalissimo.[19]

At the end of August problems with MacArthur over Formosa and Korea erupted again, for on August 20th a speech that the General had written was to have been read before a meeting of the Veterans of Foreign Wars. Advance copies had been sent to the press, and as early as August 26th copies of *U.S. News & World Report,* which had printed the speech, were in the mail. In this address MacArthur publicly challenged the Administration's policy regarding Formosa.

> Nothing could be more fallacious than the threadbare argument by those who advocate appeasement and defeatism in the Pacific that if we defend Formosa we alienate continental Asia. Those who speak thus do not understand the Orient. They do not grasp that it is in the pattern of Oriental psychology to respect and follow aggressive, resolute and dynamic leadership —to quickly turn from a leadership characterized by timidity or vacillation—and they underestimate the oriental mentality.

> Nothing in the last five years has so inspired the Far East as the American determination to preserve the bulwarks of our Pacific Ocean strategic position from future encroachment, for few of its peoples fail accurately to appraise the safeguard such determination brings to their free institutions.

> To pursue any other course would be to turn over the fruits of our Pacific victory to a potential enemy. It would shift any future battle area 5,000 miles eastward to the coasts of the American continents, our own home coasts; it would completely expose our friends in the Philippines, our friends in Australia and New Zealand, our friends in Indonesia, our friends in Japan, and other areas, to the lustful thrusts of those who stand for slavery as against liberty, for atheism as against God.[20]

Truman was very angry over the implications contained in the General's proposed address, and has charged that MacArthur "called for a military policy of aggression, based on

---

[19] Quoted in Truman, *Memoirs,* II, pp. 351–53.
[20] *U.S. News & World Report,* September 1, 1950, pp. 32–34.

Formosa's position. The whole tenor of the message was critical of the very policy which he had so recently told Harriman
he would support. There was no doubt in my mind that the
world would read it that way." Truman at this time "gave
serious thought" to replacing MacArthur with General Omar
Bradley as commander of the Far East, a change that would
leave MacArthur in charge of Japan, but not of Korea or
Formosa.[21] In an attempt to soften the impact of the MacArthur speech, Truman asked Secretary of Defense Johnson to
send a message to the General ordering him to withdraw the
statement. MacArthur complied with this directive, but the
President felt further clarification was necessary, and so sent
his Commander a copy of Ambassador to the United Nations
Austin's letter to Trygve Lie declaring that the United States
had no expansionist aim in regard to Formosa, and that the
U.S. was willing to submit the question to the Security Council.

A host of Republican senators readily saw the opportunity
to make political hay of MacArthur's apparent policy disagreement with the Truman Administration. Not only had the
General denounced (in his Veterans of Foreign Wars speech)
any policy that smacked of "timidity or vacillation," but he
further endeared himself to congressional "hawks" by predicting eventual victory in Korea. In a letter to Truman dated July
19th he stated:

> . . . the issue of battle is now fully joined and will proceed
> along lines of action in which we will not be without choice. Our
> hold upon the southern part of Korea represents a secure base.
> Our casualties despite overwhelming odds have been relatively
> light. Our strength will continually increase while that of the
> enemy will relatively decrease. His supply line is insecure. He
> has had his great chance but failed to exploit it. We are now in
> Korea in force, and with God's help we are there to stay until
> the constitutional authority of the republic is fully restored.[22]

---

[21] Truman, *Memoirs*, II, pp. 354–55.
[22] *The New York Times*, July 20, 1950, pp. 1 and 3.

That MacArthur's views were becoming sacrosanct with the Republican majority is most clearly demonstrated by the reaction to Truman's order that the General withdraw his Veterans of Foreign Wars speech. Minority Leader Wherry saw MacArthur as a figure martyred on the stake of Administration treachery. The only thing buoying up America in this time of stress, Wherry declared, is "our faith in the rugged Americanism of General MacArthur."

> Apparently there are fundamental differences over Far East–American policy between Secretary of State Dean Acheson and General MacArthur, but General MacArthur, as a good soldier, is obeying and carrying out the orders of the Commander-in-Chief as dished up to him by the bungling Acheson.

> General MacArthur knows more about what needs to be done in the Far East to correct the mistakes of Secretary Acheson than anyone in the Truman administration. And the American people have complete confidence in General MacArthur's judgment.

> The vagueness and complete lack of direction to the Administration's policies in the Far East are intolerable at a time when our boys are fighting and dying in Korea. Only our faith in the rugged Americanism of General MacArthur buoys our hopes in that conflict. Let us hear from General MacArthur, and woe to him to dares say he shall not speak.[23]

If the Republicans were well on their way toward finding a hero and a spokesman in MacArthur, they chose another General, Marshall, as their whipping boy. When Truman decided to replace Secretary of Defense Louis A. Johnson with General Marshall, several Republicans used the debate in the Senate over the nomination of Marshall to voice long-held grievances.[24] In part their complaints against the nomination

---

[23] *Congressional Record*, August 28, 1950, p. 13575.

[24] Johnson had been asked to resign on September 12th. He had been associated with two policies that put him at odds with Truman and Acheson: long before June 25th Johnson had advocated large-scale reductions in the military budget (a view highly unpopular in the post-June 25th days); and it was suspected that the Secretary was a supporter of the concept of a preventive war with Russia. See Higgins, p. 40.

were justified. At the time the Department of Defense had been set up, it was decided that only a civilian was to hold the post. Truman now proposed to waive this rule and admit Marshall back into his Cabinet. This aspect of the nomination occasioned widespread criticism; but the GOP also insisted upon using the debate over the appointment to launch a major campaign against the Roosevelt-Truman record in the area of foreign affairs. Jenner, for example, charged that Marshall's worldwide prestige "has been made possible only because the true history of this period has been torn up by the roots, locked in State Department and Hyde Park vaults and in the deep freezes of the White House and distorted and perverted and rifled and destroyed." [25]

The Administration, however, prevailed. Two votes were taken on the Marshall nomination and the first vote, tallied on September 15th, was to make Marshall an exception to the law that no military man could become the head of the Department of Defense. On this vote, the Administration triumphed over its critics by a vote of 47 to 21. Twenty of the nays came from the Republicans, but ten members of the party voted in the affirmative. On September 20th the senators voted a second time, for the purpose of actually approving Marshall as Secretary of Defense. This motion carried, 57 to 11. Every one of the nays came from the Republican side of the aisle, although fifteen Republicans voted for Marshall.[26]

The Administration's victory on the issue of Marshall's appointment to the Cabinet underscores an important characteristic of this phase of the Republican party's use of the Korean War for partisan ends. While much of the GOP leadership was backtracking from its participation in the consensus of the early days of the crisis, by mid-September it still was willing to endorse major Administration bills concerning the war and the economy.

One of the most pressing domestic problems that Truman

---

[25] *Congressional Record,* September 15, 1950, p. 14913.
[26] *Ibid.,* p. 14931. For the second vote, see *Congressional Record,* September 20, 1950, p. 15182. See Appendix, pp. 282–85.

had to deal with in July and August was that of placing the country in a position of greater preparedness while at the same time stemming the rising tide of inflation. In line with this necessity the President sent a message to Congress on July 19th outlining those powers he believed must be granted to the executive to enable the United States, to continue to resist Communist aggression in Korea. In this message Truman asked the Congress to ". . . remove the limitations on the size of the armed forces . . . authorize the establishment of priorities and allocations of materials to prevent hoarding and requisitioning of necessary supplies . . . raise taxes and restrict consumer credit, and [allocate] an additional ten billion for defense." [27]

Departing from the practice of World War II and after, Truman did not ask for price controls, mainly because his economic advisors had told him that rearmament demands did not necessarily mean that civilian output would be sharply curtailed.[28] In addition, the decision not to impose price controls was one of the ways that Truman sought to demonstrate that this was a limited, rather than an all-out war. Yet while the President did not ask for either price or wage controls, the Congress ultimately gave him discretionary power to impose them.

The controls and powers that Truman asked for in the July 19th message were incorporated in a bill entitled the Defense Production Act of 1950, drawn up by the Banking and Currency Committee headed by Senator Maybank. It was Maybank's chore to explain to the already wary Republicans that the measure actually went further than Truman's requests, particularly by granting price and wage controls (Titles IV and V of the bill). This only made the situation more sensitive since members of the GOP, although generally willing to go along with the President, very much resented greatly in-

---

[27] Truman, *Memoirs*, II, p. 348. Also see *The New York Times*, July 20, 1950, p. 14.

[28] Richard E. Neustadt, *Presidential Power: the Politics of Leadership* (New York, 1960), pp. 104–05.

creased executive control over the economy. Wherry made his opposition to this aspect of the measure clear at the outset: "We have been told by the President that the only thing confronting us is a police action in Korea . . . I think it will be very difficult for the people of this country to accept the delegation of powers requested in this bill, if all that is involved is an incident in Korea." [29]

Taft's opening remark was one of unexpected cordiality toward the proposal, for he said "I agree certainly on the general necessity of such controls." However, like Wherry, he too balked at the idea of giving additional powers to Truman and, by implication, taking such powers away from Congress: ". . . it seems to me that we are completely abdicating our authority, abdicating our duties, if we leave to the President the question of determining whether we shall turn the United States from a free economy country into, in effect, a dictated economy country." [30]

While some Republicans, such as Millikin, Thye and Ives, saw no danger in the proposals, they were expressing a minority Republican view, for most of the GOP senators agreed with Bricker when he said that "The authority to control prices, wages and distribution of consumer goods at the retail level vests in the President more arbitrary power over the lives of the American people than any other legislation past or present." [31]

It should be remembered that if the Republicans' greatest objection to the bill was the increased powers it granted to the President, they also demanded a cut in domestic spending, increased taxation, and a balanced budget—all for the purpose of easing the inflationary threat. Declaring that the proposed supplementary bill for an additional $10 billion for armaments had increased the inflationary problem in the United States, Taft insisted that the only solution to the problem was increased taxation. In his lecture to the Senate he

---

[29] *Congressional Record,* August 10, 1950, p. 12152.
[30] *Ibid.,* pp. 12156–57.
[31] *Congressional Record,* August 14, 1950, p. 12400.

managed to include a few swipes at the newfangled, "new" economics. "It has been repeatedly proved by experience that it is impossible to borrow vast sums of money and then hope by the imposition of controls to prevent the inevitable inflationary effects. Sooner or later the dike must break. If we want to stop inflation, we have to stop it at the source." [32] Later in the debate the Ohioan neatly summed up the goals of many of his party when he declared that "A balanced budget and the prevention of any continued increase in outstanding credit have long been recognized . . . as the proper weapons to prevent inflation. I think we can and should pay for the program as we go, and that if we do, price control is not necessary." [33]

Perhaps at this point a close examination of the votes taken on three major pieces of legislation—including the Defense Production Act of 1950—would be helpful in illustrating the conclusion that despite their complaints, the GOP's members by mid-September were unwilling to initiate an open break with the Administration on programs relating to the war in Korea. The three bills to be discussed here, in the order that they were voted upon, are: the General Appropriations Act, the Defense Production Act, and the Supplementary Appropriations Act.

The most interesting debates over the General Appropriations Act centered around two proposed amendments: Senator Kem's motion to reduce from $2,450,000,000 to $1,950,000,000 the amount of money granted to Western Europe; and the so-called Byrd-Bridges amendment for the purpose of bringing about a 10 percent reduction in allocations to the executive department. Senator Kem strongly defended his amendment with the argument that the aid program to Western Europe was costing the American taxpayer more and more money, yet the American people were not getting the security benefits that the Administration claimed would accrue as a result of the investment in the Economic Cooperation Administration. When the vote was taken on Kem's amendment on

[32] *Congressional Record*, July 24, 1950, p. 10824.
[33] *Congressional Record*, August 11, 1950, p. 12267.

July 31st, it lost by a vote of 12 to 59. While it is true that 10 of the 12 yeas came from the minority side of the Senate, 20 of the nays were cast by Republicans, including such party leaders as Knowland, Lodge, Saltonstall, Smith (N.J.), and Taft.

The Byrd-Bridges amendment to the General Appropriations Act was considered on August 3rd, and this time Republican demands for economy in government carried the day, for the motion received an affirmative vote of 55 to 31. Thirty-six Republicans voted for the measure—that is, every Republican present except Langer and Young. However, when one considers that this cut was authorized solely for the executive department, and that there were a number of exceptions involved, the savings brought about by the measure were not as dramatic as might first be assumed. More important is the fact that when the Administration bill itself came up for passage the $34 billion measure passed without a dissenting vote. In the House of Representatives the vote, 165–90, was complicated by the question of Spain's eligibility for Marshall Plan aid.[34]

It has already been noted that the Defense Production Act of 1950 originally incorporated both the authorizations requested by President Truman in his July 19th message, plus the price and wage controls that Maybank's Banking and Currency Committee decided that the Executive should have in this time of crisis. We have viewed the hostility that the Republicans displayed toward these new powers; yet when the bill was considered for amendment, Capehart's motion to strike out Title IV (price control) and Taft's proposal to eliminate Title V (wage control) were both defeated.[35]

---

[34] *The New York Times*, August 26, 1950, p. 1. See Appendix, pp. 285–289.

[35] Capehart's defeat, in fact, was a disaster. The vote was 6 to 75 with only Bricker, Capehart, Ecton, Kem, Taft and Williams voting for the amendment, while 27 Republicans voted against it. Taft's proposal fared much better with the GOP, but it too met with defeat, 29 to 57, with 28 of the 29 yeas coming from his Republican colleagues. Of the nays, 10 were Republican. See *Congressional Record*, August 21, 1950, p. 12899 and 12906. See Appendix, pp. 289–291.

The final bill passed by a vote of 85 to 3 in the Senate, and in the House the tally was 383–12, with 11 of the nays coming from congressional Republicans.[36]

The Supplementary Appropriations Act was passed on September 14th. This measure had been requested by Truman to pay for the cost of running the war in Korea, and also for the purpose of building our military preparedness on a global scale so as to enable us to meet "other Koreas." Here again, despite criticism of past policies, the bill was passed—this time unanimously in the Senate, and the House responded by overwhelmingly endorsing the measure, 311–1.[37] The only deference paid to Administration critics was the passage of a rider which hoped to eliminate Marshall Plan economic (but not military) aid to any nation sending to Russia or her satellites any article that could be used in the manufacture of war materiel.

The votes on these proposals have been highlighted here so as to support a conclusion that will be drawn at the close of this chapter: that while the GOP's concern over the Democrats' handling of the Korean War was growing, the party had no alternative program as yet and so continued to support the Administration overall plans.

In all of this it would be a mistake to lose sight of a statement made by Senator Wiley that was cited at the opening of this chapter. On the 12th of July the Senator told his colleagues: "I am not so sure that that feeling [of political unity] now exists to the extent it did immediately after the President sent American forces to Korea." One of the reasons for this change can be found in Minority Leader Wherry's dejected comment that "The situation in Korea is bleak." [38] Growing bitterness over the American forces' lack of success was effectively highlighted in an article by Richard Johnson of *The New York Times* and quoted by Senate Republicans.

---

[36] *The New York Times,* August 11, 1950, p. 1. See Appendix, pp. 292–294.

[37] *The New York Times,* August 27, 1950, p. 1.

[38] *Congressional Record,* July 14, 1950, p. 10172.

The average GI . . . seems not to know why he is fighting in Korea. [Johnson then quoted a nineteen-year-old corporal who said] "I keep asking myself what I am doing here. The funny thing is I can't answer my own question!" . . . The GI cannot understand why, if this is a United Nations action, he has only South Koreans with him in the battle line. He cannot understand why he was so hastily thrust from soft garrison duty posts in the Pacific or from the peaceful United States into the filth and violence of the Korean battlefields.[39]

And too, Knowland asked to have reprinted in the *Congressional Record* an article by Jim G. Lucas, of the Scripps-Howard staff, that had been printed in the *Washington Daily News*. Lucas took part in the retreat to Pusan, and the last paragraph of his article shows the bitterness and disillusionment of the American soldiers who took part in this retreat. "I can tell you this—you want to know the reason. You promise yourself you'll find out when you get home—not for a news story or an editorial but because you want to know who did this to you and who made it necessary for you to run for your life." [40]

The fact that the Communist offensive had caused American troops to run for their lives quite obviously irritated Republican (and Democratic) sensibilities. Lack of preparedness and failure to take more aggressive action were constant charges increasingly heard in congressional debates. For instance, Ferguson asked: "If Korea is a United Nations undertaking, as it most certainly is, what is the objective? Why do we not push a more vigorous, positive policy at Lake Success?" [41] This is what seems to be significant in the changed mood of the Republicans, for they were reacting to our military failures in the war and they played upon the frustration of the soldiers and the general public. After calling on the Administration for five years not to abandon Asia, they could hardly recommend a withdrawal from Korea; *hence*

---

[39] *The New York Times,* August 13, 1950, p. 1.
[40] *Congressional Record,* September 8, 1950, p. 14435.
[41] *Congressional Record,* August 14, 1950, p. 12414.

*many of the party's members were left with the politically
expedient alternative of charging that the Democrats were not
making enough of an effort to win the war.*

These Republicans, however, were expressing more than a
demand that we adopt a harder line against the Communists.

"Fight Harder! Fight Harder!"

Reprinted from *The Herblock Book* (Beacon Press, 1952)

In this period they started to voice their dissatisfaction with the entire concept of containment. This dissatisfaction was not as clearly expressed as it would be in later periods, but it was present, and it represents a further change over the party's initial response to the war in Korea. Modifying their original call for simply "holding the line" against Communism in Asia, various Republicans began calling for action *north* of the thirty-eighth parallel. Knowland suggested that the U.N. move north of the line in an attempt to reunify the country (a rather ambitious program considering the military reversals suffered by the United Nations up to this point).

> . . . for the invaders merely to move north of the thirty-eighth parallel will not mean a great deal in the final analysis. If the Republic of Korea, the United States, and the western world are to be living under a gun, in that aggression of the same type might take place three months from now or six months from now, a peace achieved under those circumstances would be a very uneasy one.[42]

Alexander Smith of the more Eastern liberal wing of the party not only called for the withdrawal of North Korean forces behind the parallel, but also the establishment by the United Nations of a provisional government to rule all of Korea until a general election could be held on the peninsula for the purpose of forming a self-governing, democratic republic.[43]

If these Senate Republicans were only willing to "suggest" that a change in the goals of the United Nations be undertaken, they were emphatic in their demands that the United States prepare for more vigorous action through a greatly improved military machine. Many on the minority side of the aisle charged that we were not building up our armed forces rapidly enough, and that we had apparently not learned from our mistakes at Pearl Harbor and South Korea. Party members

---

[42] *Congressional Record,* August 16, 1950, p. 12577.
[43] H. Alexander Smith to John Foster Dulles, August 8, 1950, Section IV, Box 100, Smith Papers.

declared that while it was not necessary for the United States to match Russia's 175 divisions, the 18 United States divisions that we would have available by the end of fiscal 1951 were insufficient to meet our responsibilities in the Far East and in Europe. And Wherry repeatedly voiced his disapproval of a $42 billion military budget which only called for an increase of 650,000 men. Universal military training plus universal military service were two solutions offered for the manpower shortage of the armed forces.

It was Henry Cabot Lodge who spearheaded the Republican effort to quicken the increase in the size of our military forces. In report after report to the Senate Lodge declared that we were not doing enough in this area. "Congress . . . has not even amended the Selective Service Act so as to make possible the procurement of enough manpower for a 3,000,000 man armed forces. Present law still effectively limits us to a total not exceeding 2,500,000 men, regardless of certain gestures to the contrary." [44]

During these two months, Republicans, despite their growing disillusionment with containment and their desire for a more positive policy, displayed great reluctance to mention the use of the atomic bomb. Only once in two months did a senator make such a suggestion, and the language Brewster used was so qualified that it displayed a genuine unwillingness to delve too deeply into the matter.

> A few days ago I ventured to suggest that the President should give General MacArthur authority, if he deemed it expedient, to use the atom bomb. As very much of an amateur in this matter, I did not venture to express an opinion as to whether or not it was wise to do so . . . I have not expressed an opinion as to whether the atom bomb should or should not be used, but merely that inasmuch as at the present time our boys are dying because of an inadequate defense, the President should have authority in his discretion to direct that the atom bomb be used.[45]

---

[44] *Congressional Record,* September 8, 1950, p. 14398.
[45] *Congressional Record,* July 17, 1950, p. 10373.

One of the major problems that Republicans faced when calling for greater vigor in the prosecution of the war was their own realization that stronger action increased the possibility of Russia's intervention in the conflict. At this time much more concern was displayed over the likelihood of Russia's entering the war than of China's although the two were naturally related since there was some fear that Russia would send the Chinese into the war just as she had sent the North Koreans. Another fear was that the Soviet Union, after she had deeply involved the United States in the Korean War, would begin to threaten other areas of the world, thus forcing the United States to dissipate her might in the process of controlling these brush fires.

The attack on the policy of containment—along with the call for an increased military buildup and the suggestion that the atomic bomb be considered—represented the Republican reaction to the Administration's program in its infancy. It was the Inchon victory (to be discussed at length in Chapter 4) which created for the GOP rather spectacular visions of what might be accomplished in the future through more aggressive policies. Yet even at this juncture one must ask to what extent this Republican dissatisfaction was a product of a genuine, nonpolitical concern for national security, and to what extent it was a means of achieving partisan ends. There are several instances where one reads the speeches of Republicans in the Congress and senses a concern that transcends political considerations. We have already mentioned Wiley's observation that "They are . . . pushing our boys back and back. If the Chinese Communists go in there with several hundred thousand men, that will constitute another important fact. Apparently the manpower available to the other side is inexhaustible. It may be that we shall be pushed out of Korea." [46] While it is impossible to know for certain, this would seem to be an expression of a genuine frustration over the imponderable and often uncontrollable difficulties of a nation engaged in the

---

[46] *Congressional Record,* July 12, 1950, p. 9995.

kind of limited war that the United States was pursuing in Korea.

And too, when others complained that Russia had caught us in a trap whereby we risked engaging in an all-out land war in Asia without forcing Russia to commit a single man herself, they were voicing a very real dilemma of the war.

Flanders offered perhaps the best statement of the agony involved in deciding what course to take in Korea.

> No one needs to be told that the people of the United States, while determined and courageous, are yet in a state of uncertainty and dismay. They are ready to go ahead. They are ready to make any sacrifice, but there is no clear or hopeful course of action spread before their eyes, as they view the world scene.

> While we meet surprise attack in unexpected places and against unexpected strength, and while we see stretching ahead of us the dismal prospects of more of these unexpected and strong attacks, time and location unknown, our courage and determination, still strong, find little to feed upon for a continuance of that strength.

> As a result of this Korean campaign, we find ourselves ruining the people we set out to protect. The fighting, the destruction, is in South Korea and only to a limited extent in North Korea. How long can the people of South Korea bless us for coming to their aid? . . . Can they afford to have us come to their aid? [47]

Yet despite the sincerity of these remarks, it would be naive to forget that 1950 was a congressional election year, and that the Korean War would loom large in that election.[48] The terms of all the representatives and of thirty-two senators were slated to expire in 1951—twelve of these Senate seats were held by the GOP (that is, the seats of Aiken, Capehart, Darby, Donnell, Gurney, Hickenlooper, Millikin, Morse, Taft, Tobey, Wiley and Young). There were, perhaps, fewer references to the coming election than might have been expected, but the

---

[47] *Congressional Record,* August 2, 1950, p. 11551.
[48] The influence of the Korean War on the 1950 elections will be discussed in Chapter 4.

very fact that the Republicans were increasing the tempo of their dissent is an indication that they would debate the war while thinking of the fall voting.

There were several direct references to the election in the debates in Congress up to September 15th. In his outburst over Truman's "gagging" of MacArthur's August 28th speech, Knowland called upon the electorate to indicate by "a solemn referendum" in November its disposition regarding our Far Eastern policy. "It is now obvious that those who have a vested interest in our past mistakes and bankrupt far-eastern policy intend to pursue their way as far as they are allowed to by the Congress and the citizens of this country. A solemn referendum by the American people on our far-eastern policy —past, present, and future—is now an urgent necessity." [49]

Brewster made a most unusual call for a referendum in November when he offered a plan for a coalition government in this time of crisis. Beginning with the observation that under the English parliamentary system it is common in times of danger for the leaders of the two main parties to join together to form a government, he reminded the Senate that F.D.R. made an attempt at this sort of thing by inviting Knox and Stimson into his Cabinet. But Brewster did not approve of this plan for America, and offered instead his own alternative. His idea of a coalition government would come about if a Republican Congress were elected to cooperate with a Democratic President who still had two years left of his term! [50]

On August 28th the Republican National Committee, headed by Guy G. Gabrielson, issued a 56-page document outlining the major areas of focus for Republicans in the upcoming elections. This blueprint for victory in November consisted of an extensive series of quotations from prominent Republicans, all in an attempt to prove that the GOP had given the Roosevelt-Truman Administration ample warning of the disaster that awaited our Far Eastern foreign policy. The

---

[49] *Congressional Record*, August 28, 1950, p. 13576.
[50] *Congressional Record*, September 5, 1950, p. 14225.

Democratic party's handling of the Korean situation was particularly stressed in this booklet.[51] Several days earlier veteran Washington reporter William S. White had written of the strategy the Republican party would use in the coming campaign: "Every great issue now being prepared for national use in November has Korea for its locale and its rationale. In this quick turnabout to face new circumstances, there is hardly a wastebasket in a party headquarters that is not filled with discarded memoranda on tactics that, a little while ago, were so firm and final." [52]

It was, then, politics as usual. The GOP was unhappy with many aspects of Truman's handling of the war by September 15th, but as yet the party had no alternative policy to offer the electorate. At this point they could only insist that the foreign policy of the opposition party had been found wanting. However, when a banner *New York Times* headline announced on September 15th: UNITED NATIONS FORCES LAND BEHIND COMMUNISTS IN KOREA; SEIZE INCHON, PORT OF SEOUL; MOVE INLAND, the party saw its opportunity to begin the formulation of an alternative position.

------

[51] *The New York Times,* August 29, 1950, p. 14.
[52] *The New York Times,* August 13, 1950, Section 4, p. 3. Also see *U.S. News & World Report,* September 1, 1950, pp. 12–13.

Chapter 4

The Offensive

The decision of the Chinese Communists to enter the Korean War was the most important event in the three-year history of that war. It is for this reason that an examination of the period between MacArthur's strategic landing at Inchon and the massive intervention of Mao Tse-tung's troops at the end of November is so vital to an understanding of the politics of this war. Significantly, as anti-Communist troops pushed steadily to the Manchurian border, and as hundreds of thousands of Chinese troops massed along the Yalu River, the American electorate increased the Republican party's representation in both the House and the Senate, although the minority party gained fewer seats than it had in the three previous midterm elections. In the House the party increased its representation by 28 seats so that the count stood 235 Democrats to 199 Republicans. In the Senate, where there were 36 contested seats, the Republicans won 18 of them, raising their number in the upper chamber to 47, a gain of five over the previous session. The GOP used this limited success to intensify its attack upon Administration policy.

❉   ❉   ❉

MacArthur initiated the United Nations offensive by his decision to take the risks involved in an amphibious landing behind the Communist lines at Inchon, the port of Seoul. The General believed that Inchon was so important because control of the port would enable him to confront the North Koreans with a two-front war while cutting off the Communist supply lines (the Inchon-Seoul area was Korea's most important rail and road complex). The success of the Inchon landing led to a spectacularly swift march north to the thirty-eighth parallel. Part of the U.N. force crossed the Han River as early as September 20th, and after intense fighting from the 15th to the 27th of September, Seoul was recaptured. On October 1st the initial wave of South Korean troops crossed the thirty-eighth parallel to pursue the retreating North Koreans.

In less than fifteen days the whole complexion of the Korean War had changed, for as a result of the General's success the United Nations altered (at least temporarily) its war aims. Once satisfied with achieving status quo ante bellum, the organization now sought the reunification of Korea, and having made the decision to cross the parallel, the possibility of Red China's entry into the war was greatly increased. Yet the temptation to exploit a great victory, plus the desire to accomplish the long-standing United Nations goal of unifying Korea, caused the policy makers to underestimate the possibility of China's entry into the conflict. These decision makers abandoned a strategy which had as its principal rationale Kennan's concept of "containment" in the hope of pursuing the more belligerent policy of "liberation." While the United States must accept the responsibility for this error in judgment, we were enthusiastically supported by Attlee's Labor government and by our Canadian allies.[1]

Once it was decided to permit the General to launch the amphibious landing, certain policy decisions had to be made regarding our future course of action. Truman approved of the following strategy on September 11, 1950:

> General MacArthur was to conduct the necessary military operations either to force the North Koreans behind the 38th parallel or to destroy their forces. If there was no indication or threat of entry of Soviet or Chinese Communist elements in force, the National Security Council recommended that General MacArthur was to extend his operations north of the parallel and to make plans for the occupation of North Korea. However, no

---

[1] Robert Leckie, *Conflict: The History of the Korean War, 1950* (New York, 1952), p. 233. Also see Higgins, pp. 52–60.

ground operations were to take place north of the 38th parallel in the event of Soviet or Chinese Communist entry.[2]

The day before Seoul was restored to Rhee, September 27th, new instructions were sent to MacArthur regarding the objectives of the war. The General was told, according to Truman's *Memoirs*, that his military objective was "'the destruction of the North Korean Armed Forces.'"

In attaining this objective he was authorized to conduct military operations north of the 38th parallel in Korea, provided that at the time of such operation there had been no entry into North Korea by major Soviet or Chinese Communist forces, no announcement of an intended entry, and no threat by Russian or Chinese Communists to counter our operations militarily in North Korea. He was also instructed that under no circumstances were any of his forces to cross the Manchuria or U.S.S.R. borders of Korea, and, as a matter of policy, no non-Korean ground forces were to be used in the provinces bordering on the Soviet Union or in the area along the Manchurian border. Similarly, support of his operations north or south of the 38th parallel by air or naval action against Manchuria or against U.S.S.R. territory was specifically ruled out.

The directive further instructed [that] "In the event of the open or covert employment of major Chinese Communist units south of the 38th parallel, you should continue the action as long as action by your forces offers a reasonable chance of successful resistance."[3]

Despite these instructions Truman remained reluctant to commit himself publicly on the question of moving north of the parallel, and on September 28th he indicated in the course of a press conference that he was not at liberty to say what the General's plans were.[4] However, it was reported two days later that the diplomats at the United Nations were in general agreement that MacArthur did have such authority: "In the absence of specific instructions to the contrary, United Na-

[2] Truman, *Memoirs*, II, p. 359.
[3] *Ibid.*, p. 360.
[4] *The New York Times*, September 29, 1950, p. 1.

tions diplomats said, General MacArthur has the power to decide on military terms for surrender—and the power to decide whether to order a crossing of the boundary line on the Thirty-eighth Parallel." [5]

On October 7th a formal resolution was passed by the General Assembly giving the Commander indirect authorization to cross the parallel and unify the country. This resolution was very much the product of American thinking. As we have seen, as early as the 27th of September Truman had told MacArthur (without specific United Nations approval) that he was free to move north of the line. The actual words contained in the text of the resolution had been chosen, for the most part, by Dean Acheson, with the approval of Truman. [6] As passed, the resolution's key provisions were:

(1) All appropriate steps be taken to ensure conditions of stability throughout Korea; (2) All constituent acts be taken, including the holding of elections, under the auspices of the United Nations, for the establishment of a unified, independent and democratic government in the sovereign state of Korea; (3) All sects and representative bodies of the population of Korea, South, and North be invited to cooperate with the organs of the United Nations in the restoration of peace, in the holding of elections and in the establishment of a unified government; and (4) United Nations forces should not remain in any part of Korea otherwise than so far as necessary for achieving the objectives specified in sub-paragraphs (a) [1] and (b) [2] above. [7]

It was at this time that Truman decided to go to Wake Island to speak personally to MacArthur. The General had been away from the United States for fourteen years, and Truman feared that his actions in the past months (particularly his great resistance to following executive directives) was an indication that he had "lost some of his contacts with the country and its people in the many years of his absence."

---

[5] *The New York Times,* September 30, 1950, p. 1.

[6] Neustadt, p. 124.

[7] *The New York Times,* October 8, 1950, pp. 1 and 6.

Truman saw growing signs that all of the General's thoughts were "wrapped up in the East. I had made efforts through Harriman and others to let him see the world-wide picture as we saw it in Washington, but I felt that we had had little success. I thought he might adjust more easily if he heard it directly from me." [8] At this conference the General assured Truman that neither Russia nor Red China would interfere in the war.

> Had they interfered in the first or second months it would have been decisive. We are no longer fearful of their intervention. We no longer stand hat in hand. The Chinese have 300,000 men in Manchuria. Of these probably not more than one hundred to one hundred and twenty-five thousand are distributed along the Yalu River. Only fifty to sixty thousand could be gotten across the Yalu River. They have no air force. Now that we have bases for our Air Force in Korea, if the Chinese tried to get down to Pyongyang, there would be the greatest slaughter. [9]

When Eisenhower came to write his *Mandate for Change* he defended the armistice that he signed ending the Korean War on the grounds that it was in line with the *original* aims of the United Nations. Very much aware that the goals of the war had been changed, Eisenhower reminded his reader that "Our nation and the United Nations went into Korea for one reason only, to repel aggression and restore the borders of the Republic of Korea—not to reunite Korea by force." [10] Yet for a time reuniting Korea by force was precisely the policy the Administration had decided to follow, and for a number of reasons: the temptations of the military victory at Inchon; the long-standing aim of the United Nations to reunite the country; Rhee's announced intention of restoring unity to his

---

[8] Truman, *Memoirs,* II, p. 363.

[9] Quoted in Richard H. Rovere and Arthur M. Schlesinger, Jr., *The MacArthur Controversy and American Foreign Policy* (New York, 1965), pp. 133–34.

[10] Dwight D. Eisenhower, *The White House Years, Vol I: Mandate for Change* (Garden City, 1963), p. 190.

nation;[11] the Democratic party's desire to exploit the September success in the November election; and Republican demands for a more aggressive policy.

It is the influence of the GOP's demands for more aggressive action that is of principal concern here. In the previous chapter Republican calls for an end to containment, a move north of the parallel, and the reunification of Korea were discussed.[12] An examination of this material forces one to the conclusion that given the storm of protest that issued forth from the policy centers of the party, it would have been exceedingly difficult for the Administration to ignore these calls for movement north of the line. Long-standing Republican complaints that the Democrats had not been sufficiently aggressive in Asia, that the initiative had been given by default to the Communists, and that all of this had resulted in a series of "disasters" that had confronted the United States in the Far East since 1945 were having their effects. Although it would be a mistake to overemphasize the influence that party critics had on the Administration's decision, with the success of the Inchon landing the GOP quickened the tempo of its demand for more resolute action. And too, because the 1950 elections loomed large in their designs, the party was anxious to identify itself with MacArthur and with his concept of victory through force of arms.

As in the past, many Republicans argued that Democratic foreign policy had practically handed Korea over to the Communists. In a national monthly, Representative Walter H. Judd of Minnesota outlined six familiar "mistakes" made by the Administration that allegedly led to the attempt by the North Koreans to conquer the South. Judd's list included the now-familiar GOP litany: granting to Russia at Yalta rights to Manchuria that were not ours to grant; the decision to divide Korea at the thirty-eighth parallel; our failure to build up a South Korean army; the 1949 withdrawal of United

---

[11] *The New York Times,* October 22, 1950, p. 1. This issue contains a letter by Rhee calling for reunification.

[12] See pp. 70–78.

States troops from Korea; Truman's January 5, 1950 announcement that we would not provide military aid to Formosa
(Judd said this was the greatest mistake of all); and Acheson's
"defense perimeter" speech.[13] Handley, who was seeking to
unseat New York's Senator Lehman (a particularly warm
supporter of Truman's policies) insisted that the United States
"invited" Stalin to attack the Republic of Korea,[14] and later in
the period Hickenlooper, fresh from an election victory in
Iowa, demanded Acheson's resignation, along with "a thor-
ough and extensive house cleaning of the whole State Department." Once again, this demand was based on the belief that
the "utterly unrealistic policies of the Administration and the
State Department with respect to the Far East was the cause
for the mess we are in." [15] Along these same lines, the *Times*
reported that the reason Senator Tydings was having such a
difficult fight in his bid for reelection was that as chairman of
the Armed Services Committee he was often held responsible
for the inability of the American forces to launch a truly
aggressive war in Korea.[16] (Tydings actually lost the election
in November.) This view was later echoed by Taft when he
wrote that the United States had received pitifully little fighting power from its investment of $50 billion for defense.[17]

Interestingly, in the weeks between the Inchon invasion and
the October 7th resolution of the United Nations there was a
definite lull in the Republican onslaught. One would suppose
that this lull came about because the Administration's decision
to back MacArthur's plans for the Inchon landing was interpreted as a sign that a new, bolder course had been taken. But
by mid-October Republican criticism was again being heard.
Truman's visit to MacArthur at Wake Island on October 15th
was undertaken because of the President's earnest desire to

---

[13] Walter H. Judd, "The Mistakes That Led to Korea," *Reader's
Digest*, November 1950, pp. 54–55.
[14] *The New York Times*, October 5, 1950, p. 27.
[15] *The New York Times*, November 23, 1950, p. 27.
[16] *The New York Times*, October 15, 1950, p. 32.
[17] Robert A. Taft, "The Dangerous Decline of Political Morality,"
Reader's Digest, November 1950, p. 154.

have his Commander understand the Administration's plans. Several Republicans, however, became convinced that the President's motives were political rather than strategic. Furthermore, it is clear that Republicans trusted MacArthur far more than they did Truman. Two days after the President's meeting with the General, Harold Stassen delivered a nationwide radio address expressing the Republican attitude toward the Wake conference. The Republican National Committee paid for the radio time.

> Any impartial observer must agree that General MacArthur is the best informed American with regard to the whole Asiatic situation. . . .

> Under our political system, no one person can really speak for the Republican party when it is in the minority in the National Government. But I am confident that I can speak for the Republican party in this one thing. If the President will place General MacArthur in supreme command of American military policy and interests in all of the Asiatic-Pacific area and will follow his advice, the President will have the united enthusiastic backing of the Republican party in this action.[18]

Stassen went on to suggest that the real reason Truman went to see the World War II hero was to help the Democratic party in November by "bask[ing] in the luster of this great military leader." [19] In a second nationwide radio address, Stassen first denounced Truman for not heeding the General's advice and then characterized the Wake Island trip as a "cleverly staged . . . political escapade to attain publicity for the campaign." [20]

Guy G. Gabrielson, Chairman of the Republican National Committee, charged that the primary reason that Truman went to Wake Island was not to "listen to this great general's views on the problems of our security in the Pacific," but rather to associate himself at election time with the victorious

---

[18] *The New York Times,* October 17, 1950, p. 6.
[19] *Ibid.*
[20] *The New York Times,* November 5, 1950, p. 38.

MacArthur.[21] Although the titular head of the GOP, Governor Thomas Dewey, did not openly charge that Truman met MacArthur for political reasons, he did indicate that it was the General's, not the President's, philosophy toward the war that he espoused. "I would hope that the President might adopt a firmer and more consistent policy [as a result of] an informative conference with General MacArthur." [22]

The General's maneuvering behind the enemy lines had clearly spread relief, hope, and encouragement in the United States, and the party was quick to respond. Senate Minority Leader Wherry forcefully expressed the new mood of the country when he told his colleagues that the tide of the war had turned. "The American armies in Korea, by the bold strategy of their commander, . . . have apparently turned the tide; they have transformed what appeared a humiliating defeat into a spectacular victory . . . the American soldiers, marines and sailors performed what may be described as a miracle." [23] Militarily, the landing at Inchon did initiate a dramatic change in the direction of the war, and the United Nations troops held their offensive position until they were overrun by a sneaker-clad Chinese army on the banks of the Yalu at the outset of a brutal Korean winter.

In all fairness to the GOP, it should be noted that the party's decidedly hawkish position was cultivated in a climate of widespread—though unwarranted—optimism concerning the imminent demise of the North Koreans. Truman recalls that MacArthur believed at this time that "the victory was won in Korea." [24] As early as September 23rd, a dispatch from Taegu declared that "The success of the United Nations arms in the last four days has about everyone in this city, from the general to the Korean houseboys, guessing how soon the war will end." It was also reported that "Most everyone asked feels certain that the Korean Republic will have been liberated

---

[21] *The New York Times,* October 27, 1950, p. 17.
[22] *The New York Times,* October 16, 1950, p. 18.
[23] *Congressional Record,* September 18, 1950, p. 14982.
[24] Truman, *Memoirs,* II, p. 365.

from the invasion forces before Christmas and many G.I.s have hopes of eating Thanksgiving dinner at home in the states." [25]

Later on, when increased resistance made it impossible for the troops to return home for Thanksgiving, there was a popular assumption—shared by MacArthur—that they would make it for Christmas. Not even the issuance of cold-weather clothing to the troops could dampen the near-holiday mood.[26]

The "Home-for-Christmas" spirit should have been deflated by the repeated warnings by Red China that that country would not sit idly by if non-Koreans crossed the parallel. In an official speech in Peking on September 30th Chou En-lai warned that the Chinese people "will not stand aside should the imperialists wantonly invade the territory of their neighbors." [27] On October 3rd the State Department began receiving messages to the effect that the Chinese were again threatening to enter the war. Chou-En-lai had told the Indian Ambassador to Peking, K. M. Panikkar, that if United Nations troops crossed the parallel China would help the North Koreans; but Panikkar also let it be known that if only South Koreans crossed the line China would not enter.[28] Viewing these warnings as "blackmail," the General Assembly passed the October 7th resolution that had been referred to in the above.[29]

Spurred on by the new aims of the General Assembly, the United Nations forces moved the war closer and closer to the Chinese border. On October 10th Wonsan was captured, and on the 19th Pyongyang, capital of North Korea, was in the hands of the United Nations forces. But as the Allies moved north, the Communist Chinese filtered south. At the end of October came the first signs of direct Chinese intervention: a

---

[25] *The New York Times,* September 24, 1950, p. 10.
[26] See Robert Leckie, *The March to Glory* (Cleveland, 1960), pp. 22–23.
[27] *The New York Times,* October 2, 1950, p. 3.
[28] K. M. Panikkar, *In Two Chinas* (London, 1955), p. 110.
[29] Truman, *Memoirs,* II, p. 362. See above, p. 82.

captured Chinese prisoner on the 26th, sixteen captured
Chinese on the 30th, and evidence on the 31st that a whole
regiment had crossed the Yalu by train two weeks earlier. The
first MIG-15's were encountered on the first day of November,
and in the early days of that month there were signs of
Chinese intervention everywhere.[30] On November 6th MacArthur sounded the alarm in a letter to the Joint Chiefs of Staff:
"Men and materiel in large force are pouring across all
bridges over the Yalu from Manchuria. This movement not
only jeopardizes but threatens the ultimate destruction of the
forces under my command."[31]

One of the most hotly debated points of the war is fought
over the question of why MacArthur, with clear warnings
early in November of Chinese intentions to intervene, stub-
bornly pursued his unification efforts. On November 6th he
was prepared to take the questionable step of sending 90
B-29's on a mission to destroy a bridge between Korea and
Manchuria across the Yalu River, but Truman instructed him
to postpone the bombings because he and the State Department feared the consequences in terms of massive Chinese
intervention. Outraged, MacArthur sent an urgent message to
the Joint Chiefs of Staff warning of the "disastrous effect, both
physical and psychological, that will result from the restrictions which you are imposing."[32]

To ask why the United Nations continued its offensive in
the face of growing evidence of Chinese participation is essentially to ask a dual question: why did Truman permit MacArthur to continue to move north, and why did the General not
heed the seemingly obvious warnings from the Chinese. Richard Neustadt's *Presidential Power* contains a fairly extensive analysis of the first question, and his conclusion is, in part,
that Truman gave MacArthur his way because he felt that
having placed him in command he should be supported as far
as possible. But Neustadt puts greater stress on the idea that

---

[30] For an account of this buildup, see Rovere and Schlesinger, p. 137.
[31] Truman, *Memoirs*, II, p. 375.
[32] Quoted in *ibid.*, p. 375.

Truman did not take the initiative in halting the General's advance because, at the urging of his advisers, he "tied himself to unification." MacArthur had done better than most had expected in the Inchon campaign and he might repeat this performance. Also, the Administration was unwilling to have it said that it was timidity in Washington, rather than aggression from Peking, which stopped the Far East Commander.[33]

Other critics of this aspect of the war have argued that while the "traditional freedom of the field commander to determine his own tactics," and MacArthur's victory at Inchon were factors in the Administration's decision not to interfere with the General, there were more compelling reasons. In particular it is believed that the President, the Joint Chiefs of Staff, and the National Security Council were "concerned lest their counter-order should arouse charges that the Administration was 'soft' in its policy toward Communist China and willing to cast . . . away the fruits of MacArthur's efforts." [34] In addition, since Inchon MacArthur's political stock had been on the rise while the Democrats' prestige, particularly after the November elections, was falling rapidly. MacArthur could count upon much congressional support at a time when the Congress was becoming increasingly skeptical of the President's handling of the war.

All of this leads to the question of the General's own decision to pursue the offensive. In his memoirs, published in 1964, MacArthur writes that "The danger was that by meeting naked force with appeasement we would not only perpetrate military disaster in Korea, but would enable Communism to make its bid for most of Asia." Still smarting under the restrictions imposed upon him by the Administration, the General continues: "This was a far larger, more complex, long-range problem than Washington seemed to comprehend." He continued to attack the British Labor government's suggestion that a buffer zone be set up between North and South Korea.

---

[33] Neustadt, pp. 143–47.
[34] Spanier, *The Truman-MacArthur Controversy*, p. 134.

Such a zone, he declared, would be "a signal to further aggression on the part of the Chinese." [35]

MacArthur reasoned that he had three alternatives: "go forward, remain immobile, or withdraw." His conclusion was that he could only choose the first of these alternatives:

> If I went forward, there was the chance that China might not intervene in force and the war would be over. If I remained immobile and waited, it would be necessary to select a defense line and dig in. But there was no terrain with natural obstacles to take advantage of, and with my scant forces it would be impossible to establish a defense in depth against the overwhelming numbers of Chinese. . . . If I withdrew it would be in contradiction to my orders and would destroy any opportunity to bring the Korean War to a successful end. . . .
>
> I concluded that the best "posture of security" was to go forward. This would deny the enemy the selection of the time and place of his attack, and the accumulation of additional forces from Manchuria. It would be simultaneously a mopping-up of the defeated North Korean force and a reconnaissance in force to probe the intentions of the Chinese. If our forward movement should prematurely expose Chinese involvement, my troops would have the necessary freedom of action to escape its jaws.[36]

In a 1953 statement issued in response to Eisenhower's decision to remove the Seventh Fleet from the Formosa Straits MacArthur insisted that he risked the advance to the Yalu because he believed it would enable him to bomb the Chinese supply lines in Manchuria if the Chinese Communists entered the war.[37]

It is now clear that the decision to move north after the Inchon success impelled China to enter the war. Neither China's desire to defend her hydroelectric plant on the Yalu nor pressures from Russia were the causes of her entry. What did induce her to intervene is bound up in a multitude of interrelated causes: her desire to preserve North Korea as a

---

[35] Douglas MacArthur, *Reminiscences* (New York, 1964), pp. 370–71.
[36] *Ibid.*, pp. 371–72.
[37] *The New York Times,* February 1, 1953, p. 7.

"Hello—U.N.?—"

Reprinted from *The Herblock Book* (Beacon Press, 1952)

political, rather than a territorial, entity; her hope of dissuading Japan from signing the impending peace treaty with the United States by showing Japan the potential of China's destructive strength; Mao's awareness that his prestige in Asia was at stake; and China's desire to keep the "imperialistic"

United States from further encroachments upon Asian territory.[38] To draw the conclusion from all of this that MacArthur
lost stature in the eyes of his admirers within the Republican
party because of his disastrous error in judgment is to fly in
the face of the available evidence. Later chapters will demonstrate the extent to which the charisma of MacArthur kept its
hold on the party. If, in the General's words, the conflict had
become "an entirely new war" with the introduction of the
Chinese troops, the party was never prepared to lay the blame
for this eventuality at its hero's door.

* * *

This is primarily a political history of the Korean War, and
so considerable attention must be paid to the way in which
the war influenced the outcome of the November 7, 1950
elections, and conversely, how the Administration's handling
of the war was influenced by the GOP victory. As was noted
toward the end of the previous chapter, while the Republicans
displayed some sincere, nonpolitical concern over the manner
in which the Truman Administration was conducting the war,
they were nevertheless very much aware of the potential
political effect of this explosive issue. Senator Lodge was at
best visionary when he wrote that a minority party must
"Appraise the past solely as a help in avoiding mistakes for the
future [and] make constructive suggestions for the future."
The role of the opposition toward the majority party, Lodge
continued, is "To support them when they are right and to
oppose them when they are wrong—to be the voice of con-
science though not of power." [39]

Though not the voice of power before the November election (or after, for that matter) the Republicans clearly aspired
to that position. The Korean issue in particular and foreign
policy in general were not the sole issues in the campaign. Yet
they did constitute very serious issues, as Taft noted when he

---

[38] Allen S. Whiting, *China Crosses the Yalu* (New York, 1960), pp.
150–61.
[39] *The New York Times*, September 17, 1950, Sec. 6, p. 58.

said that "People certainly cannot fail to see that the Democratic Administration has been in control of our foreign policy for the last eighteen years. How can they escape the results that have come from that policy?" [40] When Republican National Chairman Gabrielson was asked on September 15th if MacArthur's success at Inchon would greatly influence the campaign, he replied that it would not. "It still leaves the question of why we got into it at all. . . . The people will realize that it was the Administration's blundering and appeasement that brought it about." [41]

On balance one is led to conclude that Korea figured as a very substantial issue in the 1950 campaign, even though James Reston's thesis that Inchon had taken some teeth out of the Republican attack is often convincing. "Last time, sure of victory, they [the GOP] sat back on their fat prestige and were beaten. This time they counted heavily on the Korean War to bring them through and again they were robbed of a major issue by the successful Inchon landing, directed by their own darling, General Douglas MacArthur." [42] Reston also suggested that the electorate was less interested in Korea and Communism than in jobs, houses and new schools, and that the GOP's bark about foreign policy was far worse than its bite. "On the political stump they sound angry enough to make Senator Joe McCarthy Secretary of State, but in general they do not have the courage of their prejudices and do not really take their own campaign oratory at face value." [43] And too, a featured editorial in the somewhat conservative *Saturday Evening Post* complained that the GOP should have stressed foreign affairs far more than it did in the campaign.[44]

Yet Reston and his supporters seem to have underestimated

<hr />

[40] *The New York Times*, September 21, 1950, p. 17.
[41] *The New York Times*, September 16, 1950, p. 34.
[42] *The New York Times*, November 1, 1950, p. 39.
[43] *The New York Times*, November 4, 1950, p. 7. Also see *The New York Times*, November 1, 1950, p. 39 and *The New York Times*, November 3, 1950, p. 16.
[44] "Has G.O.P. Played Rough Enough to Win an Election," *Saturday Evening Post*, November 4, 1950, p. 10.

the extent to which the Korean War was an issue in this election. On October 15th a reporter covering the Myers-Duff senatorial race in Pennsylvania wrote that "Pennsylvania casualties, 1,509 at the beginning of the week, topped those of any other state. Republicans are making a big issue of the Korean war, linking it to what they hold are other failures of Administration foreign policy in the Far East. Their emphasis now is on this nation's unpreparedness at the start of the fighting." [45] In the bitterly contested California race between Nixon and Mrs. Douglas, the *Times* reported in mid-October that the debate over the Korean War had started a trend favoring the underdog Nixon. In South Dakota it was reported that the Korean conflict was "the top issue in the state, ranking above farm programs, highways, rural electrification and local problems." [46]

Truman did relatively little campaigning in the election, but on November 4th he delivered his sole campaign speech on behalf of all the Democratic hopefuls. On the same evening Harold Stassen addressed the nation in support of the GOP candidates. Stassen's major emphasis was clearly on the Korean War, although at the end of his speech he did mention inflation, the national debt, and the "soundness" of the record of the Eightieth Congress. The Korean War, Stassen said, was

> the direct and terrible result of five years of building up Chinese Communist strength through the blinded, blundering American-Asiatic policy under the present national Administration.
>
> It has been five years of coddling Chinese Communists, five years of undermining General MacArthur, five years of snubbing friendly freedom-loving Asiatics, and five years of appeasing the arch-Communist, Mao-Tse-tung.
>
> And the whole burden of redeeming the blunders in blood is thrust upon American armed forces weakened by a short-sighted, socialistically inclined national Administration . . .[47]

---

[45] *The New York Times,* October 15, 1950, p. 75.
[46] *The New York Times,* October 20, 1950, p. 18.
[47] *The New York Times,* November 5, 1950, p. 38.

MacArthur's letter of November 6th, charging that the Chinese Communists had intervened in the Korean War by crossing the Yalu, apparently gave the Republicans an eleventh hour boost in their attempt to parlay the war issue into an election victory. Reasoning (correctly) that the entry of Chinese Communist troops into the war would be a great political blow to Truman's party, Gabrielson charged that the Democrats were engaged in an "obvious attempt" to prevent voters from learning "that Chinese Communist divisions are pouring into North Korea, inflicting heavy casualties on our troops." [48] In line with this latest development, in the last hours of the campaign Senators Flanders, Ives, and Smith (N.J.), along with Mrs. Wendell L. Willkie, issued a statement condemning this nation's handling of foreign affairs. Our problems in Korea arose, they insisted, because the Administration's policy had been "dominated by a small willful group in the State Department intent upon appeasing the Chinese Communist revolution." [49]

From the beginning of the campaign *The Nation* was convinced that the GOP was attacking the war for purely political advantage. Reasoning that the GOP's plan to wage a campaign on the issue of Communism was destroyed by the Administration's strong stand in Northeast Asia, the magazine's editors saw that the party was faced with two alternatives. Either it could adopt the isolationist stance of Colonel McCormick, or it could decide to support "the fight passively, while aggressively attempting to fix the blame wholly and solely on the Administration." [50] Quite obviously they chose the second road.

With the November 7th returns counted, the Republicans increased their representation in the House by 28 seats and in the Senate by five. This compared rather unfavorably with the party's performance in the three previous midterm elections:

---

[48] *The New York Times*, November 6, 1950, p. 1.
[49] *The New York Times*, November 7, 1950, p. 17.
[50] "The G.O.P. and Korea," *The Nation*, September 2, 1950, pp. 199–200.

in 1938 the Democrats lost 71 seats in the House and six in the
Senate; in 1942 the majority party's loss was 45 in the House
and nine in the Senate; and in 1946 the GOP picked up 55
seats in the House and 12 in the Senate. While the party did
not win control of either house in 1950, they did add to the
luster of their victory by winning handsomely in certain key
races. For example, Dirksen toppled the Majority Leader and
Administration spokesman, Scott Lucas, and Robert Taft, no
friend of our foreign policy, won by 430,000 votes over Ferguson despite a monumental effort by the CIO to defeat him. In
California Mrs. Douglas, a consistent supporter of Truman,
was buried under a half-a-million vote margin for Nixon.
Maryland's Tydings, the influential chairman of the powerful
Senate Armed Services Committee, was defeated, and in Colorado Millikin, whose race was often spoken of as an index of
the degree of resentment in the country against the Democrats, triumphed over his opponent. By the same token, the
Democrats were not without their triumphs in 1950. There
was the reelection of both Senators Benton and McMahon of
Connecticut, Hennings' victory over Donnell in Missouri, and
Lehman's victory in New York after having been badly beaten
by Ives in 1946.[51]

U.S. News & World Report did a series of revealing inter-
views of the victors and losers, and from these statements we
can get some idea of the extent to which the candidates
themselves viewed Korea as an election issue. Taft, predictably, felt that the whole Democratic involvement in Korea was
a powerful factor in his election. "They've got us in a hell of a
mess—that's the general idea. . . . I would say that it's a vote
of lack of confidence in the Administration's foreign policy
primarily." [52]

Dewey, whose gubernatorial race did not stress foreign
affairs, nevertheless found that when he spoke of Korea at the

---

[51] See Gus Tyler, "The Mid-Term Paradox," *New Republic,* November
27, 1950, pp. 14–15.

[52] " 'Why I Won'—'Why I Lost'," *U.S. News & World Report,* November 17, 1950, p. 26.

end of his campaign, the topic aroused a good deal of interest. The Governor went out of his way to stress the need for "aid to, and a stronger policy in, the Orient." [53] In Pennsylvania, Governor Duff ran against incumbent Senator Francis J. Myers and defeated the Democratic Senator. When asked if there was any specific issue that aided him, Duff said: "It was the Korean situation. I think that the average citizen that thought about the problems felt that our Asiatic policy had been badly mishandled." [54] It was Richard Nixon, fresh from his triumphant California victory, who gave the most detailed statement of the effect Korea had on his campaign and election.

> I think the major issue in my race was the issue of the Administration's foreign policy in the Far East. It was particularly clear-cut in our race due to the fact that Mrs. Douglas from the outset defended the foreign policy in the Far East. . . .
>
> I, on the other hand, took the position that, while our policy in Europe had been successful and I supported it, our policy in Asia, by reason of the fact that it resulted in a war in Korea, had been unsuccessful and that we needed new leadership in Washington which would develop a strong, consistent policy in Asia.
>
> Over and over again . . . I pointed out that, had it not been for the fall of China, the Korean War would not have happened. I put it this way—that Korea would never have happened unless China had gone Communist because the North Koreans would never dare to move south unless they had a friendly government on their northern border. [55]

A balanced analysis of the meaning of the Republican victory in these elections would of course have to include a number of other issues that were raised by the GOP. Among these are the questions of domestic Communism, "creeping socialism," high taxes, and inflation. Taft, for instance, urged

---

[53] *Ibid.*, p. 27.
[54] *Ibid.*, p. 28.
[55] *Ibid.*, p. 29.

Americans to vote for the GOP if the country was to be saved from socialism.[56]

When *U.S. News & World Report* polled 200 candidates after the election in an attempt to determine the major issues in the campaign, they found that, in order of importance, the following issues predominated: coddling of Communists, policy abroad, war and its irritations, spending and taxes, labor-leader interference, high prices, and socialism.[57] This points up an important aspect of the election: while foreign policy issues occupied the second and third places in the survey, the number one spot went to the problem of Communism in government. An examination of the statements made by Republicans during the campaign testifies to the fact that a concerted effort was made to burden the Democratic party with this stigma. But it should be remembered that it was the setbacks in our foreign policy which led to calls for a "purge."

Having carefully cultivated this "conspiracy theory," it was certain that the GOP would exploit it in the election. Leonard W. Hall, Republican Representative from New York and head of the GOP's House campaign, charged at a fund-raising dinner that the Democratic party was in the control of "fuzzy-minded pinks," [58] and the Republican National Committee's candidates' handbook had as its central thesis the idea that a dark conspiracy was at the root of our international troubles.[59] McCarthy soon became the most sought-after speaker by Republican hopefuls (thus earning him the title of "Jumping Joe"). In October, McCarthy canvassed eight states on behalf of his Republican colleagues, and received 2,000 invitations to speak—more than all other senators *combined*.[60] Ironically, nearly five months after the Truman Administration committed United States troops to Korea, Taft told an audience that a Republican sweep would remove from power those who have

---

[56] Robert A. Taft, "The Dangerous Decline of Political Morality," *Reader's Digest,* November, 1950, p. 154.

[57] " 'Why I Won'—Why I Lost'," p. 33.

[58] *The New York Times,* October 1, 1950, p. 82.

[59] *The New York Times,* October 31, 1950, p. 22.

[60] "G.O.P. and McCarthyism," *New Republic,* October 30, 1950, p. 7.

shown "continued sympathy for Communism and Socialism." [61]

The most complete analysis of the 1950 congressional election is to be found in a comprehensive study edited by William N. McPhee and William A. Glaser. This work, published twelve years after that election, contends that while the 1950 race did not produce a unified Republican party, "it did strengthen the party as a whole and it did provide an impetus to the various factions who would compete for the presidential nomination at the 1952 convention." [62] The study further concludes that it was in this election that the New Deal majority was in its final stage of dissolution and that the results of the congressional elections foreshadowed the return of the Republicans to power two years later. "A shifting of leaders and of issues took place, and the result was a weakening of the national Democratic party and a strengthening of its opposition." [63]

Turning more specifically to the actual issues involved in the election, the McPhee and Glaser study concludes that 1950 was a time of testing and choosing of issues that would be used in later elections, and that it was at this time that the three great election issues of 1952—Korea, Communism, and corruption—rose to the forefront. "Because nearly all the victorious Republicans in 1950 had campaigned against Korea, Communism and corruption, and because later circumstances would underscore these issues further, these topics soon came to dominate American politics." [64] Hence while these students of the election are unwilling to identify Korea as *the* central issue in these 1950 elections, they do consider the war of major importance in the contest.

What, then, did the Republican victory in November portend for the future? The election results were proof to many in

---

[61] Robert Taft, "And If We Are Elected to Office," *Collier's* November 4, 1950, p. 51.

[62] William N. McPhee and William A. Glaser, ed., *Public Opinion and Congressional Elections* (New York, 1962), pp. 281–82.

[63] *Ibid.*, p. 274.

[64] *Ibid.*, pp. 277–78.

the GOP that there were no benefits to be gained from "me-tooism." These Republicans now felt freer to criticize Admin-istration policy, and the patched-over attempt to retain a bipartisan approach to foreign affairs became even more diffi-cult to sustain. If the liberal and internationalist wing of the party wished to continue to support the Administration, they would definitely be outside of the power center of he GOP. It was Taft and Millikin, aided by the "conspiracy group"— Wherry, Jenner, Malone, and McCarthy—and the pro-For-mosa group—Knowland, Bridges and Smith (N.J.)—who were in the ascendancy. To this must be added the fact that Senator Vandenberg, an internationalist who had been foreign policy leader of the Senate Republicans until illness forced him to leave the Congress, would no longer act as a balance against those who wished to limit American participation in world affairs. The strength of this anti-internationalist wing of the party can be gauged by the results of a nationwide poll of Republican state chairmen to determine their choice for the GOP Presidential nomination in 1952. Robert Taft won the "overwhelming" approval of this group.[65]

This limited upheaval within the GOP made it inevitable that the party's reaction to the Korean War would be affected. However, since the election occurred early in November (at about the same time that news was being received of Chinese infiltration into Korea) one must consider the possibility that part of this change in attitude *may* have come about as a result of the increased fear of full-scale Chinese participation in the war. By the same token, it should be noted that there was a definite lull in Chinese action from November 6th until the major offensive of November 25–27th, and that there was a good deal of confidence in the country at this time that Mac-Arthur's "Home-by-Christmas" offensive would be successful. As we have seen, this optimism was shared by Republicans.[66]

---

[65] *The New York Times,* November 12, 1950, p. 75.

[66] In addition to the material presented in the above, see Herbert Hoover, "Where We Are Now," *Vital Speeches,* November 1, 1950, p. 38.

Therefore, while one should remember that to an extent China's potential for upsetting the Korean applecart was on many minds, prior to November 27th it was primarily the election gains that were influencing the mood of the GOP.

Perhaps most important of all, the election results caused the party leadership to assume a harder line toward a possible peace settlement. Their historic attitude toward Asia, along with their belief that they had received a mandate from the electorate to oppose Democratic "weakness," led these Republicans to become increasingly hostile to Administration plans to wage a limited war for limited objectives. An indication of this change of mood can perhaps be gained by examining the way in which several Republicans spoke about an eventual peace settlement before and after the election. On October 1st, Stassen, speaking at a dinner of the General Society for the War of 1812, displayed a general willingness to go along with United Nations plans for peace negotiations. "It is right and it is wise that the administration and the terms of the Korean peace should be in the hands of the United Nations . . . Provided that their solutions shall be in the sincere interest of the future freedom and . . . progress of the people of Korea and not be used as a pawn in an appeasement deal with the Communist leadership of China or Russia." [67] Ten days later Dulles, considered by many to be the foreign affairs spokesman of the party, stated that he believed the "dominant elements" of the GOP would support the United Nations peace plan, part of which included a United States' sponsored proposal giving the General Assembly power to use armed force against an aggressor in the event that the Security Council failed to do so. (This resolution passed on November 3rd.) Dulles also announced that Governor Dewey had come out in favor of the plan.[68]

Yet after the election Knowland made it perfectly clear that his party would be most skeptical of any solutions for the war that were sponsored by the Democratic party.

---

[67] *The New York Times,* October 1, 1950, p. 66.
[68] *The New York Times,* October 10, 1950, p. 11.

Talk of seating the Reds in the United Nations is appeasement. Talk of establishing a neutral zone in Korea is appeasement. Waiting around for Mao Tse-tung to become a Tito is appeasement. The same people who told the United States Mao was only an agrarian reformer are now telling us Mao is a Tito. They are either badly misinformed or deliberately misinforming the American people. They are as wrong now as they were before.[69]

At a press conference the following day, Millikin declared that a successful bipartisan foreign policy was impossible until Republicans "are consulted freely and widely before final decisions are made." He also referred to past State Department policies as weeds that grow in the night, "Bad foreign policy weeds—Achesonian jackassery weeds." [70] But despite its enmity toward the Administration's program, there is insufficient evidence that the GOP had a meaningful alternative. There was still a glaring lack of positive proposals and a strong tendency to sit back and take issue with any Administration action that could be labeled appeasement.

❁　❁　❁

The crossing of the thirty-eighth parallel and the November elections were by far the two most important events in the ten-week period here under discussion. But two related issues, the perennial question of a seat for Red China in the United Nations and the debate over the security of Formosa, also occupied Republicans at this time. On September 19th the United Nations rejected both the Indian and the Russian motions to admit Red China into the world body. The Indian motion was the simpler of the two, for it proposed to admit Red China without mentioning Nationalist China. This was rejected by a vote of 33 to 16, with 10 abstentions. The defeat of the Indian motion was followed by a proposal by Russia to expel Nationalist China from the international organization. The vote was 30 to 10 against the motion, with eight absten-

---

[69] *The New York Times,* November 24, 1950, p. 4.
[70] *The New York Times,* November 25, 1950, p. 6.

tions. Russia then moved to admit Red China; this motion was also turned back, this time 37 to 13, with eight abstentions.

The day after the defeat of these motions, Knowland denounced the Administration's half-hearted handling of the proposals. "Our position is that we will vote against the rape of the Republic of China but will not try to influence others to the same course and that we will not use our veto when the matter finally comes before the Security Council." [71] Knowland was aided by Styles Bridges when the latter referred to a "blueprint" drafted by Acheson and the British Foreign Office to "arrange the entry of Communist China into the United Nations." [72]

> In Malik's first statement to the United Nations Security Council, he made clear that a settlement of the Korean issue could be made without the loss of a single American life if Communist China were admitted to the United Nations. That blackmail was righly turned down. Now, in the hour of triumph—after the loss of thousands of American lives and the payment in American blood of over 2,000 casualties—a blueprint for a grand sell-out is being carried out. [73]

This agitation surrounding Formosa, though long-standing, was intensified because of the decision of the Security Council to debate the Communist Chinese charge that in protecting Formosa, the United States was engaging in an act of aggression. On September 29th the Council passed a resolution stating that on the first meeting of the body after November 15th it would take up the Communist Chinese charge. It was also decided that a representative of Red China would be invited to the Council's meeting. The motion was passed by a vote of seven to three, with China, Cuba, and the United States voting in the negative. Passage of this motion, coupled with Bridges' warning that the State Department had a "blueprint" for the admission of Red China, led Republicans to

---

[71] *Congressional Record*, September 20, 1950, p. 15172.
[72] *The New York Times*, October 4, 1950, p. 10.
[73] *The Department of State Bulletin*, October 16, 1950, p. 609.

declare that Communist China would be admitted to the U.N. through the "back door," thus betraying Formosa. The ranking Republican on the Foreign Relations Committee wrote that ". . . this great sell-out now under way will jeopardize a bipartisan foreign policy. The State Department is giving away everything won by the blood of our youths and marks a major step toward turning Asia over to the Communists." [74]

Before and after the September 29th decision of the Security Council the Senate Republicans kept the Formosa issue alive. On September 20th, the "Senator from Formosa" charged that with British and French support, there was a plan afoot to make a United Nations trusteeship out of the Island.[75] Knowland was absolutely unrelenting in his pursuit of a proper role in world affairs for Chiang Kai-shek, and continued to call upon Acheson to accept Chiang's offer of troops so that the non-Communists of Asia could help combat aggression.[76] Visiting the island at the end of November, Knowland became even more vehement in his demands that Nationalist China be "unleashed" against the Communists on the mainland.

> I don't believe you can defend any island bastion if you allow a build-up to take place across the channel. Attacking the mainland would be more defense than aggression . . . if an invasion should take place the United States would take such action in cooperation with other free countries as required . . . Let the Reds guess what that means. Let them do some wondering for a change. But I should not remove the Seventh Fleet too far from the Far East.[77]

Bridges and Knowland were not the only Republicans who were assailing the Administration for its stance toward Nationalist China; Taft wrote in *Collier's* early in November that the government had failed thus far to adopt a consistent policy in its handling of Formosa. "In January, Secretary of

[74] *Ibid.*
[75] *Congressional Record,* September 20, 1950, p. 15172.
[76] *The New York Times,* November 7, 1950, p. 9.
[77] *The New York Times,* November 24, 1950, p. 4.

State Acheson ridiculed the proposal that we defend Formosa. In June, the President sent the Seventh Fleet to protect it. In August, he slapped down General MacArthur for suggesting that Formosa is of vital military importance in our line of defense in the Far East. Do we keep the Communists out of Formosa or don't we?" [78]

✿   ✿   ✿

The ten-week period from September 15th to November 27th was a time of great importance for the Republican party in their attempt to formulate a response to the Korean conflict. The party's favorite, General MacArthur, scored a dramatic victory at Inchon and temporarily turned the tide of the war. The thirty-eighth parallel was crossed, thus satisfying (for a while) those in the party calling for a more aggressive policy. Red China's attempt to join the United Nations was again foiled, and the GOP won a considerable, though by no means overwhelming, victory in the November elections. Finally, the Republicans, along with the rest of America, heard the shocking reports of Chinese hordes crossing the Yalu and slaughtering American troops. General MacArthur informed Washington on November 28th that Peking's entry into the war

> has shattered the high hopes we entertained that the intervention of the Chinese was only of a token nature on a volunteer and individual basis as publicly announced, and that therefore the war in Korea could be brought to a rapid close by our movement to the international boundary. . . . It now appears to have been the enemy's intent, in breaking off contact with our forces two weeks ago, to secure the time necessary surreptitiously to build up for a later surprise assault upon our lines in overwhelming force, taking advantage of the freezing of all rivers and roadbeds which would have materially reduced the

---

[78] Taft, "And If We Are Elected to Office," p. 51. For further evidence of the continued interest in Formosa and the Nationalists see H. Alexander Smith to George Gallup, October 31, 1950, Section IV, Box 105, Smith Papers.

effectiveness of our air interdiction and permitted a greatly accelerated forward movement of enemy reinforcements and supplies.[79]

The Republican party at last had at its disposal the weapons for a full-scale dissent. The most vocal elements within the party interpreted their election gains as an indication of widespread distrust of Administration policy. There was now proof of Truman's unwillingness to endorse MacArthur's plans to escalate the war. And finally, with the intervention of Chinese troops, there was dramatic evidence that once again Democratic policy had led to disaster in the Far East.

---

[79] *The New York Times,* November 29, 1950, p. 4.

Chapter 5

The New War

The entry of Communist Chinese troops into the Korean War late in November, along with their spectacular military success against the United Nations forces, was a great humiliation to the United States, whose men comprised 90 percent of the U.N. force. In the four-month period between the November onslaught and the dismissal of MacArthur the following April, the GOP hardened its resolve to oppose the Administration's handling of all phases of foreign policy and continued to use the Korean War for its own political advantage. But in saying this, one must recognize a deep division within the party itself on these issues. The bulk of the GOP, led by Taft, alternately called for both militancy on a scale advocated by MacArthur and withdrawal; decided that the Korean intervention was a monumental blunder; attacked the United Nations and our allies; and demanded at least a limited disengagement from our involvement in the defense of Europe. The more Eastern liberal wing of the party, headed by Dewey and Dulles, tended to move against the current of Mid- and Far Western predispositions (it was only as the 1952 elections neared that some of these Easterners, most notably Dulles, reversed their position).[1]

✿ ✿ ✿

It was not until early April that the United Nations forces, after suffering a humiliating retreat that nearly forced them

---

[1] See Chapter 8. It is, nevertheless, difficult to generalize about these matters because some members of the so-called Eastern wing of the party, such as Senator Smith of New Jersey, warmly supported MacArthur's proposals. For example, see "Memorandum of a Meeting between H. Alexander Smith and Ambassador Austin," December 27, 1950, Section IV, Box 101, Smith Papers.

off the southern tip of the peninsula, established and were holding an irregular line roughly corresponding to the old thirty-eighth parallel division. This line was achieved in the course of a dramatic sweep by anti-Communist forces down and then half-way up the peninsula. Within one week of the Chinese assault, the center of the United Nations line had retreated fifty miles to the south. By the 5th of December the United States Eighth Army was forced to abandon Pyong-yang, and on the 10th the First Marine Division, almost miraculously, broke out of a trap set for them at the Chosin Reservoir, thus freeing 10,000 men to join the X Corps in the march south to Hungnam. Still in retreat, between December 11th and the 14th the United Nations conducted a massive amphibious operation which moved 105,000 military person-nel, 91,000 Korean refugees, 17,500 vehicles, and 350,000 tons of cargo out of Hungnam, the evacuation point.

As the year ended, the Communists seemed certain of mov-ing south of the thirty-eighth parallel, and so on January 1st General Matthew Ridgway ordered a further retreat. Thus, on the 4th of January Seoul once again changed hands, and for the second time in the war was controlled by the Communists. This was perhaps the bleakest moment of this phase of the war; but while the United Nations continued to move south, by the 15th of January they were able to halt the Communist offensive. In good part this was accomplished because the United Nations supply lines shortened as those of the Commu-nists lengthened, making it increasingly difficult for them to proceed. In addition, United Nations air superiority over North Korea took much of the teeth out of the offensive. By the end of January anti-Communist troops had created a new line that ran from a point seventy miles below the parallel in the west to a point forty-five miles above the line in the east.

Despite the formation of this new division, Seoul remained in enemy hands until March 14th when, for the fourth and last time, it again changed command and was restored to Rhee. By the end of March the main elements of the United Nations forces had been reunited, and this is where the military situation of the war rested at the time of the MacArthur dismissal on April 11th.

One might expect that this terrible reversal, which sent the anti-Communist forces reeling south of the parallel, would have created within the GOP a considerable loss of confidence in the leadership of MacArthur. Nothing could be further from the truth, for the General remained a favorite of the party, and its members constantly berated the Administration for not taking his advice concerning the proper (and honorable) way to victory. The so-called "Truman-MacArthur controversy" centered around two divergent ways of handling the "new war" that was created by the Chinese intervention. MacArthur's view, put in simplest terms, was that the Administration, through the Joint Chiefs of Staff, had placed intolerable burdens upon him in his direction of the war against the Communists. To secure victory, MacArthur proposed that the United States Navy blockade the Chinese coast; that China's industrial centers, supply bases, and communication network be bombed from the air; that Chiang Kai-shek's offer of the use of his Nationalist troops in Korea be accepted; and that the possibility of a counterinvasion by Chiang against the mainland of China be at least considered.[2] The Commander thus rejected the idea that we were still engaged in a limited war, and suggested that we fight the Communists with every means at our disposal.

Truman, on the other hand, was by no means willing to abandon the idea that we were still fighting a limited war in Korea. Taking the position that policy changes had to be determined by the United Nations, inquiries were made (significantly only among those nations who had actually committed troops to the conflict) concerning the General's plans. It was found that the Allies were not willing to go along with MacArthur's proposals.[3] Aside from the opinion of the Allies,

---

[2] See the December 30, 1950 letter by MacArthur to the Joint Chiefs of Staff reprinted in MacArthur, *Reminiscences*, p. 379.

[3] Truman, *Memoirs*, II, p. 382.

Truman was personally in sharp disagreement with his Commander's strategy.

> I have never been able to make myself believe that MacArthur, seasoned soldier that he was, did not realize that the "introduction of Chinese Nationalist forces into South China" would be an act of war; or that he, who had had a front-row seat at world events for thirty-five years, did not realize that the Chinese people would react to the bombing of their cities in exactly the same manner as the people of the United States reacted to the bombing of Pearl Harbor; or that, with his knowledge of the East, he could have overlooked the fact that after he had bombed the cities of China there would still be vast flows of materials from Russia so that, if he wanted to be consistent, his next step would have to be the bombardment of Vladivostok and the Trans-Siberian Railroad! But because I was sure that MacArthur could not possibly have overlooked these considerations, I was left with just one simple conclusion: *General Mac-Arthur was ready to risk general war, I was not.*[4]

Despite its defense of its position, the Administration was seen as shortsighted and unrealistic in its continued determination to fight the war as a limited encounter when, as many Republicans saw it, the entry of the Chinese had transformed the conflict into a full-fledged war. Enthusiastically endorsing the General's request for permission to strike back at the Chinese, Senator Cain expressed the wish of the bulk of the Republicans.

> General MacArthur ought immediately to be given the right to strike wherever military necessity dictates, behind the Yalu River, or anywhere else . . .

> We are now at the war stage. We are at war in every sense of that word, and the euphonious language of the diplomats to the contrary notwithstanding . . .

> I think our troops ought to have immediate authority to strike at the supply lines, at the heart, at the marshalling areas, of the

---

[4] *Ibid.,* pp. 415–16. Emphasis mine.

enemy. Until that is done . . . we can only expect an accumulation in Korea of one disaster after another disaster . . .[5]

Several days later Capehart expressed his bewilderment over the Administration's insistence upon having the nation believe that the conflict was simply a "police action" rather than a war,[6] while Knowland, also belittling the whole idea of a police action, advanced a policy closely resembling MacArthur's. "Our strength is air and naval power. We should place, in conjunction with the Navy of the Republic of China, an immediate naval blockade against the entire China coast, and should not permit the entry or exit of a vessel of any nationality. . . . With air power we should strike at the war plants that are supplying the Communist aggressor." [7]

McCarthy was even more explicit in his support of the General's strategy, for he declared early in December that the Commander "should be immediately given the authority to hit the Chinese Communists wherever, whenever, and however he thinks it necessary so long as they are killing American men." [8] In a late December meeting with Warren R. Austin, the United States Ambassador to the U.N., Senator Smith strongly urged the bombing of North Korean and Manchurian factories and power plants. He also suggested that anti-Communist Orientals be employed in the fight against the Chinese Communists (it is obvious that Smith had in mind the use of Chiang's Nationalist troops).[9]

Even in late March, well after the Communist offensive had been halted, the General's ideas still enjoyed wide popularity. Hickenlooper made the following statement on March 30th: "Our forces in Korea are hampered terrifically by the insistence on the part of the State Department and the Administration that General MacArthur must not do what any military

---

[5] *Congressional Record*, November 28, 1950, p. 15940.
[6] *Congressional Record*, November 30, 1950, p. 15982.
[7] *Congressional Record*, December 4, 1950, p. 16199.
[8] *Congressional Record*, December 6, 1950, p. 16332.
[9] "Memorandum of a meeting between H. Alexander Smith and Warren R. Austin," December 27, 1950, Section IV, Box 101, Smith Papers.

commander has to do if he is to gain ultimate victory, namely, assault the enemy's sources of supply . . . [and] hit the enemy where he lives." [10] Two days before Truman's dramatic dismissal of the Commander, Malone declared that MacArthur had been "denied the right . . . of any field commander since the United States has been a nation . . . when a war is in progress, to win the war or come home with his troops. He must win it in any way he can, under the rules of warfare." [11] At the same time, Watkins, Knowland, and Thye introduced the following resolution to enable the Senate to obtain firsthand information from the General on the situation in the Far East.

> Resolved, That a special bipartisan committee of twelve members of Senate and House of Representatives of the United States be appointed to meet with General MacArthur in Tokyo, to solicit his views on strategy in the world-wide struggle against communism, including conduct of the United Nations effort in Korea, and to make such other observations and to conduct such other interviews in the area of the Far East as it may determine to be necessary and desirable, and to report on the same to the respective Houses of Congress. [12]

Truman's dismissal of the United Nations Commander two days later rendered the resolution meaningless. However on April 19th the GOP got its report from MacArthur—in the Capitol itself.

While the Truman Administration bore the brunt of Republican partiality for MacArthur's plan for winning the war, the United Nations, as the official agency conducting the anti-Communist effort, was under constant attack by the GOP for its part in this "disaster." There were essentially two reasons why these Republicans were hostile to the international organization: (1) the fact that it took the U.N. until February to brand Red China an aggressor in Korea; and (2) the fact that the United Nations, like the Democratic Administration, was

---

[10] *Congressional Record,* March 30, 1951, p. 3126.

[11] *Congressional Record,* April 9, 1951, p. 3629.

[12] *Congressional Record,* April 9, 1951, p. 3562.

hampering MacArthur in his execution of the war. Former President Hoover verbalized the first of these dissatisfactions when he declared that "It is clear that the United Nations is in a fog of debate and indecision on whether to appease or not to appease [the Chinese Communists]" [13] Taft, while in fundamental agreement with this aspect of Hoover's message, declared that the reason the organization could not make up its mind was that it did not have the power to deal effectively with aggressors: ". . . the United Nations has proved that it is not only an utterly ineffective weapon to check military aggression, but that it is actually a trap for those nations which rely upon it as an organization to secure action against aggressors . . . the veto power changed the whole nature of the organization and reduced the United Nations organization to a consulting body." [14] While these attacks were being launched, the United States government was seeking to revive a motion, tabled on January 20th, which would condemn Communist China as an aggressor in Korea. Finally, on February 1st, a resolution was passed by a vote of 44–7–9 stating "that the Central People's Government of the People's Republic of China, by giving direct aid and assistance to those who were already commiting aggression in Korea and by engaging in hostilities against the United Nations forces there, has itself engaged in aggression in Korea." [15]

The Republicans' second complaint with the U.N. was that it was not permitting MacArthur to attain victory in Korea, and thus had become, as Jenner put it, "a debating society death trap for American GI's." "[The] President of the United States today continues to serve as a puppet for the war-breeding, inhuman absurdity called the United Nations, while American GI's continue to fight, suffer, and die under inhuman conditions." [16] The martyrdom of MacArthur, in the eyes of his

[13] *Vital Speeches*, January 1, 1951, p. 166.
[14] *Congressional Record*, January 5, 1951, p. 61.
[15] *The New York Times*, February 2, 1951, p. 3.
[16] *Congressional Record*, December 13, 1950, p. 16675 and January 8, 1951, pp. 101–02.

Republican party supporters, is best brought out by an impassioned statement by Cain, who pictured the General as a tragic figure suffering because of the impotence of a defunct world organization. "As of this minute General MacArthur is as tragic a figure as is to be found in all history. He is required seven days out of every week to send his men forth to die without offering to those who fight the prospect of eventual victory . . . there is little ahead but frustration and futility." [17] As Knowland saw it, the solution for this intolerable situation was to cut the ties between the General and the United Nations, "permit strategic bombing . . . blockade the Chinese coast . . . and . . . free the hands of the Republic of China" —essentially the Commander's formula.[18]

Implicit in this insistence that the Administration follow the direction of MacArthur was the demand that anti-Communist troops once again move north of the thirty-eighth parallel. (It will be recalled that by the end of January some stabilization had occurred along a line that roughly approximated that of the thirty-eighth Parallel, although Seoul was still in Communist hands.) It is therefore not surprising to note Knowland's warning on the Senate floor that stopping at the parallel would guarantee to the Communists of North Korea "the opportunity to build up a Korean government north of the thirty-eighth parallel, and it will make military operations very difficult if this limitation is placed upon General MacArthur and General Ridgway. . . . The fact of the matter is that Korea cannot exist economically or politically if divided at the thirty-eighth parallel." It was later pointed out that with Korea divided the danger of another invasion from the north will always exist.[19] And too, Ferguson warned that even to debate the question of crossing the parallel was advantageous to the Communists.[20]

---

[17] *Congressional Record*, March 15, 1951, p. 2557.
[18] *Congressional Record*, January 11, 1951, p. 173.
[19] *Congressional Record*, February 12, 1951, p. 1245 and March 15, 1951, p. 2546.
[20] *Congressional Record*, March 30, 1951, p. 3117.

An important qualification must now be made concerning the party's response to the Chinese intervention. *It is patently contradictory but nevertheless true that at the very time that members of the GOP were expressing their willingness to have this government follow MacArthur to the brink of war with Peking they were advocating withdrawal from Korea.* At the root of this call for withdrawal was the growing conviction among party members that the United States had made a tragic blunder in intervening in Korea. The bipartisan support of June and July, the feeling that our "do nothing" policy toward the Far East had been reversed by Truman's decision, was rapidly vanishing. Secondly, the fact that the war was not being won in an absolute military sense, and (more importantly) the feeling that we had been abandoned by our would-be allies, triggered a strong desire to withdraw from Korea altogether. Both of these attitudes were most prevalent among Republicans from the Middle and Far West. There was little, if any, support at this time from Eastern Republicans for either the belief that American entry was a catastrophic mistake, or for the view that we should leave Korea.

Let us examine the contention that Truman should never have made his fateful decision of June 25th. The opening statement of this growing conviction was made by Taft in his first major foreign policy address of the Eighty-second Congress. Taft, it will be remembered, had reservations in June about the constitutionality of the President's actions, but was in general agreement with what had been done. Now he stated that we were "sucked into the Korean War, as a representative of the United Nations, by a delusion as to power which never has existed under the Charter. . . . The President simply usurped authority, in violation of the laws and the Constitution, when he sent troops to Korea to carry out the resolution of the United Nations in an undeclared war." [21]

When Truman pointed out in his State of the Union message of 1951 that "It is in the Far East that we have taken up

---

[21] *Congressional Record,* January 5, 1951, p. 60.

arms, under the United Nations, to preserve the principle of independence for free nations," [22] Jenner declared that the truth of the matter was that Truman had "blundered, tricked, [and] betrayed us into a war." [23] Carlson sided with Jenner, declaring that the "snap decision" by the President was the cause of our present difficulties." [24] Even more novel was Wiley's discovery that "Korea was a trap for us, of course; and I believe that we fell into it. I believe that the Russians purposely had their representatives keep away from the United Nations [!]" [25] Butler and Wiley were in firm agreement on this point, and the former declared "It is pitiful that we have not been properly supported in Korea by the other members of the United Nations, and *it seems apparent that the Korean incident was a carefully calculated trap* to employ American military strength far from home and farther from Europe." [26]

Equally interesting was a colloquy held between Watkins and Kem, during the course of which they agreed that if the question of sending United States troops into Korea had been submitted to Congress in June, such troops might not have entered the conflict. "At least there would not have been an impetuous, impulsive action, which resulted in sending American boys into Korea actually unprepared. Some Member of the Congress would have wanted to know what our state of preparedness was." Aided by more accurate intelligence reports, the Congress "could have anticipated what actually happened; we could have learned that China would ultimately come into the situation and that there would be a chain of events leading up to world war III." [27]

After his return from the Far East, Dulles made a broadcast to the nation on March 1st, in which he expressed his whole-hearted support of the United Nations effort and the support

[22] Truman, *Public Papers,* 1951, p. 10.
[23] *Congressional Record,* January 8, 1951, p. 101.
[24] *Congressional Record,* January 11, 1951, p. A97.
[25] *Congressional Record,* January 25, 1951, p. 714.
[26] *Congressional Record,* January 22, 1951, p. 515. Emphasis mine.
[27] *Congressional Record,* March 1, 1951, p. 1767.

given to it by the United States.[28] But the Dulles speech failed to stem the Republican criticism of our intervention, as Watkins' address to the Senate toward the end of the month indicates.

It is true that at first many of our people thought that the Korean intervention was a great action by our President. It seemed to show a great deal of courage and determination. It never occurred to our people, in their elation over an action that seemed to signify an end to a long history of appeasement, that the President's action was not entirely proper in point of law and that *it was a mistake both in policy and in fact.*[29]

The June intervention, warmly embraced by the vast majority of Republicans at the outset, had thus become "The President's gamble . . . which led to such disastrous results."[30] Coupled with this idea was the growing belief that since the United Nations and the allies would not permit the United States to conduct the war "the American way" (that is, MacArthur's way and the party's way) we should abandon the peninsula. In the closing days of the Eighty-first Congress, Malone argued that we should try first to win the war by using Chinese Nationalist troops and American sea and air power. Failing this, we should

completely abandon Korea and China—with all of its possible consequences and repercussions . . .

We can then establish our first line of defense through Japan, Formosa, Okinawa, Guam, the Philippines, Indonesia, New Guinea, and Australia, using ground troops recruited from *those* countries.

If all of these suggestions are discarded, then we can come home and defend the Western Hemisphere. We must be prepared to defend this continent in any case.[31]

---

[28] This speech reprinted in *Congressional Record,* March 2, 1951, pp. 1812–13.

[29] *Congressional Record,* March 27, 1951, p. 3002. Emphasis mine.

[30] *Congressional Record,* March 30, 1951, p. 3155.

[31] *Congressional Record,* December 14, 1950, p. 19719. Emphasis mine.

The next time this idea arose was in Hoover's so-called
Gibraltar speech (part of which was quoted above). "It is
clear," he said, "that the United Nations are defeated in
Korea. It is also clear that other non-Communist nations did
not or could not substantially respond to the United Nations
call for arms to Korea. It is clear that the United Nations
cannot mobilize substantial military forces." Hoover's solution
was not only withdrawal from Korea, but withdrawal to our
own "quarter of the world." [32] Even Wayne Morse, who at this
point in his career was quite friendly toward the foreign
policies of Democratic administrations, agreed with former
President Hoover's views on withdrawal from Korea! [33] Taft, at
least in early January, was not as willing as was Morse to
commit himself to such a sharp deviation from present policy,
although he did insist that we seriously consider the possibility of leaving the peninsula to its own fate. "I do not know
enough about the military situation to know whether we can
maintain our position in Korea, but certainly we should not
jeopardize our Army there to the extent of risking its destruction. It is far better to fall back to a defensible position in
Japan and Formosa than to maintain a Korean position which
would surely be indefensible in any third world war." [34] Later
in the month Taft became more explicit by saying that "Since
we can no longer rely upon the United Nations, it is obvious
that we cannot for some years hope to resist Chinese aggression in Korea, and it seems to me that we could retire as we
have already retired from Hungnam." [35]

Temperamentally less cautious than the Ohioan, Jenner
challenged his colleagues with the following taunt: "If the
Members of Congress have a shred of courage and patriotism
left, they will lay down an ultimatum to the President, demanding either a declaration of war or the bringing back of
American GI's to home shores." [36] Finally, Capehart and Lan-

---

[32] *Vital Speeches*, January 1, 1951, p. 166.
[33] *Congressional Record*, December 21, 1950, p. 17087.
[34] *Congressional Record*, January 5, 1951, p. 62.
[35] *Congressional Record*, January 23, 1951, p. 587.
[36] *Congressional Record*, January 8, 1951, p. 101.

ger were in basic agreement with Malone's idea that if we did not get the kind of cooperation from the United Nations and the Allies that we required, "we could completely abandon Korea and China." [37]

Despite this wave of Republican Senate sentiment for a general retreat from Korea, it would be a serious mistake to conclude that party members were ready to repudiate the entire Far East. If many were executing an about-face in their attitude toward the Korean War, their interest in Formosa and the fate of mainland China remained very much alive. It was, therefore, not surprising that the Asialationist group within the party hotly attacked a British proposal to engineer a speedy truce at the expense of making some concessions to the Red Chinese. In January the British Commonwealth Prime Ministers sponsored in the United Nations a resolution calling for a cease-fire to be followed by a conference between the United States, England, Russia, and Communist China to discuss the disposition of the island of Formosa and the question of Red China's admission to the United Nations. This resolution passed the U.N.'s Political Committee on January 13th by a vote of 50–7–1, with the United States voting for the proposal.[38] The Chinese Communists then made it doubly hard for the Administration to deal with this latest development by replying that such a cease-fire must be accompanied by the automatic transfer of Formosa to the Peking government and by the immediate assurance that Red China would be given its "rightful place" in the United Nations.[39] In addition, it was demanded that all foreign troops be withdrawn from Korea and that the Koreans be left to settle their own problems.[40]

In line with Republican demands for increased aid to For-

---

[37] *Congressional Record*, February 5, 1951, p. 990. Also see *Congressional Record*, January 11, 1951, p. 171 and *Congressional Record*, February 5, 1951, p. 1014.

[38] *The New York Times*, January 1, 1951, p. 1.

[39] *The New York Times*, January 23, 1951, p. 1.

[40] *Ibid.*

mosa, the Administration (in January and February of 1951) increased its appropriations for the support of United States troops on the island, and in March the Truman government reacted positively to a Joint Chiefs of Staff recommendation that a military assistance advisory group be established to aid Chiang. Later, $300 million in military aid was recommended, along with a Pentagon announcement that Formosa was sharing equal priority with Western Europe in the receipt of arms shipments. Finally, on May 18th the Assistant Secretary of State for Far Eastern Affairs, Dean Rusk, announced that "We recognize the National Government of the Republic of China, even though the territory under its control is severely restricted. We believe it more authentically represents the views of the great body of the people of China, particularly the historic demand for independence from foreign control. That government will continue to receive important aid and assistance from the United States." [41] This statement, coupled with later assurances given Chiang at the time of the MacArthur hearings that the United States would continue to strenuously oppose Peking's membership in the United Nations, put an end to a long-standing Administration attempt to cut its ties with the island.

The fact that the United States voted for the January plan linking a cease-fire proposal with Russian and Communist Chinese participation in a general Far Eastern "summit" conference was a matter of great consternation to many in the party. The following is part of a letter from Knowland to Dean Rusk:

A considerable number of us in the Senate have been quite concerned over the implications of the American support of the latest cease-fire proposal at Lake Success. As I understand the situation from reading the press dispatches, this latest proposal does not require the Chinese Communists to either get out of all

---

[41] Quoted in United States Congress. *Military Situation in the Far East.* Hearings before the Joint Senate Committee on Armed Services and Foreign Relations, 82nd Congress, 1st Session (Washington, 1951), pp. 3191–92.

of Korea or even to get back north of the thirty-eighth parallel before they participate in the conference. In addition, as I understand it, the nations which definitely will participate in the conference on the settlement of far eastern questions are the Soviet Union, Communist China, Great Britain, and the United States. It looks like a "packed jury." Great Britain has not only recognized Communist China but has consistently thrown obstacles in the way of having the United Nations declare Communist China the aggressor that she is.[42]

When Smith of New Jersey heard of the terms of the cease-fire offer, he proposed that the United Nations take a completely opposite course of action: brand Red China as an aggressor; have all nations now extending recognition to that country withdraw such recognition; and take military and economic sanctions against the Chinese Communists. These proposals were in line with a list of alternative approaches to our Far Eastern policy which Smith had drawn up in December. In this earlier list he called for the bombing of Manchuria, an economic blockade of Communist China, and the use of Chiang's troops in the Korean War.[43] The most complete statement of Republican opposition to this attempt to end the war was voiced by the party's strong man, Taft, while speaking at a meeting of the Ohio Society of New York.

> To admit that an outrageous aggression such as that of the Chinese Communists can be the basis for admission into the United Nations is not only an abject acceptance of American defeat, but it destroys the whole moral basis of the United Nations. To discuss the surrender of Formosa to the United Nations is a weakening of our entire military position in the Far East, a betrayal of the Nationalist Government of China, and a surrender of the only considerable armed force in the Far East which remains to oppose further Communist aggression.
>
> The proposal is even worse when we consider that the Nationalist Government is not to be represented in the conference, nor

---

[42] *Congressional Record,* January 15, 1951, p. 225.
[43] "Memo Re Possible Alternative Approaches to Far Eastern Policy," December 26, 1950, Section IV, Box 101, Smith Papers.

is the established Government of the Republic of Korea to be recognized.[44]

If the Administration's handling of the cease-fire proposal was denounced, it at least won praise for the new face of its Formosa policy. The extent to which these policy changes were in line with GOP designs can be determined by an examination of the demands made by Republicans between June and November (as outlined in earlier chapters). Yet even while adjustments were made in our Formosa policy, Asialationist Republicans were raising the ante. In a major foreign policy speech of January 5th, Taft voiced the belief that our anti-Communist policy should "involve the support of Chiang Kai-shek on Formosa and the providing of arms and other assistance which might enable him to defend himself and contest with the Chinese Communists in China itself at least until peace is made with them." [45] So great were Republican hopes that Chiang might be able to wrest power back from Mao Tse-tung that Millikin and Knowland had a serious discussion on the Senate floor about the possibility of United States participation in a Nationalist attack on the Chinese mainland. Knowland agreed that Chiang would need some equipment, but insisted that manpower was not needed, in part because of the Nationalists' own resources and in part because of his belief that "large numbers" of Americans and Britons would volunteer for Chiang.[46] Hickenlooper, also against sending American troops to aid Chiang, agreed that equipment could and should be sent.[47] Even Taft, who tended to be less militant, not only supported the idea of furnishing arms to Chiang, but declared that "If this brings war between the United States and the Chinese Communists, it is nothing different from what we now have—in fact, it would be a much less dangerous war to us, much less fatal to our men, and

---

[44] *Congressional Record*, January 23, 1951, p. 587.
[45] *Congressional Record*, January 5, 1951, p. 61.
[46] *Congressional Record*, January 11, 1951, p. 171.
[47] *Ibid.*, p. 172.

much less expensive in materiel." [48] Months later, in a letter to K. C. Wu of the Taiwan Provisional Government, Smith (N.J.) refused to endorse Wu's suggestion that the American navy and air force be used as part of a counterrevolution in South China. However, Smith did advocate the sending of war materiel to support such a counterrevolution.[49]

The depth of this increased militancy (often accompanied by a contradictory appeal for withdrawal from Korea) can be gauged by the party members' response to Truman's mentioning in the course of his November 30th news conference the possibility of America's use of the atom bomb. In answer to a question concerning America's response to the Chinese intervention, Truman told a reporter that "we will take whatever steps necessary to meet the military situation, just as we always have." When asked if that would include the use of the atomic bomb, the President replied: "That includes every weapon that we have. . . . There has always been active consideration of its use." [50] Within four days Prime Minister Clement Attlee was in Washington to receive clarification and assurances from the President. The official communique issued at the end of the Attlee visit had one paragraph devoted to the use of the atomic bomb. It read: "The President stated that it was his hope that world conditions would never call for the use of the atomic bomb. The President told the Prime Minister that it was also his desire to keep the Prime Minister at all times informed of developments which might bring about a change in the situation." [51]

But for months after Attlee left, many Republicans remained convinced that Truman had made secret agreements with the Prime Minister, promising that the bomb would not be used. Republicans voiced the fear that the Truman-Attlee announcement made it impossible for the United States to

---

[48] *Congressional Record*, January 23, 1951, p. 587.
[49] H. Alexander Smith to K. C. Wu, February 14, 1951, Section IV, Box 107, Smith Papers.
[50] Truman, *Public Papers, 1950*, p. 727.
[51] Truman, *Memoirs*, II, p. 413.

threaten to use the bomb, and reacted by the submission of a resolution (S. Res. 371—sponsored by Kem in the name of twenty-four of his fellow Republicans) which said in effect that any agreements made by the two heads of state should be in the form of treaties—as such they would be subject to Senate ratification—and not executive agreements.[52] The resolution suffered the fate of many such Republican moves: it was submitted to the Senate Foreign Relations Committee, never to emerge. This is not to say that the GOP (at this point) was demanding that the bomb be actually used in Korea. Relatively few (six) Republican senators even spoke on the subject in this period, and while Brewster did believe that MacArthur should be given the final say on its use,[53] Hickenlooper's statement on the subject perhaps best reflects the general note of wariness displayed by the party hawks. "I am not saying that it should be used or that it should not be used, but I say that is a matter for local, on-the-ground evaluation as to . . . the decisiveness of the results of the use of that weapon. Whenever it can be materially decisive for victory, I say it should be used. If it is not a decisive weapon, then undoubtedly there are other weapons which might be used, I assume."[54]

If there was a good deal of doubt as to whether or not the bomb should be employed, the Republicans were emphatic in their conviction that this should be purely an American decision. Typical was the remark that Truman "should make it clear to Mr. Attlee that we have no intention of giving him or anyone else a veto over the use of the atomic weapon. We are not going to be destroyed as a Nation, or permit a free world of free men to be destroyed, while someone else is passing judgment on whether or not aggression is really aggression."[55] This desire to have the United States make the major policy decisions concerning the running of the war was the product

---

[52] *The New York Times,* December 7, 1950, p. 1.
[53] *Congressional Record,* December 1, 1950, p. 16159.
[54] *Congressional Record,* December 8, 1950, p. 16514.
[55] *Congressional Record,* December 4, 1950, p. 16199.

of the deepening hostility toward both the Allies and the United Nations that was outlined in earlier chapters. While more militant Republicans such as Malone and Knowland continued to speak out sharply against the Allies, Kem perhaps summarized the feeling of his wing of the party when he said that the United States needs "friends with cool heads, not cold feet." [56]

* * *

Taiwan, then, was to be preserved at almost any cost, and Korea was to be either unified or abandoned. The growing conviction within the party's ranks that the Korean situation had been terribly bungled had considerable influence on what became known as the "Great Debate" of the Eighty-second Congress—a debate initiated by Truman's December 19th decision to send ground troops to Europe as part of this country's implementation of the North Atlantic Pact. On the surface, the issue concerned which branch of the government should have the final say on sending troops to Europe, but on a more profound level was the question of whether or not the United States should adopt a policy of neoisolationism. The results of the November elections (which the Republicans saw as a mandate for change); the humiliating defeat of MacArthur on the Korea-Manchuria border; and now the decision of Truman to take it upon himself as Commander-in-Chief to send American ground troops to Europe in peacetime touched off a monumental debate in the Congress and the nation. While Truman and most of the Democrats defended the move as a means of ensuring greater security for the United States and our allies, Republican spokesmen were outraged that an administration that (in the opinion of the party) consistently ignored the Far East in favor of Europe, should send troops to the North Atlantic countries at a time when a shooting war was in progress in Asia.

---

[56] *Congressional Record,* March 1, 1951, p. 1766. Also see *Congressional Record,* December 14, 1950, p. 16718 and *Congressional Record,* January 11, 1951, p. 166.

It is obviously not the province of this study to discuss in detail the intricate arguments surrounding the debate on the Truman plan to commit American ground troops to Europe; that is a book in itself. What will be attempted here is an examination of the means by which the growing resistance of the Republican party toward our participation in Korea greatly added to the determination of the party hierarchy not to let Truman have a free hand again in the execution of foreign policy. It has been noted that the growing opposition toward the Administration's Far Eastern policies was essentially formulated by Republicans from the Middle and Far West who provided the bulk of the opposition. This same general qualification should be applied to the analysis below.

Taft's January 5th foreign policy address had as its thesis the maxim that only a fool makes a mistake twice. Summing up one section of his remarks, Taft said "What I object to is undertaking to fight that battle [against Communism] primarily on the vast land areas of the continent of Europe or the continent of Asia where we are at the greatest possible disadvantage in a war with Russia. . . . We could not have a better lesson than has been taught us in Korea." [57] Another party spokesman, Minority Leader Wherry, declared "Before us in Korea we have an immediate object lesson. We are hopelessly outnumbered, and we are compelled to take appalling losses. But these Korean losses are almost negligible compared to what we would suffer if our ground forces received the full weight of the Red Army in Europe." [58] Several days later Watkins, a close follower of Wherry in these matters, stated his opposition to the sending of troops on constitutional grounds, but beneath the surface of his demands lurked the spirit of Korea.

> The President is waging war in Korea. It is an undeclared war into which the United States has been taken by the unilateral action of the President without consulting the Congress. The

---

[57] *Congressional Record*, January 5, 1951, p. 61.
[58] *Congressional Record*, January 16, 1951, p. 341.

President's action . . . is an outright violation of the letter and the spirit of the Constitution of the United States. . . .

I say to the Senate in all seriousness that if the President is now permitted to order American armies into Europe without consulting Congress, we will wake up one of these days and find that we have again been taken into all-out large-scale war on the order of the President in violation of the spirit as well as the letter of the Constitution.[59]

Some, like Capehart, turned the argument around, stating that the failure of the Allies to aid us in Korea was proof that even if we did send forces to protect Western Europe, Europe would not rouse itself from its lethargy and aid us in our attempt to save the continent from Soviet domination. Wiley and Cain shared his conviction that the European leaders would sit back and let America supply the bulk of their defense. And fearing a repetition of our experience in Korea with the Allies, Knowland suggested that if troops are sent to Europe, ratios should be established indicating the number of divisions Europe would supply for each Yankee division.[60]

Another reason the GOP reacted adversely to the announced troop commitment to Europe was its lack of confidence in Truman himself. Watkins statement of this mistrust was quite representative:

I have felt all along that it would be dangerous to permit the President to continue asserting his power to do these things, because no one would know in the future what he might do next. The President has shown a disposition to be very impulsive in his actions. I think the action in Korea was the result of an impulsive rather than a considered judgment. I think it would be very dangerous and unsafe under the present circumstances to acquiesce in the President's contention that he has the power to do these things. I think it is unsafe any time, and I think it is illegal any time, for him to do it; but under the

---

[59] *Congressional Record*, January 22, 1951, p. 537.
[60] *Congressional Record*, March 19, 1951, p. 2671. Also see *Congressional Record*, February 8, 1951, p. 1168 and *Congressional Record*, March 7, 1951, pp. A1307–08.

peculiar circumstances of today, in view of the way the President has been acting, I think it would be highly dangerous as a matter of fact.[61]

This attitude was supported by a Gallup poll published on April 3rd. Gallup, who at this time directed the American Institute of Public Opinion, undertook an analysis of the response of Americans to the following question: "At the present time, do you think Congress should have the right to limit the number of troops which can be sent to Europe or do you think the number of troops which can be sent should be left up to the President and his advisers?" The results were:

Congress..........	58 percent
President..........	31 percent
Both..............	1 percent
No opinion........	10 percent
Total	100 percent [62]

While these raw scores are enlightening, Gallup's evaluation of these results supports the idea that Korea greatly influenced the party's hostility to further troop commitments to Europe.

Taft's position is that if there is no limit on the Presidential power to dispatch troops abroad, it would "practically destroy the power of Congress over foreign relations."

He and other Republicans charge that Mr. Truman's own action in sending troops to Korea last summer was arbitrary and not well thought out.

The Korean episode may, in fact, have a bearing on the public's apparent wish to have Congress act as watchdog on the troops issue.

In January and again in February the weight of opinion, as measured in institute surveys, was that our entry into the Korean War was a mistake.[63]

---

[61] *Congressional Record,* March 29, 1951, p. 3085.
[62] Reprinted in *Congressional Record,* April 2, 1951, p. 3173.
[63] Reprinted in *ibid.*

While a full-scale analysis of the GOP's attitude toward Europe will not be attempted in this chapter, certain key events in the Great Debate will be outlined to suggest the pattern of Republican thought at this time. It must be remembered that a deep cleavage did exist in the party: *of the various possible philosophies regarding American participa-*

"See Any Knaves Approaching The Moat, Sire?"

Reprinted from *The Herblock Book* (Beacon Press, 1952)

tion in world affairs, Republicans ranged over a broad area which was bounded by Hoover's concept of the creation of a Gibraltar of the Western Hemisphere, to the desire of a small group of Eastern Republicans (particularly Dewey) for wide participation in world affairs. Having said this, one must nevertheless conclude that the Republican party as a whole was clearly moving toward a more isolationist position. The bipartisan support of such Democratic foreign policies as the Truman Doctrine, Marshall Plan and NATO was clearly undermined by what the Republican majority considered to be the fiasco in the Far East.

The internationalists, nevertheless, did try to influence their party's attitude toward our worldwide commitments and deplored the party's isolationist tendencies toward Europe. In the course of a speech to the New York County Lawyers Association in mid-December, Governor Dewey made a dramatic appeal for the strengthening of American military might, placing his emphasis on the need for ground troops. "In a world of brute force, there is freedom only for the brave. If we are not prepared to fight for our freedom, then we shall surely lose it. If we are prepared to fight, we still could win. . . . We may even hope to bring Russia to her senses and to bring peace to the world." [64] Again on the 11th of February the Governor supported the belief that it was up to the President and his advisers to decide where troops should be sent, since this was "a job for experts and not for politicians." Yet he did concede the obvious fact that Congress constitutionally had "absolute power" over how many troops should be raised, the total number of troops, and the allocation of funds for their support. Dewey expressed the belief that the rise of isolationism in the United States would encourage Stalin in his designs and would lead the European nations to remain neutral in a possible war between the U.S.S.R. and the United States. [65]

---

[64] *Vital Speeches,* January 1, 1951, p. 168.
[65] *The New York Times,* February 12, 1951, p. 8.

Truman sent General Eisenhower to Europe in January to determine the extent of the need for American ground forces, and on February 1st, when the enormously popular (and at this time apparently nonpartisan) general returned, he made a series of recommendations to a joint meeting of the Congress. These included: (1) that no congressional limitation be placed on the number of troops the United States could send to Europe; (2) that the Congress not attempt to establish a ratio between the number of divisions Europe had in the field and the number America would send; (3) that the United States begin sending to Western Europe military equipment on a scale comparable to that delivered under the World War II lend-lease program.[66]

A powerful Republican voice advocating the cause of internationalism against the mainstream of his party was that of John Foster Dulles, who declared at a meeting of the American Association for the United Nations that

> It is possible to plan, on paper, and describe in words, what it seems should be an impregnable defense, a China Wall, a Maginot Line, a Rock of Gibraltar, an Atlantic and Pacific Moat. But the mood that plans such a defense carries within itself the seeds of its own collapse. A defense that accepts encirclement quickly decomposes. That has been proved a thousand times.

> A United States which could be an inactive spectator while the barbarians overran and desecrated the cradle of our Christian civilization would not be the kind of a United States which could defend itself. . . .

> Around the rim of the captive world the free world can create enough economic and political vigor, enough military strength and enough will to resist so that these areas cannot be cheaply conquered by subversive methods, by trumped up "civil wars" or even by satellite attacks.[67]

In addition to these personal statements made by some leading GOP members, one finds that in vote after vote taken

---

[66] *Vital Speeches,* February 15, 1951, pp. 258–62.
[67] *The New York Times,* December 30, 1950, p. 4.

in the upper chamber Eastern Republicans like Aiken, Brewster, Duff, Flanders, Ives, Lodge, Saltonstall, Smith (N.J.), and Tobey supported those measures which advocated participation in European affairs, rather than withdrawal from them. This group, obviously, was not convinced that the Korean venture was such a disaster or that it was reason to terminate their party's cooperation with the Democrats.

Despite these efforts, the more isolationist-minded of he party would not be moved. The initial, and perhaps most famous, reaction to Truman's December 19th decision to send additional troops to Europe was former President Hoover's speech delivered the following day. In this address the former Chief Executive called for the creation of a hemispheric Gibraltar through the application of our air and naval forces: "The foundation of our national policies must be to preserve for the world this Western Hemisphere Gibraltar of western civilization. . . . We can, without any measure of doubt, with our own air and naval forces, hold the Atlantic and Pacific Oceans with one frontier on Britain (if she wishes to cooperate), the other on Japan, Formosa and the Philippines . . ." He further asserted that it would be a great mistake to assume Europe's responsibilities for her own defense.

> The prime obligation of defense of western continental Europe rests upon the nations of Europe. The test is whether they have the spiritual force, the will, and acceptance of unity among them by their own volition. America cannot create their spiritual forces; we cannot buy them with money. . . . To warrant our further aid they should show they have spiritual strength and unity to avail themselves of their own resources. But it must be far more than pacts, conferences, paper promises, and declarations. Today it must express itself in organized and equipped combat divisions of such huge numbers as would erect a sure dam against the Red flood. And that before we land another man or another dollar on their shores. Otherwise we shall be inviting another Korea. That would be a calamity to Europe as well as to us.[68]

---

[68] *Vital Speeches,* January 1, 1951, p. 166.

The next significant step in the attempt to formulate a Republican policy was Senator Taft's major speech on foreign affairs to the new Eighty-second Congress. In this speech Taft did not go as far as Hoover in advocating an almost total withdrawal from our global commitments, but he did suggest a greatly reduced participation in world affairs—and a participation of an entirely different nature.

> It seems obvious that the immediate problem of defending this country depends upon control of the sea and control of the air. . . .
>
> A land army is also necessary for the defense of air bases, further defense of islands near the continental shores, and for such occasional extensions of action into Europe or Asia as promise success in selected areas. But it need not be anything like as large an army as would be necessary for a land war on the continent of Europe or the continent of Asia. . . .
>
> We must not assume obligations by treaty or otherwise which require any extensive use of American land forces . . . we should be willing to assist with sea and air forces any island nations which desire our help. Among those islands are Japan, Formosa, the Philippines, Indonesia, Australia, and New Zealand; on the Atlantic side, Great Britain, of course. . . .[69]

The Republican reaction to Taft's concept of what our foreign policy should be emphasizes the nature of the Republican split. With the exception of Morse, it was the Easterners who objected to Taft's speech: Saltonstall, Lodge, Dulles, and Duff. Those who spoke in favor of Taft's policy were Carlson, Millikin, Knowland, and Kem.[70]

The third step in the development of a stance against Truman's plans for Europe's defense was the so-called "Wherry Resolution" introduced by the Minority Leader on January

[69] *Congressional Record,* January 5, 1951, pp. 60–64.

[70] *Ibid.,* p. 70; *Congressional Record,* January 11, 1951, pp. 160–61, 167, and A97; *Congressional Record,* January 16, 1951, p. 351; *Congressional Record,* February 27, 1951, pp. A1033–34; and *Congressional Record,* March 1, 1951, p. 1768.

8th. This resolution (S.Res. 8), clearly expressing that aspect of Republican thought which desired to circumscribe Truman's power to commit the United States to a situation that might lead to further warfare, stated: "Resolved, That it is the sense of the Senate that no ground forces of the United States should be assigned to duty in the European area for the purposes of the North Atlantic Treaty pending the formulation of a policy with respect thereto by the Congress." [71] Once again, we have the familiar division, with Carlson, Mundt, Butler, Ferguson and Taft speaking in favor of this motion and Saltonstall, Lodge, and Ives opposed.[72]

The Wherry Resolution, proposed early in January, was submitted for consideration to two Senate committees: Connally's Foreign Relations Committee and Russell's Armed Services Committee. On March 14th these committees reported back to the Congress two substitute versions of the Wherry proposal; these substitutes were identical except that one (S.Res 99 of the Foreign Relations Committee) prefaced each paragraph with "it is the sense of the Senate," while the other (S.Con.Res. 18 of the Armed Services Committee) replaced that wording with "it is the sense of the Congress." By far the most controversial of the seven-paragraph document was paragraph six:

> it is the sense of the Senate that, in the interests of sound constitutional processes, and of national unity and understanding, congressional approval should be obtained of any policy requiring the assignment of American troops abroad when such assignment is in implementation of article 3 of the North Atlantic Treaty; and the Senate hereby approves the present plans of the President and the Joint Chiefs of Staff to send four additional divisions of ground forces to Western Europe.[73]

---

[71] *Congressional Record*, January 8, 1951, p. 98.
[72] *Congressional Record*, January 11, 1951, p. A98 and 157; *Congressional Record*, January 16, 1951, p. 341; *Congressional Record*, January 17, 1951, pp. 397–98; *Congressional Record*, January 22, 1951, p. 515 and 547; *Congressional Record*, January 23, 1951, p. 572, 578.
[73] *Congressional Record*, March 14, 1951, p. 2436.

An enormous amount of Senate time was devoted to an interpretation of the meaning of this paragraph, although everyone knew that regardless of interpretations, the resolution had no legal binding force that could restrain the President—it was simply an expression of what the Senate wished him to do. Yet the debate raged. On one end of the spectrum was Wiley's clear-cut interpretation that the paragraph meant that "the President should not send further troops to Europe, above and beyond the contemplated four divisions, without action by Congress." [74] But for Smith of New Jersey it was a much more complicated directive, one which meant that congressional approval was needed only if a *policy* change were made by the Executive, since within certain limits the sending of troops to Europe would *not* constitute a policy change. The Foreign Relations Committee member did not approve of the Wherry Resolution and wished to replace it with a motion calling upon Congress to: specifically approve the sending of the four divisions; give up its plan of fixing a ratio between American and European troops; and set up a sixteen-member bipartisan committee to make policy recommendations. He also called upon the President to consult with Congress before further troop commitments are made.[75]

Because of this conflict in interpretation, and because of considerable Republican determination to express clearly their belief that Congress should play a strong role in deciding this troops-to-Europe question, Republican suspicion of paragraph six was not quelled until passage of the McClellan Amendment on April 2nd. This amendment stated that "it is the sense of the Senate that no troops in addition to such four divisions should be sent to Western Europe in implementation of the North Atlantic Treaty without further senatorial approval." [76] This was the guarantee that Republicans were waiting for, and the amendment, facing stiff Democratic opposition (de-

---

[74] *Congressional Record*, March 16, 1951, p. 2624.

[75] "Salient features of proposal by Senator Smith of New Jersey on a substitution for the Wherry Resolution," March 1, 1951, Section IV, Box 108, Smith Papers.

[76] *Congressional Record*, April 2, 1951, p. 3170.

spite its sponsor) passed by a vote of 49 to 43. The only Republicans voting against the proposal were from the East: Aiken, Duff, Flanders, Ives, Lodge, Saltonstall, Smith (N.J.), and Tobey.[77] Two days after the passage of the McClellan Amendment the Senate was able to take a vote on Senate Resolution 99; the tally was 69 yeas, 21 nays, and six not voting. The amendment was undoubtedly responsible for the fact that approximately half of the Republicans (Taft among them) voted for the resolution. Fourteen of the fifteen Eastern Republicans (Williams of Delaware was the exception) voted with the Democrats for passage of the measure. The opposition came primarily from the Republicans from the Middle and Far West.[78]

A good deal of stress has been placed thus far on the idea that recent foreign policy "failures," particularly in Korea, were responsible for this upsurge of neoisolationism within the party. While it is true that this factor must be emphasized, another—namely the great interest among Republican party members in fiscal economy—was a powerful factor in determining their attitude toward U.S. involvement in world affairs. Republican interest in economy was quite pronounced in the November to April period, and it is interesting to note that in several of their statements linking fiscal responsibility to military spending, Republicans quoted various parts of Washington's Farewell Address, which warned against the dangers of overgrown military establishments. Yet one finds the following two sentences in the address that the GOP budget-watchers seem not to have noticed: "As a very important source of strength and security, cherish public credit. One method of preserving it is to use it as sparingly as possible, avoiding occasions of expense by cultivating peace, *but remembering also that timely disbursements to prepare for danger frequently prevent much greater disbursements to repel it . . .*"

---

[77] *Ibid.*, p. 3178. See Appendix, pp. 294–296.
[78] *Congressional Record*, April 4, 1951, p. 3382. See Appendix, pp. 296–298.

Both Hoover and Taft agreed in their major policy speeches outlined in the above that emphasis should be taken away from the use of ground forces and placed on the air force and the navy. Their economic motivation for this is clear, for as the former President said, "We could, after initial outlays for more air and Navy equipment, greatly reduce our expenditures, balance our budget, and free ourselves from the dangers of inflation and economic degeneration." [79] The Ohioan was very interested in this same problem. "The key to all the problems before this Congress lies in the size of our military budget. That determines the taxes to be levied. It determines the number of boys to be drafted. It is likely to determine whether we can maintain a reasonably free system and the value of our dollar, or whether we are to be weakened by inflation and choked by Government controls which inevitably tend to become more arbitrary and unreasonable." [80]

Republicans generally operated on the premise that the funds and manpower of the United States were strictly limited resources, and that the expenditure of these items must be undertaken with the greatest of care. Bricker, for example, was sure that we were overextending ourselves: ". . . the Acheson containment plan involves policing the 20,000 mile Soviet perimeter with American ground forces. It would bleed us white both physically and financially." [81] Another Republican who had become convinced that the Administration was derelict in the formulation of a financially feasible military policy was Ecton. "So far as I can discern, there is no plan [for defense and peace] other than to tax and tax and spend and spend and use American sons to police the wide world." [82]

With their obvious desire for a cut in expenditures, particularly those being used for defense, these Republicans were outraged by the announcement of Truman's $71,594,000,000 budget for fiscal 1952. Nor were they heartened by the Presi-

---

[79] *Vital Speeches,* January 1, 1951, p. 166. Emphasis mine.
[80] *Congressional Record,* January 5, 1951, p. 64.
[81] *Congressional Record,* February 26, 1951, p. 1582.
[82] *Congressional Record,* March 28, 1951, p. 3043.

dent's assurances that while receipts for the period were expected to be slightly over $55 billion, the $16½ billion deficit
would be covered in the form of tax increases.[83] New Hampshire's Styles Bridges quipped after hearing the terms of the
proposed budget that it reminded him of Mark Twain, who
"once made a New Year's resolution. He said in the resolution,
'This year I am going to live within my income, even if I have
to borrow money to do it.' That is typical of the Truman
approach to the budget." [84]

❋   ❋   ❋

In all, the four-month period between the Chinese intervention and MacArthur's dismissal was honeycombed with issues
that might well be used against the Democrats in the next
Presidential election. Taft, in an address to the Republican
Club of the District of Columbia in January, was very candid
in voicing his expectation that the foreign policy question
might very well determine the election outcome the following
year.

> Now is the time for all Republicans to begin to plan the
> campaign of 1952 and the best way to start is to find the reasons
> for some of the huge majorities in many States in 1950.

> I believe the decision last November was probably more af-
> fected by the concern of the people over the foreign policy of
> the United States and that in 1952 also, that may well be the
> determining factor. . . . The interest of this Congress, and very
> likely that of the people in 1952, is centered on this problem of
> meeting the threat of Communist aggression.[85]

Taft's confidence was echoed by liberal-internationalist and
conservative-isolationist Republicans. Alexander Smith wrote
to a friend in December that he had high hopes that the gains

---

[83] *The New York Times,* January 16, 1951, p. 1.
[84] *Congressional Record,* January 23, 1951, p. 587.
[85] *Congressional Record,* February 1, 1951, p. A527.

made by his party in 1950 could be parlayed into a Republican Presidential victory.[86] At a Lincoln Day address Wiley promised that just as the Republicans had rescued the nation from a great crisis at the time of the formation of the party, it would do so again in the coming election,[87] and Knowland optimistically predicted that "Nineteen hundred and fifty-two is the year for the American people to get rid of both red ink and red herrings." [88]

---

[86] H. Alexander Smith to R. Stuyvesant Pierrepont, December 21, 1950, Section IV, Box 105, Smith Papers.

[87] *Congressional Record,* February 15, 1951, p. A809.

[88] *Congressional Record,* February 19, 1951, p. A854.

Chapter 6

The President, the General, and the GOP

The period generally characterized as the Great Debate came to an unofficial end on April 4, 1951 with the successful passage of Senate Resolution 99—the "troops-to-Europe" resolution. Any hope of a renewal of bipartisan support for the Administration's handling of the war, however, was doomed by the furor that accompanied President Truman's dismissal of General MacArthur exactly one week later. It has been noted in earlier chapters that MacArthur responded to the pressures of fighting the Korean War by rejecting the very concept of a limited war while calling for total victory against the enemy. More specifically, he asked for a naval blockade, air strikes against the Chinese Communist mainland, and the use of Nationalist Chinese troops in Korea. The Administration (somewhat self-righteously in the light of its unfortunate decision to move to the Yalu after the General's success at Inchon) insisted that we had entered the Korean conflict to protect and preserve the political and territorial sovereignty of the Republic of Korea against the attacks from the Communist north. The intervention of the Chinese into the war had thus caused Truman to quickly revert to his original goal of preserving South Korea from aggression.

This clash of attitudes was in evidence from the early months of the war. The General's visit to Chiang on July 31st, it will be remembered, caused widespread alarm in Washington that he might have made offers of support to the Nationalist government which were inconsistent with the Administration's policy of discouraging the Generalissimo's ambitions to reconquer the mainland. This was only the beginning, for in August the General sent to the Veterans of Foreign Wars a speech condemning those who "do not grant that it is in the pattern of Oriental psychology to respect and follow aggressive, resolute and dynamic leadership, to quickly turn on a leadership characterized by timidity or vacillation." [1] It was at this time, Truman has written, that he gave serious thought to replacing General MacArthur with General Omar Bradley as field commander in the Far East.[2] At the very end of the year, after a full month of suffering the blows of the Chinese Communist attack, MacArthur made his famous December 30th request for a blockade, strategic bombing of Manchuria, and the use of Nationalist troops. The Joint Chiefs of Staff replied in the negative on January 9th. Two days later the Commander countered by insisting that the Administration answer the following question: given the enormous odds against holding both Japan and Korea under present restrictions, "was it the present objective of the United States political policy to maintain a military position in Korea indefinitely, for a limited time, or to minimize losses by the evacuation as soon as it could be accomplished?" [3]

These earlier challenges to Administration policy serve as a backdrop for three statements issued by MacArthur in March which were the direct cause of his dismissal, for they indicated to Truman that the General was not willing to comply with the principle of complete civilian control over the military. The first of these statements was read to the press on March 7th after the Commander had made an inspection tour of the front lines. He announced at this time that if the United Nations continued in its present policies an intolerable stalemate would occur, followed by a "savage slaughter" of anti-Communist troops at the hands of an army that had no regard for the sanctity of human life.[4] This was a clear call for a

---

[1] This speech reprinted in *U.S. News & World Report,* September 1, 1950, pp. 32–34.
[2] Truman, *Memoirs,* II, p. 355.
[3] MacArthur, *Reminiscences,* p. 381.
[4] Truman, *Memoirs,* II, p. 442.

policy change, but a rather mild one when compared to his later statements.

Just as Republican insistence upon complete "victory" in Korea made it more difficult for Truman to encourage the January attempt of the United Nations to bring about a cease-fire, in late March MacArthur blasted Administration designs to bring the conflict to a close. The General was notified on March 20th that "United Nations feeling exists that further diplomatic efforts toward settlement should be made before any advance with major forces north of the 38th parallel," but that he was to have "sufficient freedom of action for [the] next few weeks to provide security for United Nations forces and [to] maintain contact with the enemy." [5] In the meantime the United States and those members of the United Nations who had troops in Korea drafted a statement of their intentions. In part, the draft read:

> The Unified Command is prepared to enter into arrangements which would conclude the fighting and ensure against its resumption. Such arrangements would open the way for a broader settlement for Korea, including the withdrawal of foreign forces from Korea.

> The United Nations has declared the policy of the world community that the people of Korea be permitted to establish a unified, independent and democratic state. . . .

> Until satisfactory arrangements for concluding the fighting have been reached, United Nations military action must be continued.[6]

On March 24th Truman was forced to scrap this yet-undelivered message to the world because MacArthur issued one of his own, the thesis of which was in direct conflict with the plans of Truman and the United Nations. In effect, the Commander told the opposition forces that they could either capitulate or pay the price in blood.

[5] *Ibid.*, pp. 438–39.
[6] *Ibid.*, pp. 339–40.

The enemy's human wave tactics have definitely failed him as our own forces have become seasoned to this form of warfare; his tactics of infiltration are but contributing to his piecemeal losses, and he is showing less stamina than our own troops under the rigors of climate, terrain, and battle.

Of even greater significance than our tactical successes has been the clear revelation that this new enemy, Red China, of such exaggerated and vaunted military power, lacks the industrial capacity to provide adequately many critical items necessary to the conduct of modern war. . . .

The enemy, therefore, must by now be painfully aware that a decision of the United Nations to depart from its tolerant effort to contain the war to the area of Korea, through an expansion of our military operations to its coastal areas and interior bases, would doom Red China to the risk of imminent military collapse.[7]

At this juncture the President had come to a decision about the advisability of retaining the General at his post: "This was a challenge to the authority of the President under the Constitution. It also flouted the policy of the Unied Nations. By this act MacArthur left me no choice—I could no longer tolerate his insubordination." [8]

But there was one final act of insubordination that had to be endured before the final decision was announced. This involved the text of a February 12th address that House Minority Leader Joseph Martin delivered in Brooklyn, voicing his concern that ". . . in our earnest desire to protect Europe, we do not weaken our position in Asia [and suggesting] that the forces of Generalissimo Chiang Kai-shek on Formosa might be employed in the opening of a second Asiatic front to relieve the pressure on our forces in Korea." Martin sent a copy of the speech to MacArthur, along with a cover letter asking for the

---

[7] From *Reminiscences*, by General Douglas MacArthur, pp. 387–88. © 1964 Time, Inc.

[8] Truman, *Memoirs*, II, p. 442.

Commander's "views on this point, either on a confidential basis or otherwise." [9] MacArthur's confidant, Major General Courtney Whitney, has written that the General was particularly attracted to Martin's speech because it stressed "the point he had been stressing for years—the tendency in shaping national policy for the administration to focus nearly all of its attention on Europe, with only minor concern for Asia, the inability to realize that Asia would in time become the nerve center of civilization's progress and that disaster in Asia portends disaster in Europe." [10]

Answering Martin almost immediately, the Far East Commander used the opportunity of the response to launch another attack on the entire concept of limited war. "My views . . . follow the conventional pattern of meeting force with counterforce, as we have never failed to do in the past . . . if we lose the war to Communism in Asia the fall of Europe is inevitable, win it and Europe most probably will avoid war and yet preserve freedom. As you pointed out, we must win. There is no substitute for victory." [11] While MacArthur's biographer, Charles A. Willoughby, would have us believe that his subject wrote this letter in the hopes of supporting Truman's peace plans, [12] it is often assumed that the message (which was read on the House floor by Martin on April 5th) was the proverbial straw that broke the back of Truman's patience. Actually, the President writes in his *Memoirs* that he had made up his mind to assert civilian control over the military before the April date. It was the March 24th statement by the General that sealed his fate. [13]

Truman's formal announcement to the press of his decision to relieve MacArthur of his posts closely paralleled his own

---

[9] Quoted in Whitney, p. 463. For a parallel account, see MacArthur, *Reminiscences*, pp. 385–86.

[10] *Ibid.*, p. 463.

[11] MacArthur, *Reminiscences*, p. 386.

[12] Charles A. Willoughby, *MacArthur, 1941–1951* (New York, 1954), p. 422.

[13] Truman, *Memoirs*, II, pp. 445–48.

deep conviction on the subject: "Full and vigorous debate on matters of national policy is a vital element in the constitutional system of our free democracy. It is fundamental, however, that military commanders must be governed by the policies and directives issued to them in the manner provided by our laws and Constitution. In time of crisis, the consideration is particularly compelling." [14] For the purposes of this study, it is the impact that the dismissal and return of MacArthur had on the nature of the GOP's response to the Korean War that is of primary import. There were, after all, millions of Americans who viewed the situation as Major General Whitney did when he wrote that his colleague had been the "victim . . . of this infamous purge . . . he had . . . become the first captain in all history to be so shamefully treated, and by the hand of the leader of those for whom he was even then fighting in a forlorn hope against desperate odds resulting from our self-imposed military disadvantages." [15]

The Republican party immediately grasped the tremendous opportunity that presented itself by the abrupt removal of this universally popular military figure. Herbert Hoover wired MacArthur to "fly home as quickly as possible before Truman and Marshall and their propagandists can smear you." [16] House Minority Leader Martin moved with lightning speed too; by 10 o'clock in the morning of April 11th (the press conference announcing the removal had been held a mere nine hours earlier) Martin had gathered Taft, Wherry, and a host of Republican leaders into his office and informed the reporters present that a Republican conference had already been held. At this meeting it had been decided that a full-scale congressional investigation of American foreign policy would be undertaken, and that MacArthur would be asked to address the Congress. Finally, it was dramatically announced that "In addition the question of possible impeachments was

---

[14] *Ibid.*, p. 449.
[15] Whitney, p. 472.
[16] This episode related in Rees, p. 221.

discussed." [17] Since more than one was in the offing, one might guess that at least Acheson, and possibly Marshall, might be tried along with the Chief Executive.

The physical return of the almost mythical MacArthur after a nearly fourteen-year absence aroused a hysteria that had rarely, if ever, been witnessed in the United States. The General was mobbed by an enormous, demonstrative crowd upon his arrival in San Francisco on the 17th—many of those who showed up for the demonstration carried signs reading "Mac-Arthur for President." Two days later he addressed the Congress, disclaiming in the course of his speech any partisan intent, yet attacking the Administration's entire handling of the Korean War:

> . . . once war is forced upon us, there is no other alternative than to apply every available means to bring it to a swift end. War's very object is victory—not prolonged indecision. In war, indeed, there can be no substitute for victory. There are some who for varying reasons would appease Red China. They are blind to history's clear lesson. For history teaches with unmistakable emphasis that appeasement but begets new and bloodier war. It points to no single instance where the end has justified that means—where appeasement has led to more than a sham peace. Like blackmail, it lays the basis for new and successively greater demands, until, as in blackmail, violence becomes the only other alternative. . . .[18]

The effect of the speech was sensational. White reports in the *Citadel* that a highly respected senator (unnamed) told him after the speech "I have never feared more for the institutions of the country. I honestly felt that if the speech had gone on much longer there might have been a march on the White House." [19] Perhaps the most emotional response of all came

---

[17] *The New York Times*, April 12, 1951, p. 3. For additional Republican support for the impeachments see *Congressional Record*, April 11, 1951, p. 3723; *Congressional Record*, April 23, 1951, p. 4287; and *Congressional Record*, June 14, 1951, pp. 6708, 6753.

[18] MacArthur, *Reminiscences*, p. 404.

[19] Quoted in White, *Citadel*, p. 241.

from Representative Dewey Short of Missouri who exclaimed "We heard God speak here today, God in the flesh, the voice of God." [20] Congressional mail from constituents ran very heavy, with New Jersey's Senator Smith receiving over 5,000 letters.[21]

From this triumph MacArthur was welcomed to New York, his home until his death. An estimated one million persons stood along the seventeen-mile route from International Airport to the Waldorf-Astoria Hotel. The ticker-tape parade given in his honor set a new standard for this New York ritual; before MacArthur's salute Lindbergh's 1927 parade was the model against which all others were measured. Moreover, popular enthusiasm for the General was a long time dying. Louis Harris of the Elmo Roper poll service reports that "Easily the two most popular generals during the war had been Eisenhower and MacArthur. The two outstripped in popularity all other prominent military leaders combined. By 1952, Eisenhower and MacArthur rated first and second as the most admired living Americans." [22] J. Edgar Hoover, Eleanor Roosevelt, and Bernard Baruch occupied the third, fourth, and fifth places respectively.

The GOP's reaction to the MacArthur dismissal was understandably violent—particularly because of the party's great partiality to the General, who had for months been indirectly supporting their demands for a more aggressive policy in the Far East. Only hours after hearing of Truman's decision, Wherry declared that "the action of the President in summarily relieving General of the Army Douglas MacArthur of his

---

[20] This episode related in Rees, p. 227.

[21] For information on the volume of mail to Senator Smith see folder entitled "Foreign Relations Committee—General MacArthur," Section IV, Box 106, Smith Papers.

[22] Louis Harris, *Is There a Republican Majority?* (New York, 1954), p. 56. Harris reports, however, that while MacArthur was greatly admired, his stock dropped once Americans considered him for the White House. While Eisenhower emerged first in order of preference for President in 1952, MacArthur was in fifth place, trailing Senator Taft, President Truman, and Senator Kefauver. See Harris, pp. 56–57.

command . . . has precipitated a situation fraught with danger to the national defense and has struck a blow to the national unity that is so vital in these perilous days." The following day the Minority Leader delivered a radio address in which he told his listeners that "The pygmies cannot bring down this giant, this tower of strength and deserving idol of the American people. . . . Compare the monumental record of General MacArthur with that of his accusers, with the record of moral decay, greed, corruption, and confusion of these weaklings in the Truman administration." [23] Knowland called the General "a rock of Gibraltar against the further spread of communism in the East," [24] and Smith of New Jersey told members of the United States United Nations delegation that Truman had made a disastrous error in thinking that the so-called Martin letter was cause for dismissal.[25] Lodge was hardly one to be unduly critical of Administration policies, yet even he was clearly astonished by Truman's behavior and told a meeting of the Republican 21 Club of Massachusetts that "It seems to be inexcusable that the President never called General MacArthur to Washington for consultation. Actions which are so crude and so impulsive shake one's confidence profoundly, for how can one have faith in a Commander in Chief who so obviously cannot command himself." [26]

At a meeting of the Republican National Committee in Tulsa on May 11th, a full month after the removal, Millikin continued to voice the party's hostility toward the President's decision: "Out of the fineness of his character and accomplishments he [MacArthur] symbolized the whole complex of the people's revolt over everything that has been ignoble and stupid, that has jeopardized the Nation's solvency and security and has shamed the morals by which we would live and be

[23] *Congressional Record*, April 13, 1951, p. A2107. For the earlier statement see *Congressional Record*, April 11, 1951, p. 3712.
[24] *Congressional Record*, April 11, 1951, p. 3727.
[25] "Memo of Meeting with Mr. Ernest Gross, Deputy Representative to the United Nations for the United States," Section IV, Box 106, Smith Papers.
[26] *Congressional Record*, April 30, 1951, p. A2501.

governed." [27] To Hoover, the GOP's idol was the "reincarnation of St. Paul into a great general of the Army who has come out of the East." [28] (It is interesting to note that privately Hoover recognized that MacArthur's presentation of his ideas had caused much of the conflict. According to the former President, the General had a Napoleonic streak, was often overbearingly proud, and tended to couch his ideas in a manner resembling the King James version of the Bible. Yet he was an outstanding military genius who had accomplished much in the Far East and so should be forgiven much. [29])

Leverett Saltonstall of Massachusetts and James Duff of Pennsylvania were unique in their defense of Truman's actions; in the statement below, Duff voices his belief that the General's past actions warranted his dismissal:

> When the commander in the field publicly and repeatedly disagreed with the Commander in Chief and the Joint Chiefs of Staff he thereby created an impossible situation that had to be resolved.
>
> Supreme authority in the Armed Forces must reside somewhere. Under the Constitution of the United States it resides in the President as Commander in Chief. To permit a continuous dispute as to authority and military policy at the most critical juncture in our history is unthinkable. [30]

This raises another point, for while only Saltonstall agreed with Duff on this count there was unanimous agreement on Truman's *right* to take the action he did. As Knowland put it, "The question is not the President's right to remove MacArthur . . . The question which is raised is on the judgment of the President . . . in doing so." [31] Dewey's verdict was similar, for he said "I do not challenge the power or the right of the President under the Constitution to relieve a military com-

---

[27] *Congressional Record,* May 21, 1951, p. A3014.

[28] *The New York Times,* April 27, 1951, p. 14.

[29] "Memo—Conference with Honorable Herbert Hoover," April 14, 1951, Section IV, Box 106, Smith Papers.

[30] *Congressional Record,* April 23, 1951, p. A2323.

[31] *Congressional Record,* April 12, 1951, p. 3836.

mander. I do challenge the wisdom of the dismissal and the
shabby manner in which it was done." [32] This view was set
forth time and time again by the Republicans, and even found
its way into the Minority Report which was issued by the
Republican members of the MacArthur Hearings. This report,
signed by Bridges, Wiley, Smith (N.J.), Hickenlooper, Knowland, Cain, Brewster, and Flanders, stated "No one disputes
the President's authority and power to assign, reassign, or
remove officers of the Armed Forces of the United States." [33]
At a Waldorf-Astoria meeting Smith and Hoover agreed that
Truman had the power to remove MacArthur from command,
but they saw a more tactful alternative that the President
might have taken. It was suggested that MacArthur be kept on
as Supreme Commander of the Allied Powers (and thereby
continue to contribute to the Japanese peace settlement) but
that a shift in command be made in Korea itself.[34]

While the Chief Executive bore the brunt of this censure,
other Republicans voiced the belief that he was a figurehead
in the plot against MacArthur. Acheson and the Allies (especially England) were singled out as the masterminds behind
the scheme. Wherry made his charge against Acheson very
pointedly when he said "he, more than anyone else, I think,
has influenced the President . . . to summarily recall General
MacArthur, who has done much for our foreign policy in
Asia." [35] Capehart believed that it was the "stultifying international policies" of Acheson and the Europeans that were chiefly
responsible, while Bricker offered the theory that the "disaster" was the result of the Secretary's following "the dictates
from London rather than the people of the United States." [36]
Displaying a bit of his showman qualities, the newly elected
Everett McKinley Dirksen waved a copy of a British newspa-

---

[32] *The New York Times,* May 11, 1951, p. 4.
[33] Hearings, p. 3577.
[34] "Memo—Conference with Honorable Herbert Hoover," April 14,
1951, Section IV, Box 106, Smith Papers.
[35] *Congressional Record,* May 4, 1951, p. 4984.
[36] *Congressional Record,* April 11, 1951, p. 3754. For Capehart statement see *ibid.,* p. 3737.

per whose headline read "MacArthur Sacked," and bitterly quipped that it should have read "MacArthur sacked on the altar of British foreign policy." [37] And too, McCarthy's talent for rhetoric came to the fore when, in agreeing with the Premier of Italy that the General's dismissal was the greatest victory for British diplomacy since the end of World War II, he went on to render in vivid terms the "real" President of the United States. "Truman is the President . . . in name only . . . the real President who discharged MacArthur is a rather sinister monster conceived in the Kremlin, and then given birth to by Acheson, with Attlee and Morrison as midwives, and then nurtured into Frankenstein proportions by the Hiss crowd, who still run the State Department." [38]

With MacArthur at the crest of a great wave of enthusiasm for his views, the Republicans demanded and received a public hearing on foreign policy—and so the famous MacArthur Hearings (actually he testified for a scant three days) began on May 3rd and ended on the 25th of June. There was extensive feuding between the two parties concerning the mechanics of the hearings, with the Republicans obviously seeking to get the maximum political benefit from them. Hence the GOP argued for the appointment of a special committee—with equal representation—to conduct the sessions, while the Democrats insisted upon using the existing Senate Foreign Relations and Armed Services Committees. In addition, the Republicans fought fiercely to have the meetings open—open to the press, television cameras and the public; the Democrats wanted closed sessions in the interest of national security. When a compromise was finally worked out, the Democrats won on the point of using the standing Senate committees, and also won a partial victory in that no television cameras, broadcasting equipment, or correspondents would be permitted in the room. However, each hour transcripts of the testimony were released to the press, after they had been censored by Admiral Arthur C. Davis of the Defense Department and Adrian Fisher of the State Department.

Every Democrat present (13) voted for a closed session, and they were joined by three Republicans: Wiley, Smith (N.J.), and Tobey. The following Republicans voted for an open committee hearing: Bridges, Saltonstall, Knowland, Hickenlooper, Cain, and Flanders.[39] The Republicans were downcast, but not defeated—yet. In rather mild speeches both Cain and Malone voiced their belief that "if the people of the United States could have heard the testimony this morning, the party would be over." [40] Sneering at the Democrats' concern over secrecy, Dirksen reminded those on the other side of the aisle of the results of the secrecy at Yalta.[41] The following day, May 4th, Wherry introduced a motion to place the Ferguson bill dealing with open hearings (S.Res.137) at the top of the voting calendar. He lost by a vote of 37 to 41; McCarran was the only Democrat who crossed party lines to vote for the motion.[42]

* * *

The great controversy that raged during the MacArthur Hearings had an ideological as well as a political basis, for while arguing matters of strategy the Republican party had an eye cocked toward the 1952 election. While supporting the "MacArthur Plan" of air strikes, blockades and the like, and while attacking the concept of limited war, the Republicans were reinforcing their decision to present a more aggressive alternative to a confused and anxious electorate.

The depth of Republican support for MacArthur's way of fighting (and presumably winning) is one of the most striking aspects of the period under discussion. But here as in the Great Debate many of the Eastern Republicans—with the

---

[39] Hearings, p. 3570.
[40] Congressional Record, May 3, 1951, pp. 4899, 4901.
[41] Ibid., p. 4907.
[42] Congressional Record, May 4, 1951, p. 4974. See Appendix, pp. 298–299.

notable exception of Bridges and Smith (N.J.)—differed with their Mid- and Far Western colleagues by withholding their acceptance of MacArthur's strategy for winning the war. These Easterners were moving against a massive outpouring of support for the General's blueprint for victory. Taft, for instance, said during a major foreign policy speech on April 27th that he had "no difficulty whatever in lining . . . up with the general principles announced by General MacArthur. I believe that by such principles we may reasonably hope to end the war in Korea." [43] Bridges followed suit a week later by declaring "I think General MacArthur's views are definitely the answer in order to bring [the war] to a successful conclusion. He has presented the only positive program for China." [44] And Hickenlooper characterized the General's strategy as "the only sensible and sound program which has been proposed to end the fighting in Korea." [45] While meeting with Ambassador Austin in mid-April, Senator Smith of New Jersey argued that Truman's interpretation of MacArthur's strategy was at best naive; he also expressed great disappointment over Austin's endorsement of the President's dismissal of the Commander.[46]

The psychological appeal of the MacArthur program, of course, was that it represented a clear call for the kind of action that represented a welcome relief from the subtleties of limited war. He simply called for the full use of American power with victory as the object. Hence Wiley assured his colleagues that once the United States decided to "meet force with force . . . the outcome will be victory." [47] The Administration's repeated objection to this was that the application of such force would lead to World War III. Yet most Republican senators, at least for the record, denied that MacArthur's program involved a widening of the war. As Kem explained, its

---

[43] *Congressional Record,* April 27, 1951, p. 4590.
[44] *Congressional Record,* May 15, 1951, p. A2933.
[45] *Congressional Record,* May 31, 1951, p. 6149.
[46] "Memo on H. Alexander Smith's meeting with Ambassador Austin," April 14, 1951, Section IV, Box 106, Smith Papers.
[47] *Congressional Record,* May 9, 1951, p. 5253.

purpose was to end "a situation in which [the American troops] are shot at like sitting ducks." [48]

If the GOP had acquiesced in the concept of limited war in the early stages of the conflict, many in the party found it impossible to support the policy after the intervention of the Red Chinese. On April 11th Truman delivered a radio address which contained his defense of the broad outlines of his war strategy. "I believe that we must try to limit the war to Korea for these vital reasons: to make sure that the precious lives of our fighting men are not wasted; to see that the security of our country and the free world is not needlessly jeopardized; and to prevent a third world war." [49] On three separate occasions Taft expressed his belief that Truman was laboring under a basic inconsistency in his handling of the war since the end of November. For example, in a June 9th speech to the Republicans of Wisconsin he said that a

> strain of inconsistency was exhibited by the President in his radio speech on April 11th. He said that he had prevented world war III by moving into Korea on the theory that failure to punish aggression would have encouraged Russia to make war. But in the second half of his speech he says that he is preventing world war III by not punishing aggression when the aggressor is Communist China and waging only a soft war. If the success of aggression encourages war, then the present American policy is encouraging war. . . . The Chinese Communists have captured half of Korea and their aggression is peculiarly flagrant because it is against the United Nations itself. Yet they are perfectly safe. They can lose nothing. No bombs can be dropped on their land; no blockade can be enforced against them. The Nationalist Chinese Army is prevented from making any attempt to invade South China or build up a popular front in South China against communism. [50]

Most of the opposition to the Administration's policies came from those Republicans who enjoyed the seemingly unshaka-

---

[48] *Congressional Record,* April 26, 1951, p. 4520.
[49] Truman, *Public Papers,* p. 226.
[50] *Congressional Record,* June 12, 1951, p. A3623.

ble conviction that for all intents and purposes we were already at war with Red China. When the Democrat Robert S. Kerr of Oklahoma ended a Senate speech supporting the Administration's China policy, he said "We are not engaged in a war and we do not want to do anything to draw us into war." [51] It was this very frame of mind that the Republicans attacked so strenuously in this period. In an address to the Young Republican Club in Illinois, Wiley took the position that "there are over a half million Red Chinese troops poised for a spring offensive against some three hundred thousand United Nations troops. If that is not a full-scale war, what is?" [52] Bricker insisted that "There is no way in which we can incite them [the Chinese Communists] to do any more than they are now doing in Korea, because they are there in full strength now." [53]

This party determination to press for more vigorous action emerged in the form of a startling resolution (S.J.Res.62) declaring war on North Korea and China! Cain, the sponsor of the bill, immediately followed his motion with another (S.J.Res.63) calling upon the President to withdraw our troops from Korea.[54] This was the majority Republican sentiment in a nutshell—they could not endure the gray area in which Truman and his followers were attempting to maneuver. They rejected the Administration's plan in part because it was not the "American" way of fighting, and also because it had (for them) all of the earmarks of appeasement. The Cain proposal, however, never came up for debate.

If the main body of the GOP had become convinced that the United States was engaged in an entirely new war against the Chinese Communists, these members were unwilling to take seriously the Administration's warning of possible Russian intervention should the anti-Communist forces decide to escalate the war. At the hearings, Flanders gave the joint

---

[51] *Congressional Record,* April 12, 1951, p. 3824.
[52] *Congressional Record,* April 24, 1951, p. 4367.
[53] *Congressional Record,* April 24, 1951, p. 4367.
[54] *Congressional Record,* April 17, 1951, p. 4087.

committee his assurance that if we did bomb Manchuria we would not be any closer to world war III because "China is fighting against us an unlimited war. They hit us with all their force wherever they find us. If we undertake only those military operations which hamper or prevent Chinese operations in North Korea, it would seem to me that there is not the slightest excuse for any nation to assume that we are provoking such a direct attack on the total sources of Communist power in China, Siberia, or elsewhere." [55] While it was widely assumed at this time that Russia and China had worked out some form of mutual defense pact, Ferguson was sure that, as in the past, Russia would not abide by her treaties.[56] Senator Hickenlooper pointed out that when we announced the deployment of four divisions to Europe, Russia declared that she would consider such a move an unfriendly act; yet the troops were sent. In contrast, while the Kremlin did not announce that the bombing of Manchuria would be considered an unfriendly act, we were operating as if we had received just such an ultimatum.[57] In a series of New York meetings with the American delegation to the United Nations, Smith of the Foreign Relations Committee argued that we should bomb Manchuria even if in so doing we risked war with Russia—but it is obvious from Smith's comments that he did not believe this risk to be very great.[58]

The Secretary of State, on the other hand, saw no grounds for the belief that Russia would remain neutral in the event of a major war in Asia.

> I cannot accept the assumption that the Soviet Union will go its way regardless of what we do. . . . This view is certainly not well enough grounded to justify a gamble with the essential security of our Nation.

---

[55] Hearings, p. 1946.
[56] *Congressional Record*, April 24, 1951, p. 4355.
[57] *Ibid.*
[58] "Memo of Meeting with Mr. Ernest Gross," April 14, 1951, Section IV, Box 106, Smith Papers.

The basic premise of our foreign policy is that time is on our side if we make good use of it. That does not necessarily mean that time must bring us to a point where we can match the Soviet Union man for man and tank for tank.

What it does mean is that we need to use the time we have to build an effective deterrent force.[59]

And too, Secretary of Defense Marshall's forthright condemnation of MacArthur's entire approach to the war was based largely on his belief that it would lead us to war not only with Red China, but with Russia, and would thus leave other strategic parts of the world exposed to attack. What Marshall greatly feared was that Soviet troops in Middle and Eastern Europe would invade Western Europe once we were heavily engaged in the Far East.[60] Acheson took a similar position:

. . . it is the judgment of the President's military advisers that the proposed enlargement of our military action would not exercise a prompt and decisive effect in bringing the hostilities to an end. To this judgment there must be added a recognition of the grave risks and other disadvantages of this alternative course.

Against the dubious advantages of spreading the war in an initially limited manner to the mainland of China, there must be measured the risk of a general war in China, the risk of Soviet intervention, and of world war III, as well as the probable effects upon the solidarity of the free world coalition.[61]

At the formal hearings the Republicans continued to have a strong and willing ally in MacArthur, who voiced his objection to a program which advocated that the United States "go on indefinitely and indefinitely, neither to win nor lose." [62] While questioning the General, Saltonstall read an April 15th statement of Dean Rusk to the effect that "What we are trying

---

[59] Hearings, pp. 1719–20.
[60] *Ibid.*, p. 325.
[61] Hearings, p. 1718.
[62] *Ibid.*, pp. 67–68.

to do is maintain peace and security without a general war. . . . At the same time, we are trying to prevent a general conflagration which would consume the very things we are now trying to defend." [63] When asked for his reaction to this program, the General voiced his total disagreement with such a plan for ending the hostilities in Korea.

> That policy, as you have read it, seems to me to introduce a new concept into military operations—the concept of appeasement, the concept that when you use force, you can limit that force . . .

> If that is the concept of a continued and indefinite campaign in Korea, with no definite purpose of stopping it until the enemy gets tired or you yield to his terms, I think that introduces into the military sphere a political control such as I have never known in my life or have ever studied.[64]

To the end of the hearings the Republican members of the joint committee sided with the former Far East Commander and said so in no uncertain terms in their minority report.

> The enemy in Korea fought with no holds barred. They had no Navy or they would have used it. They had a small air force, which was steadily expanded as the war went on and the full strength of this air force was thrown into battle.

> We did have inescapable handicaps; witnesses testified to our limitations. But the idea of not exploiting the resources available in the face of an enemy exerting all his power is to us indefensible.[65]

Closely associated with Republican complaints that the Administration had failed to recognize that Communist China was at war with the United States was the repeated charge that we had maneuvered ourselves into a stalemate position— we would neither win nor lose the war, we would only increase our casualties. The most complete statement of the

---

[63] *Ibid.*, p. 39.
[64] Hearings, pp. 39–40.
[65] *Ibid.*, p. 3585.

party's opposition to this kind of war was contained in Taft's major foreign policy address of April 27th in which he countered Truman's nationwide address of the 11th of April. The President had expressed the belief that if sufficiently heavy casualties were inflicted upon the enemy it "may discourage the Chinese Communists from continuing their attack." The President also contended that if the Communists are not allowed to make further gains on the peninsula "they may recognize the folly of continuing their aggression. A peaceful settlement may then be possible." [66] Taft saw this as a blueprint for a "stalemate war" that "makes a joke of the United Nations ban against aggression, and encourages aggression everywhere else."

> As I see it, the plan which is proposed by the President is an impossible plan. The American people will not stand for it. Psychologically, no one will stand for it. We are either going to fight a more aggressive war against China, or else we are going to have an appeasement peace. The choice which this country has is between Acheson and MacArthur. That is the only issue. . . . Sooner or later, psychologically, we are going to have to go one way or the other; and what I fear is that we may go the Acheson way.[67]

Among the many who made protests similar to that of Taft were Capehart, Butler (Md.), and Millikin. While the tone and phraseology differed in each case, the basic idea of each was that the Korean War was getting nowhere under the Truman strategy and that there was not a shred of hope of accomplishing anything. Yet when Bridges suggested to Air Force General Vandenberg that we might use our air power to drive the Communists back and win the war, Vandenberg informed the committee of the weakness of that branch of the military. "The shoestring United States Air Force that we are operating today, in view of our global commitments, must not be utilized until it is larger for anything except holding it intact as

---

[66] Truman, *Public Papers,* p. 226.
[67] *Congressional Record,* April 27, 1951, pp. 4588–89.

nearly as possible against a major threat, against a major power." [68]

It was also at the hearings that General Omar N. Bradley, the chairman of the Joint Chiefs of Staff, made his famous "wrong war" statement in support of the Administration's handling of the conflict. In light of his position as Chairman of the Joint Chiefs of Staff, Bradley's analysis of the situation is particularly revealing.

> Korea, in spite of the importance of the engagement, must be looked upon with proper perspective. It is just one engagement just one phase of the battle. . . . As long as we keep the conflict within its present scope, we are holding to a minimum the forces we must commit and tie down. . . . We have recommended against enlarging the war. The course of action often described as a "limited war" with Red China would increase the risk we are taking by engaging too much of our power in an area that is not the critical strategic prize.

> Red China is not the powerful nation seeking to dominate the world. Frankly, in the opinion of the Joint Chiefs of Staff, this strategy would involve us in the wrong war, at the wrong place, at the wrong time, and with the wrong enemy.[69]

But after over two million words of testimony, the GOP Senate representation was far from convinced that Truman's plan for ending the war had any merit, a fact that became forcefully apparent in the Minority Report. After once again endorsing the plan of the former Commander, the Republican group wrote that by contrast "The Truman Administration had no plan to win. It offered the vague concept of limiting the war's area while permitting unlimited casualties. The immoral, un-Christian idea of killing Chinese until the Moscow puppets sue for peace is unacceptable. The corollary of suffering American casualties at the present rate is also unacceptable." [70]

Somewhat related to this great unrest over the running of

---

[68] Hearings, p. 1393.
[69] Hearings, pp. 730–32.
[70] *Ibid.*, p. 3590.

"We've Been Using More Of A Roundish One"

Reprinted from *The Herblock Book* (Beacon Press, 1952)

the war was the long-standing Republican belief that European security was being strengthened at the expense of Asian security. Taft was the major spokesman of this point of view, and on many occasions in these three months he denounced official policy on this score. He explained to a meeting of The American Assembly that his quarrel was "with those who wished to go all out in Europe, even beyond our capacity, and at the same time refuse to apply our general program and strategy to the Far East." More specifically, he contended that in the midst of a "bitter and dangerous war, the administration refuses to fight that war with all the means at its command on the theory that we might incite Russia to start a third world war. But in Europe we have not hesitated to risk a third world war over and over again." [71] Knowland, who had made a cult of defending the interest of Asia, insisted that such partiality must end: "I do not believe we can meet the global menace of communism by closing the door to it in Europe and leaving the door wide open in Asia." [72] And Butler declared that "the people of Maryland want to know what kind of foreign policy it is that rushed troops to meet a threatened aggression in Europe while it is providing a sanctuary for aggressors on the Korean peninsula." [73] At the conclusion of the MacArthur Hearings the Republican representation once again raised the question of the amount of aid furnished to Europe in relation to Asia.

> While granting the importance of Europe and while recognizing the military and economic potential of that continent, we cannot help but feel that there has been a myopia approaching blindness whenever we have dealt with matters in the Pacific.

> There has never been the same amount of effort expended on behalf of Asiatic matters by the State Department as there has been toward those of Europe. It is unfortunate, but true, that the State Department has been affected by a group who have interpreted Asiatic problems to the advantage of Russia rather than of the United States.[74]

Thus the majority of Senate Republicans would not acknowledge the extent of Democratic involvement in the Far East by its engagement in a shooting war in Asia, and they would not accept Bradley's suggestion that Europe, and not

---

[71] *Congressional Record*, May 22, 1951, p. A3073.
[72] *Congressional Record*, April 24, 1951, p. 4350.
[73] *Congressional Record*, May 10, 1951, p. 5275.
[74] Hearings, p. 3596.

the Far East, was the "critical strategic prize" for the Communists.

The disagreement over the means of achieving "victory" or of ending the war in Korea was, of necessity, related to the differences existing as to the goals of the war. Put in very general terms, the Republicans were strongly of the opinion that the goal of the United Nations was to unify Korea, and that only when this was accomplished could an honorable peace be achieved. Long before the opening of the hearings the Administration had reverted back to its original premise that the object of the international organization was to drive the Communists north of the thirty-eight parallel, thus successfully repelling the original aggression. The *military* intent of the U.N. was to repel the aggressor; the *political* objective of the United Nations for the past five years had been to unify the country. But the United Nations did not go to war in pursuit of this political objective. It would, undoubtedly, have been wiser to have resisted the temptation in September of moving north of the parallel, but once the massive retreat of the winter of 1950–51 was undertaken, no directives were given to again move north of the line.

Despite the statements by the United Nations of its aims in prosecuting the Korean War, the GOP persistently maintained that Korea must be unified. Once again they were supported here by MacArthur who, on the first day of his testimony before the joint Senate committee, waved aside a good deal of evidence to the contrary and made the astounding statement that his "mission was to clear out all North Korea, to unify it and liberalize it." [75] In a radio address on April 12th Wherry insisted that our troops "were sent there originally to liberate all of Korea, take the offensive, and punish the North Koreans and their helpers into submission." [76] He went on to charge that Truman had changed this original design and had substituted it with a plan for a holding action along the thirty-eighth

---

[75] Hearings, p. 19.
[76] *Congressional Record*, April 13, 1951, p. A2107.

parallel. When Cain and the Democrat Kerr appeared on the American Forum of the Air, Cain insisted that "on the 27th day of June 1950 . . . the United States of America and 52 other free nations of this world, members all of the United Nations, signed a solemn resolution that their mission in Korea was to be that of expelling the enemy, whoever that enemy might be, from Korea, and making Korea a free, a united, and a self-controlled nation." [77] Cain made a similar statement at the hearings, and tried, but failed, to get General Albert C. Wedemeyer to agree with him.[78]

The best and most complete expression of the difference of opinion existing between the two parties on this crucial issue is to be found in a colloquy engaged in by Secretary Acheson and Senator Smith (N.J.) in the course of the joint committee's meeting. Their statements are reproduced here at length because the hostility of many Republicans toward signing a treaty that guaranteed less than the unification of the peninsula continued into the days of the Eisenhower Administration.

> Smith: You probably will agree that we are faced with defiance of the United Nations by Communist China and that we have to resolve that defiance if the United Nations is really going to continue to succeed at all in its international obligations.

> Acheson: I am aware of that, sir.

> Smith: That is the reason I am trying to get clearly in my head just what we are driving at. I admit I am still a little bit confused that we are thinking possibly in terms of stopping where we began. If we stop where we began, say on the Thirty-eighth or near the line across there, and leave it where it was when the outbreak began last June, I have great difficulty in justifying the casualties, which, as was brought out here, are some 141,000, counting combat and other casualties in this operation.

---

[77] *Congressional Record,* May 8, 1951, p. A2705.
[78] Hearings, p. 2518.

Acheson: Senator, if you accomplish what you started out to do, I don't think that is synonymous with saying you stopped where you began.

We started out to do two things. One is repel the armed attack and the other is to restore peace and security in the area. Now, if we do those two things, we have done what we started out to do, and I should think that is success.

Smith: Well, that is what I wanted to get clear in my own mind. You think that if we stopped them at the Thirty-eighth and pushed them back to where they began and if we restored peace and security in South Korea, that is all we are expected to do in order to assert the prestige of the United Nations?

Acheson: That is the military objective of the United Nations, as laid down by the United Nations itself.

There is also the political objective of the United Nations, which is creating a free, independent and democratic Korea, and the United Nations will continue to do that and I hope it will be able to do that.

Smith: But you don't suggest, do you, that by force of arms we stop fighting at the Thirty-eighth parallel, and the political dispute will go on, back and forth, with Russia and the Communists just as before?

That is what is confusing me.

Acheson: Well, I think that what you are referring to, Senator, are the inherent difficulties of the situation; but those difficulties existed before the United Nations acted, and we hope they may be less after it is successful in obtaining its objectives.[79]

This question of the ultimate goal of the United Nations leads to one of the most controversial, and certainly one of the most difficult questions that the Republicans were asking at this time. Put in simplest terms they now wanted to know who was in charge of the Korean operation, the United States or the United Nations. The problem is a thorny one for several reasons, one of which is the fact that the Security Council on

---

[79] Hearings, p. 1786.

June 25th and June 27th took the action it did only after strong pressure by the United States. More important, it is now clear that Truman committed American forces to Korea several hours *before* the formal passage of the June 27th resolution of the Security Council requesting member nations to send aid.[80] The disproportionate number of American troops in Korea (about 90 percent of the entire United Nations force) was another problem. Finally, when Truman removed MacArthur, he not only removed him from his duties as a General in the United States Army; of necessity MacArthur was automatically removed from his United Nations post. Should not the U.N. have been consulted?

Mundt presented what would appear to be the most complete argument for the view that since the President sent troops into Korea before United Nations authorization was received, the United Nations had no control over those troops.

> . . . it is incontrovertibly clear from the chronology of events at the United Nations, that the action of President Truman in ordering troops into Korea preceded the adoption of the resolution by the Security Council of the United Nations. It was an action taken by the President, acting for himself as Chief Executive of the United States, and it was not taken in pursuance of a resolution which had previously been adopted. The United Nations resolution, as a matter of fact, was adopted in support of an action already undertaken at the order of the President.

> It would seem to follow inevitably, therefore, that the United States has the authority, the power, and the responsibility to set the pattern for this war, to determine what tactics can bring it to the earliest and most honorable conclusion, and to decide what methods are best designed to protect the lives of the American boys who figure so overwhelmingly in the total number of non-Asiatic troops engaged in this gruesome conflict.[81]

Four Republican senators—Knowland, Hickenlooper, Ferguson, and Brewster—conducted a colloquy in which they began with a different premise than Mundt but ended with

---

[80] See discussion of this question in Chapter 2.
[81] *Congressional Record,* May 9, 1951, pp. 5238–43.

the idea that there was no need to consult with the United
Nations on matters of policy. It was in the course of this
discussion that Knowland pointed out that when Truman
appointed MacArthur in accordance with the United Nations
resolution of July 7th, "the United States was designated in
fact as the operating agency for the United Nations, and . . .
therefore the responsibility for military operations flows
through the United States high command . . . in effect we are
the operating agents from a military point of view." [82]

By the time the Minority Report was issued, the signers had
a clear picture of where the power in Korea rested—with the
United States. The trouble, they said, was that we were not
exercising that rightful authority. "It would appear that the
allied commander . . . would have, subject to the approval of
the Joint Chiefs and the Commander in Chief, sufficient
authority to take whatever measures might appear desirable to
successfully carry out the military mission in Korea. . . . It
appears that the United States has been unduly apprehensive
of the opinions of our allies in carrying out its command
authority." [83]

The last of the general policy questions discussed at this
time concerned the island of Formosa, whose Nationalist
troops, MacArthur argued, should have been used both to
fight in Korea and to launch an attack on Southern China. The
staunchest Republican supporter of the first of these plans was
Knowland, who insisted at the hearings that there should be a
larger percentage of Asiatic troops fighting in Korea. Both
Knowland and Smith (N.J.) stressed the point that it was very
much to the benefit of the Nationalists that Communism be
halted in Asia, and that the troops contributing to the anti-
Communist effort in Asia should not be limited to those sent
by the Philippines and Thailand.[84]

---

[82] *Congressional Record,* May 31, 1951, pp. 6146–47.

[83] Hearings, p. 3583.

[84] "H. Alexander Smith to Robert A. Lovett, Deputy Secretary of
Defense," August 1, 1951, Section IV, Box 105, Smith Papers. For
Knowland statement see Hearings, p. 3049.

While this demand that Nationalist forces be used in Korea
had been made since the start of the war, the idea that Chiang
should invade Southern China had remained dormant. Capehart questioned Truman's authority in interposing the Seventh
Fleet between Formosa and the mainland; what right, he
asked, did the head of one sovereign nation have to tell
another sovereign nation that it could not fight to regain its
own country?[85] This time the Eastern liberal wing of the
party gave support to the Asialationists, for Dewey insisted
that "The President should immediately withdraw the order
he had no right to issue prohibiting Chiang from aiding guer-
rillas on the mainland and using his own troops in any way he
deems fit. When American boys are being killed, we should
stop being so fussy about who helps us kill our enemies."[86]
Taft and Smith went considerably further than Dewey by
suggesting that in addition to lifting the ban on Nationalist
attacks on the mainland the United States should provide
material assistance to Chiang's troops. It will be remembered
that in a letter to K. C. Wu of the Taiwan government in
February Smith assured his friend that he was in favor of all
military support of an invasion of the mainland short of actual
intervention by the American navy and air force.[87] Taft's
advice was that we should provide "logistical aid . . . that is,
means of transportation, airplanes, arms—whatever they desire. But so far as troops are concerned, I would not send an
American soldier to the mainland of China."[88] In an extension
of these remarks in a speech to the Republicans of Indiana,
the Ohioan again expressed great confidence in the presence of
a huge underground movement in China which would welcome the Generalissimo with open arms.[89]

The Administration countered these assumptions through

---

[85] *Congressional Record,* April 24, 1951, pp. 4360. Also see *Congressional Record,* May 2, 1951, p. 4841.

[86] *The New York Times,* May 11, 1951, p. 4.

[87] "H. Alexander Smith to K. C. Wu," February 14, 1951, Section IV,
Box 107, Smith Papers.

[88] *Congressional Record,* April 27, 1951, p. 4581.

[89] *Congressional Record,* July 5, 1951, pp. A4299–4300.

General George Marshall, now Secretary of Defense, who pointedly stated at the hearings that he did not believe that the widely acclaimed Nationalist Army was capable of accomplishing the grandiose plans that the Republicans were formulating. In fact, Marshall reported that the Joint Chiefs of Staff were of the opinion that based on past performance of these troops in the Chinese civil war, they would not be effective in either Korea or in China itself.[90] But Formosa and the Nationalist Army, as we shall see, remained a vital issue in the Korean controversy.

With the GOP now closely identified with MacArthur's formula for victory in Korea, the Republicans looked upon the Administration's attempts to negotiate a peace treaty with great disfavor, resentment, and suspicion. By far the greatest difficulty the Administration experienced was the GOP's refusal to publicly accept its assurances that the terms of the January peace attempts—particularly the section containing the provision for a Far Eastern summitlike conference in which Russia, Red China, England, and the United States would participate—had been scrapped. Assurances were given by the Administration that the fate of Formosa and the possibility of a U.N. seat for Red China were not to be discussed, but party members remained unconvinced. So deeply ingrained were these suspicions that they were not allayed by the publication of Ridgway's message to the commander of the Communist forces in which the new commander made it plain that discussions were to deal only with the cessation of hostilities.[91] Many Republicans remained convinced, at least for the sake of their audience, that Ridgway and the Administration were withholding the complete terms of the truce offer. Jenner declared that "we [are] going along in a phony peace move in which we will surrender to the Communists everything for which our men have died," [92] while California's Richard Nixon complained that "The only

---

[90] Hearings, p. 337.
[91] The New York Times, June 30, 1951, p. 1.
[92] Congressional Record, April 11, 1951, p. 3723.

plan the administration can offer to bring the war to an end is one of bare-faced appeasement, because recognition of Red China and giving up Formosa to Communist China is nothing but appeasement." [93] Taft voiced his distrust of Truman by saying "The President uses the words 'no appeasement,' but he completely omitted from his speech any repudiation of the policy of surrendering Formosa to China or the United Nations or the policy of recognizing the Chinese Communists." [94] The most representative statement of the party's hostility toward the rumors of peace negotiations was made in mid-June by Taft:

> Apparently the President is willing to get out of the present war as best he can. The State Department apparently is still willing to discuss the surrender of Formosa and the admission of the Chinese Communists to the United Nations. It is willing to consider the retirement of American troops from Korea if the Chinese will withdraw. That would restore us to exactly the position we were in when we withdrew our troops in 1949 and set the stage for a repetition of the whole Korean tragedy. It would undoubtedly bring about the same ultimate result of a Communist Korea.

> The Administration has been moved to be somewhat more emphatic against the Chinese because of the protest against MacArthur's dismissal, but they still look longingly to such a peace. If such a peace is made, we have wasted 140,000 casualties and billions of dollars. [95]

Wherry, in a Fourth of July speech, accused the Administration of "fear that our traditional foreign policy of equal justice to all no longer is sound and that we must appease and compromise with principle and engage in power politics; fear that if we do not appease on Korea our cities will be bombed into ashes." [96] In the section of the Minority Report dealing with the up-and-coming peace talks, the main emphasis was

---

[93] *Ibid.*, p. 3758.
[94] *Congressional Record*, April 13, 1951, p. A2110.
[95] *Congressional Record*, June 12, 1951, p. A3623.
[96] *Congressional Record*, June 19, 1951, p. A3873.

placed upon the idea that stopping at the thirty-eighth parallel did not constitute victory because the objective of the United Nations would not have been fulfilled, and the threat of another Communist attack from the north would remain.[97]

Dewey was one of the very few of his party who was the least bit sanguine, at least publicly, about the peace talks; at the outset of his Far Eastern tour he said that "There is reason to believe they [the Communists] are willing to bring what they have found to be a very unprofitable venture to an end. I prayerfully hope that is true." [98]

One must now consider briefly the source of the opposition that did exist toward the pending peace talks; one must ask why the party took the stance that it did. In part, no doubt, it was because the GOP genuinely feared that an Administration willing to discuss a United Nations seat for Red China in January might discuss the identical thing in July. More important, it would seem that much of the hostility was the result of the GOP's conception of the "true" goal of the war. It was universally accepted that once the armies dug in at the parallel and peace talks began, no effort would be made by the United Nations to even consider the unification of the country by force of arms. Perhaps the greatest reason of all was that opposition to *any* Democratic peace plan, under the conditions existing in June and July of 1951, was the most politically expedient stance for the party to take. With public sentiment running against Truman it would be extremely difficult for the Administration to defend the fact that the war could honorably end where it began. Throughout the period, the Republicans for the first time displayed an active interest in the 1952 elections. For example, Wiley was blatantly partisan when he declared that it was his "firm judgment that a victory for the Republican Party in November 1952 is imperatively necessary for the future peace, prosperity, and freedom of America." [99] Lodge, speaking before the Republican 21 Club of Massachu-

---

[97] Hearings, p. 3605.
[98] *The New York Times*, July 3, 1951, p. 12.
[99] *Congressional Record*, April 17, 1951, p. 4064.

setts on April 28th, used harsh words for this particular Republican: "We meet tonight as citizens who are thoroughly aroused by the lack of foresight and general incompetence of our national leadership, who are determined decisively to rid ourselves of this administration in the coming year; and who are also determined that until the time comes that we can throw them out, we will surmount our problems here at home and present a united front to our Communist opponents." [100] Even Ives, who like Lodge generally supported Administration measures, told a New York State Republican Committee meeting that "This is where the Republican Party has its greatest opportunity and faces its greatest challenge since 1860. . . . We Republicans, solely on the basis of the Truman record, can and should win in 1952." [101] Another New Yorker, Dewey, declared in a major address on May 10th that "The confusion and bitterness in this country today are the result of the incompetence and petty politics of the Democratic administration and next year the people will throw it out. That overturn will put the destiny of the nation in firm Republican hands and will serve the cause of freedom everywhere." [102] Turning more specifically to the peace proposals, Millikin in his address to the Republican National Committee predicted that the opposition party would go down in defeat because this group of warmongers could never convince the country that it was the party of peace.

> Right now they [the Democrats] are putting soothing syrup labels on deadly poison. Their medicine men are trying to palm off that foul gang as the peace party and we are to be condemned as warmongers. Goebbels, the master liar of all times, must be spinning in his grave with envy. . . .

> By this time close to 70,000 (sic) casualties among our boys in Korea attest to the fact that they lie. It's their last big lie. They have gone too far. They have irretrievably offended the deepest emotions of our people.

---

[100] *Congressional Record*, April 30, 1951, p. A2500.
[101] *Congressional Record*, May 14, 1951, p. A2835.
[102] *The New York Times*, May 11, 1951, p. 4.

Our people are through with them. They are going to kick them out of office in 1952 and they would like to see a quicker way of doing it.[103]

At this same meeting Representative Charles Halleck gave his reason why the Democrats would be defeated in 1952: "The greatest, the most devastating indictment is that, under Democratic leadership we have failed tragically to win the peace; that six years after the most glorious victory over tyranny in the history of mankind we are again at war. While we may well argue at the moment about how best to end the war, let no one forget why we are in it. We are in it because of the greatest mismanagement and miscalculation of any great nation in all times."[104] Taft had the final word to say on the subject when he declared three days before the beginning of the peace talks that "the Nation is heartsick that for 19 months more it cannot rid itself of those whose administration is endangering the safety and the liberty of the people . . . there is no satisfactory protection against socialism at home and against war and ignominy abroad except an overwhelming Republican victory in 1952."[105]

There was much truth in Stassen's observation that the "great debate" between Truman, MacArthur, and the Republicans would not be decided at the hearings; rather, he believed that the people would choose sides according to the progress of the war on the battlefield.[106] This almost too-obvious "truth" explains the source of Republican strength in the April to July period. Americans could not tolerate the military stalemate, and so could not sympathize with General Bradley's attempt at the hearings to prove that the Korean War had not been a "pointless and inconclusive struggle." The Chairman of the Joint Chiefs of Staff testified that "The alluring prospect for the Communist conspiracy in June, 1950—the prospect of a quick and easy success which would not only win Korea for

---

[103] *Congressional Record*, May 21, 1951, p. A3013.
[104] *The New York Times*, May 13, 1951, p. 51.
[105] *Congressional Record*, July 5, 1951, p. A4300.
[106] *The New York Times*, May 15, 1951, p. 29.

the Kremlin but shake the free nations of Asia and paralyze the defense of Europe—all this has evaporated." [107] But Bradley's was the voice of the Administration, and many in the Republican hierarchy were listening to another military figure, one described by Herbert Hoover as the "reincarnation of St. Paul into a great general of the Army who has come out of the East." [108]

There is, of course, nothing very startling about a political party which is out of power criticizing the policies of the majority party and predicting its own victory in the next election. Nor is there anything wrong with an opposition party's offering an alternative direction to a nation facing a serious crisis. It is, in fact, the duty of such a party in a democracy to offer alternatives. This is not the reason why the Republican party is held up for condemnation in this study. Had the party been consistent in its advocacy of the MacArthur position its sincerity would not be subject to question. The major element in the GOP offered no such consistent alternative. They first supported the American intervention, then retreated from the implications of that support; they steadfastly called for American withdrawal from the Korean War, then passionately associated themselves with the "no substitute for victory" philosophy of MacArthur. Finally, in a period still to be discussed, the party nominated for the Presidency a military hero whose platform lacked any concrete program for peace even as it disavowed both unification and an all-out military victory. Criticism by the Republican party during the Korean War was justifiable; but when the nature of a party's dissent indicates that its members are motivated more by political expediency than by a desire to present a consistent and viable alternative to Administration policies, then censure is in order.

---

[107] Hearings, p. 1716–17.
[108] See p. 150.

Chapter 7

*Negotiated Peace and
Deterrent Power*

The second year of the Korean War was the least eventful period of the entire conflict. It was a year that lacked the drama of the Chinese intervention, the MacArthur dismissal, or the Presidential election. However, it does constitute an important phase in the development of Republican thought, in part because it represented a hardening of the party's resolve to accept a military victory rather than a negotiated peace; and too, the second year of the war witnessed the formulation of a new anti-Communist strategy offered by the party. This strategy was represented by the twin concepts of deterrent power and liberation. Of obvious significance was Eisenhower's resignation from his NATO post, his decision to become a contender for the 1952 Republican nomination, and his refusal to support the GOP's contention that an all-out military victory must be achieved in Korea. Ironically, the Republican party nominated the General despite his avowed disenchantment with the party's current solutions for ending the Korean War.

* * *

The United Nations Command (UNC) delegation, led by Vice-Admiral Turner Joy, began negotiations with the Communists at Kaesong on July 10, 1951, two days after the first meeting of the liaison group. The UNC had three overall objectives: to establish a cease-fire along a line of contact that was militarily defensible; to call into existence a joint commission to supervise the truce; and to convince the Communists that these were military rather than political talks—that the sole objective of the talks was a cessation of hostilities. For its part, the Communist delegation, headed by Nam Il, favored the thirty-eighth parallel as the line of demarcation and called for the removal of all foreign troops from the peninsula. Both General Ridgway and Admiral Joy saw these two issues as essentially political in nature, since to agree to the thirty-eighth parallel would have meant the recognition of the pre-1950 division of the country. Finally, while the July 1951 line of contact was militarily defensible, the old parallel was not.

Despite these early differences (which plagued the negotiators for months) the two sides were able to agree on a working agenda for the talks by the end of July. The agenda contained five items:

1. Adoption of an agenda.
2. Fixing a military demarcation line between both sides so as to establish a demilitarized zone as a basic condition for a cease-fire.
3. Concrete arrangements for the realization of a cease-fire and an armistice, including the composition, authority, and functions of a supervising organization.
4. Arrangements relating to prisoners of war (POW's).
5. Recommendations to the governments of the countries concerned on both sides.

That it took the negotiators several weeks to agree upon an agenda foreshadowed future frustrations; these initial conferences were characterized by a series of interruptions as each side sought to influence the outcome of the talks. This pattern began on August 4th when a group of Chinese soldiers blocked the path of the United Nations delegation; in retaliation, Ridgway broke off the talks for six days, after which they resumed, though they remained deadlocked. Two weeks later the Communists accused the United Nations forces of dropping a napalm bomb in the conference area and Ridgway, irritated once again by the Communists' lack of good faith, refused to send the delegation into the conference tent. The General's main strategy here was to move the talks to an area that would be more neutral than Kaesong. When the Communists agreed to meet at Panmunjom the talks were finally resumed on October 25th. A week later General Nam Il consented to the U.N.'s concept that the "line of contact" was to serve as the demarcation line between the two sectors. While both sides continued to disagree about the location of such a line, this was a major victory for the anti-Communist position. While sporadic advances were made in the "peace tent," the shelling continued across the new division, often accompanied by heavy casualties (a fact, as shall be demonstrated, that the Republicans continually used against the Administration). Perhaps as important as this constant warfare was the continuous escalation of military strength by both sides. While the Republicans often complained that the Communists were using the negotiations as a method of diverting attention from their military buildup, it should be remembered that as early as August 1951, the United Nations forces numbered in excess of 550,000.

The opposition, of course, was not idle. An important step was taken by the Communists in strengthening their position when an agreement was signed on November 27th—at the suggestion of the UNC—to the effect that the line of contact as of that date, as decided upon by staff officers of both sides, was to be considered the demarcation line *if* the two sides could agree to an armistice within thirty days. Since nothing was to be gained by an advance in territory should an armistice be signed within a month's time, the Communists used this breathing spell to heavily reinforce their defensive network.

Such agreements—and the peace talks themselves—led many Republicans to the conclusion that the Administration was plotting to end the war at all costs, regardless of our military position in the area. This objection to our failure to fight an offensive war while negotiating is strongly supported by Henry A. Kissinger in his influential *Nuclear Weapons and Foreign Policy*. It is Kissinger's contention that the Administration made a substantial military error in deciding at the outset of the talks that only a defensive war would be fought. The error, the author suggests, was in the underlying assumption that the peace talks were somehow independent of the military position occupied by each side.

> Our decision to stop military operations, except those of a purely defensive nature, at the *very beginning* of the armistice negotiations reflected our conviction that the process of negotiation operated on its own inherent logic independently of the military pressures brought to bear. But by stopping military operations we removed the only Chinese incentive for a settlement; we produced the frustration of two years of inconclusive negotiations. In short, our insistence on divorcing force from diplomacy caused our power to lack purpose and our negotiations to lack force.[1]

Despite the difficulties inherent in these negotiations, by the spring of 1952 all items on the agenda had been agreed to with the exception of the prisoners of war question, the Communists' desire to rehabilitate the air fields in North Korea, and the question of including Russia as a member of the Neutral Nations Supervisory Commission. Clearly the most important of these three issues was that concerning the prisoners of war, which deadlocked the negotiations for fifteen months. The core of the problem was the Communists' demand for automatic repatriation of all POW's while the United Nations insisted that it would only agree to voluntary repatriation. On May 7, 1952 Truman made the following statement on the POW issue: ". . . there shall not be a forced repatriation of prisoners of war—as the Communists have insisted. To agree to forced repatriation would be unthinkable. It would be repugnant to the fundamental moral and humanitarian principles which underlie our action in Korea. To return these prisoners of war in our hands by force would result in misery and bloodshed to the eternal dishonor of the United States and of the U.N."[2]

While this position won the acceptance of the Republican party, there was another aspect of the POW question which

---

[1] Kissinger, pp. 50–51. Emphasis his.
[2] Truman, *Memoirs*, II, p. 461.

heightened the public's ever-increasing hostility toward the war, thus making it an even greater political liability. At the end of 1951 the Communists released a list of prisoners that were being detained; the list contained 11,559 names, 3,200 of which were Americans. With growing horror the nation realized that according to figures of the United Nations almost 100,000 members of the UNC had been captured, and of these 11,224 were American. The vast discrepancy in the two sets of figures represented those who had apparently been either murdered or had died in Communist POW camps. These details were hardly calculated to increase the American public's sympathy for the war.[3]

While there was almost constant firing across the line of contact during the peace talks, the Republicans bitterly complained that the United States refused to fight an offensive war. Yet the navy and the air force under the UNC were employed in this period in such a way that would be hard to characterize as merely "defensive," Kissinger notwithstanding. The navy undertook a large-scale blockade of North Korea, preventing Chinese and Russian supplies from reaching that portion of the peninsula by the water route (a good many Republicans continually demanded that this blockade be extended to Red China so as to prevent her receipt and delivery of vital war materiel). The naval blockade left the supply routes on land open to the interdiction strategy of the air force, although there were problems here that were never solved. One of the primary difficulties in the plan to bomb and destroy vital North Korean targets was that by the fall of 1951 Soviet aid to the Red Chinese air force enabled the opposition to become quite effective in deterring the U.N.'s daylight raids. Another problem was that the Communists had an uncanny ability for repairing rail and road connections that were destroyed in the bombing raids, and were frequently able to provide alternative methods of supply (often by using runners to deliver food and ammunition).

---

[3] *Ibid.*, p. 460.

The most dramatic of our interdiction attempts began on June 23, 1952 when United States air power bombed and destroyed the North Korean hydroelectric system, including its Suiho plant on the Yalu River. As a result of this and subsequent raids on the power system, much of North Korea remained without effective electrical supply for the remainder of the war. Politically, the raids were important because of the British reaction to the bombings and the ensuing Republican hostility to the British position. Essentially the British complained that as an ally of the United States she should have been consulted before an offensive drive of this magnitude was undertaken. Much to the annoyance of the GOP, Secretary of State Acheson made some attempt to apologize; there was considerable Republican support for the view that the British attitude was further proof that our allies were uncooperative and that we must strive for a "harder line" in Asia.[4]

There were, in addition, several changes within the United Nations Command itself in this period. In May of 1952 Ridgway assumed General Eisenhower's NATO post after the General decided, as a consequence of the returns in a number of primaries, that he must reach some conclusion about his Presidential ambitions. Ridgway was replaced in Korea by General Mark W. Clark, whose *From the Danube to the Yalu* indicates that he favored a somewhat more militant course in Korea than the Administration was pursuing.

> I was in favor . . . after carefully studying the situation and discussing it with all my senior commanders, who concurred, of an all-out offensive to win the war, providing Washington could furnish me both the authority and the additional infantry divisions and air and naval support required. . . .
>
> I knew that victory would entail heavy losses, but I also was convinced, and still am, that the losses we suffered gaining victory in Korea would be far less than the losses we would have to take eventually if we failed to win militarily in Korea and

---

[4] See pp. 124–126.

waited until the Communists were ready to fight on their own terms.[5]

Along with these changes in command, the Joint Chiefs of Staff, apparently in sympathy with Admiral Joy's feeling that he had reached a permanent impasse in the negotiations at Panmunjom, agreed to his replacement by Major General William K. Harrison.

✿   ✿   ✿

The Republican party's response to the Korean War in the July 1951 to July 1952 period can be characterized by: a determination to increase pressure on the Administration to terminate its limited war policy; the conviction that the peace talks were being used by the Communists to shield an ever-increasing escalation; and the genesis of an alternative foreign policy.

As the MacArthur Hearings came to a conclusion in June of 1951, Republican enmity toward the policy of limited war remained pronounced. The Administration was accused by Senator Cain of sacrificing this country's young men on "the altar of futility . . . in a vicious war in which American forces are prevented from utilizing their maximum strength and are required to fight with inadequate numbers."[6] Lodge, who had been urging a more rapid buildup of American military strength since the outset of hostilities, finally broke with the Administration on the general philosophy of limited war late in August when he made public a copy of a report which he had submitted to Chairman Russell at the close of the MacArthur Hearings. While bringing his report to light, Lodge said that "Failure to do all in our power to support our troops is a new development in America. It is a most unhappy one, full of fateful consequences for the future. It shocks our national

---

[5] Mark W. Clark, *From the Danube to the Yalu* (New York, 1954), pp. 180–82.

[6] *Congressional Record*, August 16, 1951, p. A5185.

sense of decency." He went on to advocate the adoption of "economic, military and political" measures so as to "end the war through application of pressure on the Kremlin, and to do so as rapidly as we can." [7] On this issue Lodge was supported by the conservative wing of the party—a group that he was soon to alienate by his successful attempt to capture the Presidential nomination for General Eisenhower. Jenner declared that we were bogged down in a "treadmill war in Korea," while Malone characterized the war as "that police action which our boys are not allowed to win and which they dare not lose." [8] Although he was much more inclined to speak on domestic rather than foreign affairs, McCarthy took pains to denounce the State and Defense Departments for their fear that if we adopted a policy of victory we would become involved in a major war with Russia,[9] and Knowland told a Los Angeles audience in February that he was shocked during the hearings to listen to "witness after witness, high in the councils of our Nation, tell why we couldn't win a victory in Korea over Communist aggressors who have been designated by the U.N. as outlaws. Among the reasons given were, fear of what Communist China might do, or fear of what the Soviet Union might do, or fear of what our allies might do or say." [10]

Wayne Morse of Oregon was simply crying in the wind when he attempted to warn his colleagues of the great danger that would arise from an escalation of the war.

> When we pull back the veil of the war propaganda of those who are advocating expanding the war in Asia, we are confronted with the ugly proposal on the part of this growing war clique in the United States that we commit an act which constitutes for the first time in American history an aggressive act of war against a foreign power. I do not believe that we should push

---

[7] *Congressional Record,* August 24, 1951, p. 10609. Also see *The New York Times,* February 19, 1952, p. 5.

[8] *Congressional Record,* October 18, 1951, p. 13422, and *Congressional Record,* September 24, 1951, p. 11943.

[9] *Congressional Record,* February 6, 1952, p. 805.

[10] *Congressional Record,* February 19, 1952, p. A957.

the American people into a war through the back door. I believe that the constitutional provision for a declaration of war is still the legal process we should follow in putting this nation of ours into a war. That should have gone for Korea as well as any other possible war in Asia.[11]

Related to the Republican animosity toward fighting a "half-war" was the party's continued disenchantment with the implications of containment. It is important to note here the emphasis placed on the cost of containment, for again a good deal of the Republican criticism was centered on the economic aspects of the program. A major Republican spokesman who was particularly opposed to containment on these grounds was Taft. While agreeing with the Administration that we must not relax our efforts to halt Communist expansion, Taft insisted that "There are definite limitations on what the United States can do. We cannot undertake to engage in land warfare with Russia throughout the entire world, or meet every advance the Communists may make. . . . Already the administration seems to contemplate a total deficit spending of $50,000,000,000 during the two years at the peak of our rearming." [12] The fear that we would "ruin ourselves economically" by adhering to Kennan's program was also voiced by Flanders in the course of an address before the Dallas Council of World Affairs.

> The Korean campaign is indeed a preview . . . of the difficulties in which we will find ourselves in any endeavor to contain the Soviet Government militarily. . . . In response to that Government's challenges, we shall be frantically rushing from spot to spot, always at great expense, always with the shedding of the valuable blood of our sons, our husbands, and our brothers in this gigantic effort to contain the Soviet power militarily. . . .
>
> What gives us the most serious reasons for pausing to reflect on this containment policy is that we quite evidently may, and if

---

[11] *Congressional Record,* February 14, 1952, p. 1011.
[12] *Congressional Record,* July 30, 1951, p. A4762.

we do not reflect will, ruin ourselves economically by inflation or over-taxation or, more likely, by both together.[13]

Brewster complained that "To maintain a merely defensive position indefinitely means exhaustion of our resources, as we maintain a constant state of readiness awaiting the time when the enemy shall decide to attack," [14] and Special Ambassador John Foster Dulles, an important figure in the evolution of an alternative foreign policy in 1952, also opposed the economic implications of containment: ". . . to attempt generally a policy of military containment along 25,000 miles, with the Russians having both an immense force and interior lines, would, I suppose, be impractical as a military matter; and surely it is impractical as an economic matter." [15] The most complete statement of Dulles' position up to the time of the Republican National Convention is to be found in his now-famous *Life* article entitled "A Policy of Boldness." While his attention was focused on the evolving concept of deterrent power (to be discussed below), he did attack the economic pitfalls in the current techniques being employed to hold the line against Communism.

If you will think back over the past six years, you will see that our policies have largely involved emergency action to try to "contain" Soviet communism by checking it here or blocking it there. We are not working, sacrificing and spending in order to be able to live *without* this peril—but to live *with* it, presumably forever. . . . Our present negative policies will never end the type of sustained offensive which Soviet Communism is mounting; they will never end the peril nor bring relief from the exertions which devour our economic, political and moral vitals. Ours are treadmill policies which, at best, might perhaps keep us in the same place until we drop exhausted. . . .

The Administration's security policies would this year cost us, in money, about 60 billion, of which about 99% goes for military

---

[13] *Congressional Record*, January 23, 1952, p. A353.

[14] *Congressional Record*, April 10, 1952, pp. A2355–56.

[15] John Foster Dulles, "Can We Stop Russian Imperialism?" *United States Department of State Bulletin*, December 10, 1951, p. 939.

purposes and for equipment (which will quickly become obsolete and demand replacement indefinitely). Such gigantic expenditures unbalance our budget and require taxes so heavy that they discourage incentive. They so cheapen the dollar that savings, pensions and Social Security reserves have already lost much of their value.[16]

Even when not addressing themselves directly to the concept of containment, Taft and Dulles continually charged that Truman's foreign policy was leading to financial ruin. During his ill-fated primary fight in New Hampshire, Taft outlined his position: "As a good neighbor we desire to help the rest of the world in any reasonable way. But certainly that cannot be a primary object of foreign policy or an excuse for the wrecking of our economy at home for the terrible tragedy of war." [17] As the GOP convention neared, Tafted granted an interview to *U.S. News & World Report* during which he indicated that his opposition to both a large land army and the European aid program was based as much on domestic fiscal considerations as it was on military strategy.[18]

One of the most popular Republican remedies to relieve the financial and military burden of the Korean War was to permit the Chinese Nationalists to participate in the war effort in Asia, a remedy long advocated by the GOP. Governor Dewey, who could hardly be classified as an Administration enemy, thought that the Democrats were making a serious mistake in not integrating Formosa into the security network in the Pacific. "The island of Formosa is essential to the defense of the Philippines. . . . And yet in these troubled times our National Government has been on-again, off-again on Formosa four times in two years. We need a firm and broadly developed policy concerning Formosa, establishing its permanent position as part of the free world." [19] Along these same general

---

[16] John Foster Dulles, "A Policy of Boldness," *Life*, May 19, 1952, p. 146. Emphasis his.

[17] *The New York Times*, March 7, 1952, p. 15.

[18] "Taft," *U.S. News & World Report*," June 13, 1952, p. 100.

[19] *Congressional Record*, September 24, 1951, p. A5797.

lines Senator Watkins voiced his belief that "The American people ought to rise in their wrath and demand that all those willing to fight communism in Asia, particularly those who have special rights to carry on that fight, should be used in every battle and at every point where they can be used effectively." [20]

To move from Asia to Europe for a moment, the failure of our allies to comply with the spirit of the United Nations position toward the Communist aggressors in Korea was a constant irritant to Republicans. The GOP's reaction to this situation was to insist that the Administration take punitive measures against those nations who failed to support us in Korea. The party's opposition to the passage of the Administration-supported Battle Act (which was to replace the Republican-sponsored Kem Amendment) demonstrates the basic outlines of the Republican position on the subject of Allied cooperation. Briefly put, the Kem Amendment provided that Economic Cooperation Administration (ECA) funds would be denied to those countries shipping war materiel to Communist nations. The measure, however, gave the National Security Council the right to make certain exceptions to this rule, and the Council made broad use of this power, much to the dismay of the Republicans. In an attempt to prevent the Administration from taking such action in the future, on August 9, 1951 Kem proposed another amendment (S.1987) to tighten his previous measure. The key paragraph of the new amendment struck out the provision that exceptions could be made at the discretion of the National Security Council.[21] Three weeks later the Battle bill was introduced in the House (H.R.4550). This bill stated that the Administration had the power to determine when and if goods were to be classified as strategic, and, more importantly, to determine whether or not an ECA country would have its aid cut off because it exported such goods. The Battle Act passed the Senate on August 28th,

---

[20] *Congressional Record*, October 20, 1951, p. 13682.
[21] *Congressional Record*, August 9, 1951, p. 9714.

with the only opposition coming from a hard core of sixteen Republicans who had consistently favored the Kem Amendment.[22]

Passage of the Battle Act served to heighten the GOP's unrest over the lack of Allied participation in the war. Kem asserted his conviction that passage of the act leaves "no doubt about what is now planned by the administration. American aid to countries furnishing war materials to the Reds will not be stopped. American boys in Korea will continue to be killed and wounded by war material furnished in part by ourselves." Focusing his attention on England's trading policy with Communist nations, Malone pointed out that the enactment of the Battle bill into law raised the question of "whether we approve of Britain's arming our enemies with goods, services, and money which we are furnishing her, or whether we will, without further delay, institute a desperately needed American policy and let the British fit into our picture. Too often the British play their own game and we fall into their picture." [23]

If the Republican attitude toward Allied shipping is indicative of its desire to punish those nations not supporting United States policy in Asia, its response to English protests over this country's bombing of the North Korean power stations demonstrates the considerable support within the party for America's following a stronger course in the Far East. Upon hearing of the American attacks on the Yalu power plants late in June of 1952, both Attlee and Bevan declared that the unilateral decision was in violation of the spirit of America's pledge to consult her allies in actions of this nature. This protest from a country then shipping supplies to Red China nettled the GOP; Cain took the position that since we were the "command agent" for the United Nations, our action was in no way extraordinary. Knowland's defense of the American action

---

[22] *Congressional Record*, August 28, 1951, p. 10744. For the details of the measure, see *ibid.*, p. 10725. Also see Appendix, pp. 299–301.

[23] *Congressional Record*, September 14, 1951, p. 11358. Kem: *ibid.*, p. 11357.

closely paralleled Cain's statement, for he agreed that ". . . as the command agent we are authorized to take any steps required by military necessity, without referring the need for a particular operation to anyone." [24]

Before turning to the Republican reaction to the peace talks at Kaesong and Panmunjom, some mention should be made of the GOP's attitude toward Truman and his decision to intervene in the period under discussion here. While Truman was under increasing attack for the steps he had taken since June of 1950, up to the time of the opening of the 1952 Republican National Convention he still had some powerful Republican supporters of his June decision—notably Dulles and Dewey. But his detractors far outnumbered his supporters. Accusing the President of an "arbitrary action," Ferguson warned that "the Nation cannot afford to risk blundering into world war III through some similar episode." Taft, now in full-blown retreat from his initial position toward the war, conjured up a rather sinister picture of the President making nocturnal decisions: "The Korean war was begun by President Truman without the slightest authority from Congress or the people in a hasty decision the night of June 26, 1950. He plunged this country into a major war, when under the Constitution only Congress can declare war." Andrew Schoeppel declared that in the light of Truman's actions, "To place a United Nations label on this Korean war is a shabby and disgraceful farce," and Wiley was sure that had Truman sought the advice and consent of the Senate, "America and the world could have been saved from the horrors of Korea and the threat of a suicidal world war." [25]

But not all Republicans at this time were opposed to our role in the Korean conflict. The titular head of the party told

---

[24] *Congressional Record*, June 25, 1952, p. 8131. Cain: *ibid.*, p. 8016.

[25] *Congressional Record*, May 9, 1952, p. 4987. Ferguson: *Congressional Record*, July 30, 1951, p. 9122. Taft: *Congressional Record*, October 16, 1951, p. A6422. Also see *The New York Times*, November 18, 1951, p. 62 and November 29, 1951, p. 27. Schoeppel; *Congressional Record*, June 25, 1951, p. 8002.

the annual convention of the American Bar Association in September that he was "positive that the most astonished and incredulous man on earth was Mr. Josef Stalin when the United States did a backward summersault, announced that we would defend Korea and moved swiftly and decisively in the United Nations for action by the free nations of the world. The decision was right. It was necessary. I supported it wholeheartedly the day it was made and I still do." [26] Practically on the eve of the Republican convention Dulles' *Life* article appeared. While he wrote of his disapproval of the general philosophy behind American foreign policy, he defended Truman's June action: "In Korea, for all our failures to deter attack, we did respond nobly when the attack came. President Truman's decision that the United States should go to the defense of the Korean Republic was courageous, righteous, and in the national interest." [27] The Presidential campaign had not begun in earnest and so Dullas could afford to be generous.

❀ ❀ ❀

In examining the development of the Republican party's position toward the cease-fire and armistice attempts of the Administration, one finds that the GOP was hostile to the negotiations even before they began, in good part because of the belief that the United States, through the United Nations, was operating from a position of weakness which would lead to certain appeasement. While the party's hostility toward the Kaesong and Panmunjom talks grew from 1951 to 1953, its members never offered the Administration the slightest cooperation or encouragement, for the great majority of the Republicans clearly favored a MacArthur-styled military solution. Jenner summed up this view when he said "I am sure . . . [MacArthur] would not have ridden in a little jeep with a

---

[26] Reprinted in *Congressional Record,* September 24, 1951, p. A5797.
[27] Dulles, "A Policy of Boldness," p. 146.

small white flag flying on it into the Communist enemy territory to sit down and talk about peace. He warned that if the
United Nations stopped 'its tolerant effort to contain the war
in the area of Korea [it would] doom Red China to the risk of
military collapse.'" Two weeks after the Kaesong conference
began, New York's Senator Ives expressed grave doubt over
the advisability of our participation in talks that had been
initiated by the Communists. "Let us not be deluded by the
so-called truce or agenda connected with it or by any cease-
fire resulting from it, which may occur in Korea. . . . Let us
remember . . . that the negotiations between our forces and
the Chinese Reds and North Koreans were initially carried on
according to their terms, at their stipulated time, at their
picked location, and in their prescribed fashion." The very
idea of seeking a negotiated peace, and a seemingly disastrous
one at that, was the result of a growing "fear psychosis" which
had gripped many of our United Nations associates, according
to Knowland. This group of Allies was demanding a "peace at
any price" formula to end the war, as if unaware that such a
peace, in Knowland's opinion, would constitute "a tremendous
victory for aggressive Communism in Asia." [28]

While these statements were made within a few months of
the opening of the talks, the great Republican resistance to the
peace attempt at Panmunjom continued throughout the period. It seems clear that while the underlying cause for the
dissatisfaction was the GOP's great desire for a traditional
military victory, there were three immediate reasons for the
party's attitude toward the talks. In ascending order of importance they were: (1) the fear that along with a cease-fire, the
negotiators would agree to a United Nations seat for Red
China and Communist domination of Formosa; (2) the realization that a negotiated peace meant that the goal of a unified
Korea was doomed; and (3) the belief that the Communists
were using the talks merely as a screen to cover a massive

[28] *Congressional Record,* August 24, 1951, p. A5388. Jenner: *Congressional Record,* September 24, 1951, p. 11944. Ives: *Congressional Record,* July 24, 1951, p. A4619.

"Now, Here's A General I Have Confidence In"

Reprinted from *The Herblock Book* (Beacon Press, 1952)

military buildup behind the thirty-eighth parallel and the Yalu River.

So persistent was the Republican concern over the fate of Formosa and her position in the United Nations that the day before the formal opening of the peace talks Flanders warned the Administration not to yield "to the blackmailing attempt of Communist China to 'shoot its way into the United Nations' . . . [or to agree to] damaging arrangements as to Formosa and the Nationalist Army." Three days later Senator Martin told the annual convention of Pennsylvania Veterans of Foreign Wars that "we must make known to the world that we will not permit Formosa to fall into the hands of Communist China. We must make known to Russia and every other nation that we will not permit any aggressor to shoot his way into the United Nations over the bodies of American boys." As always, the major spokesman for Formosa in the Congress was Knowland, who warned that the American public and the Congress would not tolerate any compromise over Formosa: ". . . there must be no Far-Eastern Munich which betrays either the free people of Korea or of Formosa to the Communists. . . . Our associates should be told in language that is so clear that no one can misunderstand that if they vote Red China into membership, as some of them tonight are negotiating to do, that on that day the United States will withdraw." [29]

If the fate of Formosa was a rallying point for the Republicans in their assault on the Administration's attempts to reach a negotiated settlement, an even greater and more fundamental issue was raised over the question of unifying Korea. Truman's assertion in his 1952 State of the Union message that "we went into the fight to preserve the Republic of Korea" [30] was but another attempt by the President to make clear that our original aim was the protection of South Korea, and not the unification of the entire peninsula. It was necessary to continually remind the country (and particularly the Republican party) of this because the GOP loudly insisted that our 1950 aim was indeed unification. The party would not agree that the unification attempt in October and November of 1950

---

[29] *Congressional Record,* February 7, 1952, A721. Flanders: *Congressional Record,* July 9, 1951, p. 7769. Martin: *Congressional Record,* July 30, 1951, p. A4756.

[30] Truman, *Public Papers, 1952,* p. 12.

was a temporary shift in policy which represented a terrible tactical error. Party members constantly asserted that the Yalu River was Korea's historic boundary, and as such must be restored. That the country had been divided after World War II, and remained divided at the time of the North Korean assault, was studiously ignored by the party's spokesmen.

A week after the opening of the Kaesong talks, Cain made a lengthy presentation of the view that it was the entry of Red China into the war that caused the United States and the United Nations to alter their original goal, and that the United States must not permit this altered policy to come to fruition. "A divided Korea would be a continuing and amazingly costly liability . . . the economic life of Korea will remain disrupted and she will become an economic burden on the United States. Politically, the Republic of Korea will be faced with conditions of terror and tension until an ultimate settlement is reached." Nearly a year later Cain (who was one of the few Republicans still supporting Truman's original decision to aid the South Koreans) told the audience of the American Forum of the Air that the United States could not agree to any settlement that called for less than the unification of the peninsula.[31]

In an August address entitled "American Foreign Policy in the Far East" and delivered at Chautauqua, New York, Knowland strongly objected to an agreement that authorized a return to the status quo ante bellum: ". . . this Nation is negotiating terms of a settlement at Kaesong . . . which leaves the North Koreans in possession of most of the territory they had before their aggression and leaves the Chinese Communist aggressor free to move elsewhere when he thinks the time is right." Smith of New Jersey was similarly disposed to have the negotiators ignore the fact that at the time of the opening of hostilities Korea was in effect two nations. Smith based his argument for unification on the belief that "The United Nations had the responsibility for the entire Republic of Korea

---

[31] *Congressional Record,* May 7, 1952, p. A2778. For Cain's earlier statement see *Congressional Record,* August 16, 1951, pp. A5184–85.

and when the Commies had defied the United Nations and stayed in Korea in defiance, then the U.N. should get together and say, 'You get out,' withdraw recognition, and cut off trade, do everything to force them to recognize the authority of the United Nations." In a January radio and television address that was widely hailed by Republicans, former President Herbert Hoover attacked the armistice attempt on the grounds that "in this negotiation we have retreated from the original purpose of unity and independence for Korea to an appeasement idea of a division of Korea about where it was before." [32]

Perhaps the most interesting and revealing of all Republican attitudes on this issue was the position taken by Taft. The Ohio Senator made several comments in this period that would lead one to conclude (erroneously) that he had acquiesced to the idea of a "stalemate peace at the thirty-eighth parallel." For instance, he told the Plymouth County Republican Club in July of 1951 that ". . . there have been 80,000 American boys killed or wounded, we have destroyed the very nation to whose assistance we went and it is said that there have been a million civilian casualties. Certainly a stalemate peace at the thirty-eighth parallel is better than a stalemate war at the thirty-eighth parallel." But the Ohioan had not given up the idea of following MacArthur's program to force the Communists north of the Yalu, for in the course of a campaign swing through Tennessee he strongly denounced the Administration for not following the General's policies, "especially the bombing of Communist air fields and the use of Chinese Nationalist Government troops for diversionary raids on South China." Again in a February speech to the Republican Vermonters he spoke of winning the war in precisely the same way that MacArthur had defined victory.[33] By

---

[32] *The New York Times,* January 27, 1952, p. 42. Knowland: *Congressional Record,* August 24, 1951, p. A5388. Smith: *Congressional Record,* January 15, 1952, p. A130.

[33] Robert A. Taft, "Faults of the Present Administration," *Vital Speeches,* March 15, 1952, p. 332. Also see *Congressional Record,* July 30, 1951, p. A4762 for Plymouth County Republican Club statement and *The New York Times,* October 31, 1951, p. 21 for an account of his remarks in Tennessee.

their insistence that the United States and the United Nations had come to the relief of the Republic of Korea for the purpose of defeating the Communists and unifying the country, the GOP members deliberately sought to impress upon the American public the idea that the Panmunjom talks were nothing more than a dishonorable sellout of our objectives in the Pacific.

While the question of unification greatly influenced the Republican position toward the peace talks, the most persistent criticism of the Administration's efforts toward peace was that these efforts permitted the Communists to use the negotiations as a cover for their stepped-up mobilization program. The strength and appeal of this argument stemmed from the simple fact that it was true; *both* sides were increasing their military potential, either on the peninsula or in its immediate vicinity. The Republicans, however, took our build-up for granted while decrying similar tactics by the Communists. Typical was Cain's observation that while we were negotiating at Kaesong the Communists "used the talks as a screen behind which they moved fresh troops, more aircraft, a large quantity of artillery, and many modern tanks into the line and in reserve. That is where they are now, waiting to go against us." Cain's analysis of this buildup in Korea was based on a trip to the area in the winter of 1951–52. Upon his return in January he reported to his colleagues that "it is perfectly clear to anyone who visits Korea that the Communists have increased their fire power by making available more artillery and ground forces. Worse than that, they have increased their air power by constructing airfields behind the Yalu, in North Korea, thus placing the position of the United Nations in jeopardy in the event the truce talks collapse." [34]

In a major radio address on June 1, 1952, Taft likened the United Nations attitude toward the Communist buildup to France's attitude toward Hitler at the outset of World War II.

---

[34] *Congressional Record,* January 29, 1952, p. 570. For Cain's earlier statement see *Congressional Record,* October 3, 1951, pp. 12539–40.

"Today our policy in Korea is exactly that of the French during their so-called phony war against Hitler from November 1939 to May 1940. The French waited while Hitler built up his strength. In May 1940, the French Army was destroyed. I pray God that our national administration is not preparing the same fate for our men in Korea." The following day, at his home base at Oakland, Knowland compared MacArthur's solution to the present situation in Korea in which the Communists continued to increase "their reinforcements, their artillery, and their motor transportation. Their air power has been built up to the point where they now threaten to take superiority in the air over Korea away from us." An infrequent contributor to the foreign policy debate over Korea was Kansas' Senator Andrew Schoeppel, but on the second anniversary of the Korean War he made a major foreign policy address and one of his foremost concerns was the apparent willingness of the United Nations Command to talk rather than fight while the Communists were augmenting their strength.

> Month after month our negotiators sit in the tents at Panmunjom, listening to Communist bickering and double talk. . . . In the meantime, this formidable foe reorganizes his army, brings in a Russian air force, prepares entrenched positions, and assembles artillery and self-propelled guns and tanks in vast quantities. . . .

> Vice Admiral C. Turner Joy, former chief negotiator at Panmunjom . . . stated as early as February 29, 1952, that the military advantage which the Allies held in July 1951 had been lost during the armistice talks. He warned the American people that: "We must realize that we are not negotiating from the same position of military strength as we were at the beginning, when the enemy was badly pressed, but from a position of mass stalemate." [35]

Up to the time of the Republican National Convention, Eisenhower's comments on Korea were distinctly low-keyed.

---

[35] *Congressional Record*, June 25, 1952, pp. 8002–03. Taft: *Congressional Record*, June 3, 1952, p. A3410. Knowland: *Congressional Record*, June 5, 1952, p. A3495.

The best account of his views on the war in the period between his return in May and his nomination in early July are to be found in the transcript of a June 5th press conference. At this time Eisenhower was not taking the position that the Administration had made a monumental error in permitting itself to become entangled in peace talks with an enemy that was preparing to crush the UNC; rather, he made the observation that the Communist buildup in Manchuria, particularly in the realm of air power, made it impossible for the UNC to extend the war until similar strides were made in the same direction by the UNC.[36] Yet the General's position here was far from representative of the GOP's reaction to the Communists' tactics in Korea during the Panmunjom talks. Much more typical in spirit and tone was Hoover's ominous warning toward the conclusion of his January 27th address to the nation: ". . . during these negotiations the Chinese have built up a great air force. What the outcome may be we do not know."[37]

To measure the effect of the Republican attack on the peace talks one must consider that the nation by July of 1952 had been at war for two years, and had been frustrated in both its attempts to win the war and negotiate the peace. The Republicans, in effect, were saying that if the Administration continues its present policies the Communists will continue to mobilize, evenually break off negotiations, and finally confront us with overwhelming military superiority in Korea and the Far East. But there was an alternative to this catastrophe: the solution was to be found, or so the GOP would have the nation believe, in the emerging Republican strategy for peace through the development of deterrent power.

✿   ✿   ✿

The development of an alternative Republican foreign policy involved two distinct problems. The party's immediate

[36] *The New York Times,* June 6, 1952, p. 10. For a more complete view, see pp. 215–217.

[37] *The New York Times,* January 28, 1952, p. 6.

concern was to find a solution for ending the Korean War; at the same time, it attempted to offer recommendations for the prevention of the further spread of Communism. As has been demonstrated, by June of 1951 the GOP had largely rejected the Democratic policies of limited war and containment as inadequate for conducting or preventing wars. And too, so far as the Korean War was concerned, the very idea of a negotiated settlement had become anathema. Given the Republican contention that the only solution to the crisis was a decisive military victory, the party still had to offer some alternative to containment, and by the time the Republican National Convention met in July, the basic outlines of deterrent power and liberation—the GOP's answer to containment—had been set forth.

While Dulles is generally credited with having developed the concept of deterrent power (and he was the major advocate of this program), Taft had been offering a very similar idea for some time. In *A Foreign Policy for Americans* Taft wrote:

> It seems to me that by reasonable alliance with Britain, Australia and Canada the control of sea and air can establish a power which never can be challenged by Russia and which can to a great extent protect Europe, and it has been protected now for five years through fear of what sea and air power can accomplish against Russia. There is no need for a specific line of defense in every section of the world, but we can exercise a power for peace over a vast area. If the Russians realize that our power in the final outcome of war cannot be challenged except on the continent of Eurasia, and perhaps not there in the final issue, and that it can do real damage to their own nation with the atomic bomb and otherwise, their purpose of military aggression in Eurasia itself may well wither.[38]

That Taft's formulation of deterrent power was restricted rather narrowly to the development and use of a powerful air force (with its attendant ability to hurl atom bombs at an

---

[38] Robert A. Taft, *A Foreign Policy for Americans* (Garden City, 1951), p. 79.

aggressive Russia) is clear from his responses during an interview that was conducted by *U.S. News & World Report* and published in June 1952. "Control of the air . . . is the only possible insurance of peace, and Russia must know that certain kinds of aggression will be met by an air attack . . . The ability of our Air Force to deliver atom bombs on Russia should never be open to question, and today it is being questioned, even by our own experts. Until it is fully established we cannot be certain of peace." [39]

The more definitive statement of this evolving concept of deterrent power was to come from Special Ambassador John Foster Dulles. Two factors should be recognized in examining this new concept—the desire of the GOP to formulate a less expensive foreign program, and the *dis*inclination of party members to sanction that part of MacArthur's program that entailed the United States' fighting wars "Alone, if necessary." [40] If deterrent power was to be less expensive than containment, it also envisioned a *multilateral* threat to Russian expansion. As early as November of 1951 Dulles outlined for the Advertising Council of Detroit his ideas for stemming the Communist threat.

> Let the free nations combine to create a striking force of great power and then rely more and more upon the deterrent of that punishing power, and less and less upon a series of many local area defenses. That means having, at whatever are the convenient places, the capacity to hit Russia's interior lines of communication with such disruptive power that its highly centralized despotic police state will fall apart. Russian militarists will not invite that by sending the Red armies to capture other peoples' lands. [41]

---

[39] "Taft," *U.S. News and World Report*, June 13, 1952, p. 100.

[40] At the hearings, MacArthur said: "If the other nations of the world haven't got enough sense to see where appeasement leads after the appeasement which led to the second World War in Europe, if they can't see exactly the road that they are following in Asia, why then, we had better protect ourselves and go it alone." Hearings, p. 42.

[41] John Foster Dulles, "Can We Stop Russian Imperialism?," *Vital Speeches*, December 10, 1951, p. 940.

It was in May of 1952, however, that Dulles made his major statements on the subject and refined the policy that he would later support as Secretary of State. On May 5th he told a Far Eastern Conference audience in Paris that

> It is not possible to create, through the vast Asian sector of the frontier of freedom, the kind of local defense which is being created here in Western Europe. The cost of that would be prohibitive. So long as Soviet and Chinese Communist leaders can pick the time, place and method of aggression, anywhere in Asia, and so long as we only rush ground troops to meet it at the time they select, at the place they select, and with the weapons they select, we are at a disadvantage which can be fatal.
>
> On the other hand, the free world possesses, particularly in sea and air power, the capacity to hit the aggressor where it hurts, at times and places of our own choosing. If a potential aggressor knew in advance that his aggression would bring that answer, then I am convinced that he would not commit aggression. . . .
>
> That could be done within the framework of the United Nations Charter and perhaps with the help of such agencies as the Peace Observation Commission. If it were done that way, it would, on the one hand, impress more strongly the potential aggressors, and, on the other hand, give reassurance that no single free world nation would recklessly take action which might have grave consequences for many.[42]

A week later he was invited to address the National Conference of Christians and Jews, and once again Dulles voiced his belief that "The only deterrent that will, at bearable cost, protect the entire frontier of freedom is the organization of striking power to hit any aggressor—where it hurts—if he should commit himself to armed aggression anywhere." [43] The most extensive statement of Dulles' position as of July, 1952 is to be found in his article entitled "A Policy of Boldness." Significantly, Dulles began the piece with an account of the

---

[42] John Foster Dulles, "Far Eastern Problems: Defense through Deterrent Power," *Vital Speeches,* June 1, 1951, p. 494.
[43] Reprinted in *Congressional Record,* May 14, 1952, p. 5147.

fearsome consequences stemming from the Democratic Administration's "gigantic expenditures" for defense. The remedy for this was a foreign policy which afforded a greater degree of security at a lower price. "There is one solution and only one: that is for the free world to develop the will and organize the means to retaliate instantly against open aggression by Red armies, so that, if it occurred anywhere, we could and would strike back where it hurts, by means of our choosing." Dulles argued that such a community punishing power would not provoke Russia to attack: ". . . the Kremlin has not used its Red armies for open military conquest even in these past years when there was no military obstacles in their path." Finally, the future Secretary of State emphasized that his plan definitely included the use of atomic weapons.

> Today atomic energy, coupled with strategic air and sea power, provides the community of free nations with vast new possibilities of organizing a community power to stop open aggression before it starts and reduce, to the vanishing point, the risk of general war. So far these weapons are merely part of national arsenals for use in fighting general war when it has come. If that catastrophe occurs, it will be because we have allowed these new and awesome forces to become the ordinary killing tools of the soldiers when, in the hands of the statesmen, they could serve as effective political weapons in defense of the peace.[44]

The other Republican alternative for halting the spread of Communism was that of liberation. Once again, it was Dulles in his *Life* article who first outlined the general design of this program. The somewhat dubious assumption underlying this policy was that the very suggestion by the United States that it looked forward to the eventual freedom of satellite countries from Mother Russia would greatly speed up the process of separation.

> Liberation from the yoke of Moscow will not occur for a very long time, and courage in neighboring lands will not be sustained, *unless the United States makes it publicly known that it*

---

[44] Dulles, "A Policy of Boldness," pp. 146 and 151–52.

wants and expects liberation to occur. The mere statement of that wish and expectation would change, in an electrifying way, the mood of the captive peoples. It would put heavy new burdens on the jailors and create new opportunities for liberation. . . .

We could make it clear, on the highest authority of the President and the Congress, that United States policy seeks as one of its peaceful goals the eventual restoration of genuine independence in the nations of Europe and Asia now dominated by Moscow, and that we will not be a party to any "deal" confirming the rule of Soviet despotism over the alien peoples which it now dominates. . . .

We do not want a series of bloody uprisings and reprisals. There can be peaceful separation from Moscow, as Tito showed, and enslavement can be made so unprofitable that the master will let go his grip.[45]

These then were the alternatives that the Republican party offered the American people after two frustrating years of war and negotiation in Korea: the hope of a decisive military victory on the peninsula plus the vision of an inexpensive but effective method of deterring further attempts by the Communists to extend their control to the free areas of the world. It was a singularly attractive prospect.

✿ ✿ ✿

As was to be expected in an election year, the Republicans were particularly interested from January through July of 1952 in the probable effect that the foreign policy issue would have on the November race, and party members made it absolutely clear that they would not heed Truman's appeal to

---

[45] *Ibid.*, pp. 154–57. Emphasis his. Smith (N.J.) proved to be a warm supporter of his friend Dulles' concept of liberation, for he believed that containment was an immoral attempt to condone the status quo and thereby condemn the captive peoples of the world to endless supression. The road to peace was through the granting of all peoples a climate of freedom in which they could develop and express their national characters. Untitled draft of a speech dated July 2, 1952. Folder: Convention: 1952. Section VII, Box 207, Smith Papers.

confine politics to the three-mile limit. Knowland told the Republican National Committee gathered in January that "despite the President's speech some weeks ago in Washington, I do not agree with him that foreign policy should not be a subject of campaign discussion. To the contrary, I am firmly convinced that this administration is as vulnerable on its foreign policy as it is on its domestic policy." [46] Earlier, in November, Taft listed the three most important election issues of the coming year as the growth of the federal bureaucracy, the Administration's attempts to introduce socialism into the American economy, and the conduct of our foreign policy. Of the three, the Ohioan said foreign policy would most influence the election. [47]

Shortly after his defeat in the New Hampshire primaries, Taft addressed the Women's National Republican Club, and by the conclusion of the address few could doubt the extent of his rejection of the "me-too" approach of Governor Dewey in 1948. It was equally clear that the Korean crisis had a great deal to do with this decision. He charged that even during the late 1940's, when bipartisanship in foreign affairs was at its height, Senator Vandenberg, the Republican leader in this field, was not consulted on Far Eastern problems. Taft declared that the Democrats could not expect any cooperation now in their attempt to keep Korea out of the election. In his West Virginia primary race the Ohio Senator once again rejected any possibility of cooperation with the Democrats on the Korea issue. He accused the President of hypocrisy in his call for bipartisan support, charging that since 1948 Truman had made "secrecy and arbitrary power . . . the keystone" of his foreign policy. [48]

House Minority Leader Martin, in basic agreement with Taft's position, declared that there was one advantage to come from our failures in Korea: The American people would see that they had no alternative but to defeat the Democratic

---

[46] *Congressional Record*, January 24, 1952, p. A377.
[47] *The New York Times*, November 1, 1951, p. 25.
[48] *The New York Times*, February 5, 1952, p. 22.

leadership in 1952. "They know we can never avert a third world war so long as we follow policies and leadership that have destroyed the balance of power in the world. They know what any sandlot ball player can tell you—in a losing game, you yank the pitcher and put in a new one." Kem spoke of the Korean War as the proverbial straw that would break the back of the public's twenty-year support of Democratic administrations, and Iowa's Bourke Hickenlooper told his Senate colleagues on March 10th that "it is up to every candidate to justify to the American people the part he has played in this terrible reign of disaster, which has ruined the lives of so many American youths in Korea." Warning the American people that when they choose a President they also choose a Commander-in-Chief, Dirksen intoned soberly: "They have forgotten that in other days. That thought needs to be revitalized, and it needs to be refreshed in their recollections when they exercise their responsibilities as voters." [49]

The Administration was thus forewarned, at least a year before the election, that the Republicans would seek to parlay the unpopular war into an election victory. While their strategy and success in this attempt will be discussed in Chapter 8, there is one facet of the Republican-Democratic clash that received much attention before the July nominating convention. The Administration had been emphasizing the fact that the American people were enjoying an unparalleled prosperity, while the opposition charged that this prosperity had at its foundation the coffins of the Korean War dead. In his *The Revolt of the Moderates,* Samuel Lubell reports that "surprising numbers of voters came to resent the prevailing prosperity as being 'bought by the lives of our boys in Korea.' The feeling was general that the Korean War was all that stood in the way of an economic recession. From accepting that belief, many persons moved on emotionally to where they felt something

---

[49] *Congressional Record,* March 19, 1952, p. 2503. Martin: *The New York Times,* February 12, 1952, p. 28. Kem: *Congressional Record,* February 27, 1952, p. 1542. Hickenlooper: *Congressional Record,* March 10, 1952, p. 2042.

immoral and guilt-laden in the 'you never had it better' argument of the Democrats." [50]

The Republicans played upon these feelings of guilt, for they constantly reminded the public that the Korean War, not Democratic economic know-how, was responsible for the good times. Jenner put it this way: "Every Fair Deal dollar is dripping with the warm blood of 1,037,513 American casualties in World War II and 109,000 casualties in the Korean police action. The Republican Party doesn't want or believe in that kind of 'prosperity.'" Thirteen months before the election, Senator Martin told the Ohio Federation of Republican Women's Organizations that "if we can attain prosperity only through the tragedies of war, paying for it in the lives of our boys who are dying in Korea, I want to say right now that the price is too high." Cain appeared on the American Forum of the Air in May, voicing his belief that "I personally want no more prosperity of the kind we have today, which is based on and built out of what? Out of war, out of blood, out of deficits, out of stimulated inflation . . . out of taxes, and out of debt. . . . Pull the rug out from under Korea and N.A.T.O. today and our fictitious prosperity would crumble and engulf two millions of the innocent in misery." Of a somewhat different nature was Schoeppel's charge that the Administration was deliberately prolonging the Korean War so that it could sustain its "much publicized prosperity"! [51]

While this chapter has sought to deliniate the stance that the Republican party had assumed toward the Korean War by the time the nominating convention began its search for a standard-bearer, it must be noted that the two major contenders for the GOP nomination, Taft and Eisenhower, differed greatly over the possible use of the Korea issue in the campaign. Taft, obviously, was completely hostile to the Adminis-

---

[50] Samuel Lubell, *Revolt of the Moderates* (New York, 1956), p. 40.

[51] *Congressional Record,* June 25, 1952, pp. 8003–04. Jenner: *Congressional Record,* April 9, 1952, p. A2250. Martin: *Congressional Record,* October 18, 1951, p. A6510. Schoeppel: *Congressional Record,* May 7, 1952, p. A2278.

tration's strategy and from the outset was determined to use the war to win the election. While Eisenhower would soon take a harder line toward Korea, up to the time of the convention he saw no panaceas for ending the war. The General made the following statement a month before the nominations began:

> I do not have any prescription for bringing the thing to a decisive end because with the build-up that is apparently taking place on the other side of the Yalu in that region I would not think from this that it would be possible for our forces to carry through a decisive attack, which we would call tactical or strategic victory on the ground.
>
> But I do not believe that we can, in the idealogical war we are waging, retreat from the area we occupy, and therefore I believe we have got to stand firm and to stand right there and try to get a decent armistice out of it. In other words, I do not believe that in the present situation there is any clean-cut answer to bringing the Korean war to a successful conclusion.[52]

When Eisenhower met with the delegations from Oregon and Arizona on June 18th, he broke publicly with the Taft position. The General's refusal to advocate an escalation of the war, and thereby condone the MacArthur-Taft strategy, was a critical juncture in the party's political history. The General warned the assembled delegates that seeking a military victory on the peninsula would mean risking a general war. Having thus struck a serious blow to the very heart of the GOP position, Eisenhower further shocked the conservative-Asialationist wing of his party by proclaiming that since Chiang Kai-shek's Nationalist forces were needed on Formosa there was no justification for their deployment in Korea. While advocating the introduction of more South Korean troops into the war, he cautioned members of the party to remember that Japan was "the real outpost of our civilization" in the Far East and must not be jeopardized by ill-advised ventures in Korea and Formosa.[53]

---

[52] *The New York Times,* June 6, 1952, p. 10.
[53] *The New York Times,* June 19, 1952, p. 14.

Thus at the outset of the nominating convention the Republican party was faced with a serious dilemma. That Truman and the Democrats had been seriously weakened by the public's reaction to the Korean conflict was certain. But how were the Republicans to capitalize on this disaster that befell the majority party? Taft was calling for a course of action that had total victory or a war with Red China in the offing at the very time that the enormously popular General Eisenhower was advocating a policy that often bore disturbing resemblances to the Truman-Acheson strategy. In time Eisenhower would become far more militant, but in July 1952 the GOP, caught between the General and the Senator, wondered which path led to the White House.

Chapter 8

The Korean War and
the Election of 1952

The 1952 election afforded the Republicans their greatest opportunity to exploit the Korean War for partisan advantage. The party rose to the occasion, and its standard-bearer, General of the Army Dwight D. Eisenhower, abandoned his position of acquiescence toward the Administration's handling of the Korean War and quickly recognized the political potency of the war once he embarked on the campaign trail. Nevertheless, Eisenhower wisely steered clear of Taft's rather confused attempt to reconcile Hoover's neoisolationism with MacArthur's militancy. Charting a middle course between these two positions, the GOP candidate was successful in his "crusade" to convince America that he (and those who earned his support) was uniquely suited to bring the war to an honorable conclusion.

One does not attempt a history of the 1952 election in a single chapter. Our present concern is with the ways in which the Republican party, and Eisenhower in particular, used the war in the Far East as a means of winning widespread public support for the GOP ticket. If this method does not make for a balanced picture of the election (and it certainly does not) it would seem to serve the purposes of this work, for the GOP's "marketing" of the Korean War is central to the theme.

The outcome of the 1952 election was the result of dozens of factors, of which the Korean War was only one; consequently it would be foolhardy not to recognize some of the more vital issues affecting the final decision on November 4th. There were many so-called "trailer" issues—those which were, to an extent, related to the war. Such factors would include charges of Communism in the federal government, high taxation, inflation, and the "war prosperity." Other elements affecting the campaign were the great popularity of Eisenhower as a war hero; the constant charge of corruption in the federal government (symbolized, as Nixon saw it, by the Democratic mink coat as opposed to the Republican cloth coat); the fear of a growing bureaucracy; warnings of a socialized economy; the split in the Republican party between the Taft and Eisenhower wings; and the charge that Stevenson was a hand-picked stand-in for Truman. Because of the close relationship of some of these issues to the Korean War itself they will be mentioned throughout this chapter.

One would expect, and indeed one finds, considerable disagreement concerning the role and importance of the Korean War in the 1952 election. There are those, such as pollsters Lubell, Harris, and Roper, who contend that the war was the greatest issue making for the Republican triumph. Samuel Lubell in *Revolt of the Moderates* writes that ". . . the frustrations over Korea were the most important single propellent behind Eisenhower's sweep . . . the angriest condemnation of the Truman administration from traditionally Democratic voters were provoked by the grievances that rose out of the Korean War—higher taxes and higher prices and the drafting of 'our sons' for 'a useless war.'" [1]

Louis Harris, one-time research executive with Elmo Roper, has written a detailed work on the election entitled *Is There a Republican Majority?*; his conclusion is that Korea was the most important issue in the 1952 contest. "If one were to find a single, basic root cause out of which the impatience and protest of 1952 grew," Harris writes, "it would have to be the failure of the Administration to bring the Korean fighting to a successful close. There were other issues which also aroused partisan sentiments in the heat of that campaign. There was none on which Eisenhower was to score so heavily." [2]

The Roper polls, undertaken for NBC, support the views of these commentators. The Roper group conducted six separate

---

[1] Lubell, p. 265. Also see p. 39.
[2] Louis Harris, *Is There a Republican Majority?* (New York, 1954), pp. 23–27.

surveys between January and October in an attempt to discover what percentage of the population viewed the Korean
War as one of the most important problems facing the country, and the rise in concern during this nine-month period is
striking.[3]

January	25
March	29
June	30
September	33
Mid-October	39
Late October	52

Significantly, a Roper poll conducted in June also discovered that the public had no clear view of what should be done
to end the Korean stalemate. Only 30 percent of those questioned had any faith in the negotiations, while 70 percent did
not foresee a settlement. Thirty percent believed that we
should take a sufficiently militant stance in Korea to drive the
Communists north of the Yalu while less than 20 percent of
those polled wanted the United States to withdraw from the
struggle.[4]

Harris' finding is supported by Graebner's contention that
"Korea was the Achilles heel in the Democratic record and the
General exploited it skillfully."[5] And in *Korea and the Fall of
MacArthur*, Trumbull Higgins draws a parallel between the
dismissal of one general and the election of another: "As a
direct consequence of MacArthur's recall, the Republicans in
1952 managed to reap the political benefits of each of their
mutually inconsistent criticisms of the Democrats [that the
Administration would not end the war and would not escalate
it]. In the furious struggle which terminated his active military career, Douglas MacArthur had, at least, greatly aided in
electing another Republican general as President of the
United States."[6]

[3] *Ibid.*, p. 25.
[4] Harris, p. 26.
[5] Graebner, p. 106.
[6] Higgins, p. 183.

The impression that one receives of the importance of the Korean War in the 1952 election is startlingly different if one reads the conclusions reached by the Survey Research Center of the University of Michigan. This group, headed by Angus Campbell, found domestic issues to be of far greater concern to the voter in 1952 than foreign policy, or more specifically, the Korean War. As the table reproduced below indicates, while only 3 percent of those interviewed responded favorably to the Democratic party's management of the war, an astoundingly low 13 percent felt that the GOP had the ability to handle the war.

Favorable Perceptions of Republican and Democratic Parties

Favorable References	Mentioned in connection with	
	Republican Party	Democratic Party
Party leaders	13%	7%
Party identification: traditional party allegiance	8	11
Domestic policies and issues	33	43
Foreign policy: ability to handle Korean War	13	3
Association with certain groups (working people, farmers, etc.)	2	32
"Time for a change"	13	—
Made no favorable references	49	35
	1,614	1,614

The Center's report further undermines the position of those who choose to view the war as a vote of confidence for the

Table 4.3, "Favorable Perceptions of Republican and Democratic Parties" in *The Voter Decides* by Angus Campbell et al. (Harper and Row, 1954). Reprinted by permission. Note that the columns total more than 100 percent because some people gave more than one reason for liking the Democratic or Republican party.

foreign policy proposals of the Republican party by concluding that public confidence in Eisenhower the man, rather than in the Republican party generally, was the reason many voters believed that the new administration would settle the Korean problem.

> . . . foreign policy, to the extent that it was a party issue, was almost exclusively a pro-Republican issue; but . . . foreign policy was much more a pro-Eisenhower than a pro-Republican party issue. Whereas many more people responded favorably to Eisenhower in terms of the foreign situation than in terms of what he might do on the domestic scene, the reverse was true of the favorable perceptions of the Republican party: many more people mentioned favoring the Republican party because of the domestic situation (clean up corruption, lower taxes, etc.) than because of its ability to do something about the foreign situation and the Korean War. The favorable perception of Eisenhower in this area, then, was not just a symptom of dissatisfaction with the Korean War, nor a mere echo of the public's reaction to the Republican party. Eisenhower, because of his background and experience, seems to have been perceived as a person peculiarly able to cope with the nation's international problems.[8]

In at least one sense this question of the influence of the voting on the actual outcome of the election is secondary to the theme of this work. Essentially we are concerned here with the GOP's "marketing" of the war—that is, how much of an attempt did the party make to transform popular discontent over our Asian policies into votes. It is this attempt, rather than the success or failure of the attempt, that is of primary importance. If the objective of this chapter is defined in this manner, there can be very little doubt that the Republican party and General Eisenhower tried their utmost to enter the White House by a road that led through the hills of Korea.

Truman's later blast against Eisenhower's use of the Korea issue to gain the Presidency was as righteous as it was unreasonable. The former President charged in his *Memoirs* that "when our struggle in Korea was appropriated for partisan

---

[8] *Ibid.*, pp. 56–58.

political purposes at a time when we were negotiating for an armistice in the face of a most stubborn and tricky foe, I felt that we had reached a situation that was politically and morally intolerable. I could understand certain extreme isolationists using Korea as a political weapon, but I will never understand how a responsible military man, fully familiar with the extreme delicacy of our negotiations to end hostilities, could use this tragedy for political advantage." [9]

The hope of the Democratic party to keep Korea out of the campaign was all the more naive because of the military position of the United Nation forces at the time of the election. By the beginning of October two offensives were launched on the peninsula, representing the heaviest fighting in a year. On October 6th the Communists began a ten-day attack, falling back only after an entire division had been destroyed. Mark Clark then ordered a United Nations counterattack to begin on October 14th—this resulted in a two-week ordeal which took the lives of 8,000 UNC forces and 12,000 Communist troops. The seeming hopelessness of the war, as demonstrated by these battles, strengthened the Republicans' hand and helped plunge Truman's Gallup poll rating to a new low.

※   ※   ※

Encouraged by a series of primary victories and pressured by Republican leaders (particularly Senator Henry Cabot Lodge), Eisenhower decided in late May to return to the United States and seek the Republican Presidential nomination. Two general attitudes characterized Eisenhower's approach to foreign affairs in the weeks between his return from Paris and his nomination as the GOP standard-bearer: his unwillingness to criticize the Administration's Korea policy, and his growing alienation from Taft's concept of what our foreign policy should encompass. At his first news conference

---

[9] Truman, *Memoirs*, II, p. 501.

after his return, the General made it emphatically clear to reporters that he had no magic formula for concluding the conflict in Korea.

> I do not have any prescription for bringing this thing to a decisive end because with the build-up that is apparently taking place on the other side of the Yalu . . . I would not think from this that it would be possible for our forces to carry through a decisive attack, which we would call tactical or strategic victory on the ground. . . . In other words, I do not believe that in the present situation there is any clean-cut answer to bringing the Korean War to a successful conclusion.[10]

This attitude was, of course, a marked departure from the stance taken by Taft and his Republican colleagues, who had been calling for everything from withdrawal to escalation— sometimes simultaneously. Meeting with the New Jersey delegation on June 12th, Eisenhower insisted that the war "can't be settled by extending it. . . . If we can't stop this one we certainly can't stop a bigger one." Bombing beyond the Yalu, he was convinced, would make matters worse since the "Yalu has become a political symbol and to do so would be to extend the war." [11]

While battling the General for the party's designation, Taft contended that Eisenhower would not make an effective candidate because of his too-close association with Administration politics. In the course of a nationwide broadcast on June 1st Taft told his audience that he was ". . . interested in the fact that my Republican opponents in this campaign have spent their whole time attacking my position whenever I differed with the Administration—apparently they are defending and they approve everything Mr. Acheson has done, and apparently they want to see a campaign run on a me-too basis. They seem to be afraid that a direct attack on the Administration is some attack on General Eisenhower." [12]

---

[10] *The New York Times,* June 6, 1952, p. 10.
[11] *The New York Times,* June 13, 1952, p. 13.
[12] *The New York Times,* June 2, 1952, p. 14.

Two weeks later, while meeting the Oregon and Arizona delegations, Eisenhower publicly broke with the Taft-MacArthur attitude toward the war. He told the delegates that an attempt to unify Korea and win a traditional military victory on the peninsula would run the risk of provoking World War III. He also warned that there was not sufficient evidence that Chiang's troops, if transferred to Korea, would make a significant difference in the course of the war. The troops, he believed, were more valuable for the security of Formosa itself.[13] Obviously bruised by this frontal attack on the main tenets of his position, Taft issued a statement the following day to the effect that Eisenhower was unwilling or unable to "condemn at all at any point the foreign policy of Mr. Truman which has gotten this country into the tremendously difficult problem we have today." [14]

There was more to the Taft-Eisenhower rift than disagreement over a solution for the Korean War. The two sides fought a bitter battle over the seating of delegates from Georgia, Louisiana, Texas, and Mississippi; with Lodge at the helm the general's forces eventually prevailed in their attempt to seat pro-Eisenhower delegations, giving a great psychological boost to the campaign to nominate the general. While the fight over delegate strength was a powerful divisive force within the party, the foreign policy battle between the Taft and Eisenhower wings also made for a great deal of disunity. The general's camp fought fiercely to overturn the decision to have MacArthur (an avowed Taft man) deliver the keynote speech at the convention, though the Taft side prevailed on this issue. More important, in a radio and television address on June 23rd Eisenhower, having already dissociated himself from Taft's attitude toward Korea the week before, launched a full-scale denunciation of several of the Senator's positions on foreign policy and voiced strong opposition to Taft's belief that we could effectively rely on air, rather than ground

---

[13] *The New York Times,* June 19, 1952, p. 14.
[14] *The New York Times,* June 22, 1952, Sec. 4, p. 1.

forces. "The bleak scene of an America surrounded by a savage wolf pack could be our lot if we heed the false prophets of living alone—who preach that we need do nothing except maintain a destructive retaliatory force for use in the event the Russian army should march." While Taft had repeatedly called the United Nations a "failure," Eisenhower reassured the country of his faith in the organization: ". . . there must be no wavering in our support of the United Nations. Some regard the United Nations in terms of its short-comings, and would reduce our support for it to a reluctant minimum. . . . The United Nations is an instrument of peace. Our aim must be to make it more vital and effective." And in a rather blunt reference to Taft's early opposition to NATO, the General said "There must be no wavering in our support for the North Atlantic Alliance. Even those who blindly opposed its launching admit that it has stopped the spread of communism in Europe and the Mediterranean." [15]

Hence it would appear that August Heckscher was quite right when he wrote in the *Foreign Policy Bulletin* a month before the election that one must question Taft's contention that the "differences on foreign policy between himself and General Eisenhower are 'matters of degree.' " [16] As a matter of fact, throughout the campaign Taft, although he went on a speaking tour in behalf of Eisenhower's election, made it clear that he and his former rival had not settled all of their differences.[17]

Once the Republican National Convention convened in Chicago on July 7th, considerable effort was expended on the molding of the foreign policy plank. The three main authors of the GOP's platform were Senator Eugene Millikin of Colorado; Clarence Budington Kelland, National Committeeman

---

[15] *The New York Times,* June 24, 1952, p. 20.
[16] August Heckscher, "The Republican Record," *Foreign Policy Bulletin,* October 1, 1952, p. 4.
[17] *The New York Times,* September 13, 1952, p. 6. Also see *The New York Times,* September 27, 1952, p. 9.

from Arizona; and John Foster Dulles. Both Millikin and Kelland were avowed Taft supporters, while Dulles, the central figure drawing up the foreign policy plank for the party, was more closely associated with Eisenhower. The formal reading of the platform was undertaken by Senator Millikin on July 19th; seven items in the document were closely related to the party's "marketing" of the war. Past mistakes that led to the June 1950 invasion by the North Koreans were outlined as follows:

> In South Korea they withdrew our occupation troops in the face of the aggressive, poised-for-action Communist military strength on the northern border. They publicly announced that Korea was no concern of ours. Then when the Communist forces acted to take what seemed to have been invited, they committed this nation to fight back under the most unfavorable conditions. Already the tragic cost is over 110,000 American casualties.

The Republicans then charged that the Administration, having needlessly encouraged the aggression, refused to fight an honorable war: ". . . by their hampering orders they produced stalemates and ignominious bartering with our enemies, and they offer no hope of victory." Associated with the party's hostility toward a stalemated war was its opposition to containment: "They profess to be following a defensive policy of 'containment' of Russian communism which has not contained it . . . 'containment' . . . abandons countless human beings to a despotism and godless terrorism which in turn enables the rulers to forge the captives into a weapon for our destruction."

The platform's alternative to containment was Dulles' concept of liberation.

> The Government of the United States, under Republican leadership, will repudiate all commitments contained in secret understandings such as those of Yalta which aid Communist enslavements. It will be made clear, on the highest authority of the President and the Congress, that United States policy, as

one of its peaceful purposes, looks happily forward to the genuine independence of those captive peoples.

We shall again make liberty into a beacon light of hope that will penetrate the dark places.

The foreign policy plank also reflected the characteristic desire of the Republicans to cut military costs. "We shall always measure our foreign commitments so that they can be borne without endangering the economic health or sound finances of the United States. Stalin said that 'the moment for the decisive blow' would be when the free nations were isolated and were in a state of 'practical bankruptcy.' " We shall not allow ourselves to be isolated and economically strangled and we shall not let ourselves go bankrupt."

By cutting the cost of our defense system and commitments abroad, the party believed that it would be able to place the domestic economy on a sounder footing. "They claim prosperity, but the appearance of economic health is created by war expenditures, waste and extravagance, planned emergencies and war crisis. They have debauched our money by cutting in half the purchasing power of our dollar."

Finally, under a separate heading of National Defense, the platform outlined the Dulles program of deterrent power. Interestingly, before July Dulles had always mentioned this strategy in connection with other Western powers; but the 1952 platform, by omitting this qualification, would seem to imply that the United States was to develop this deterrent power unilaterally.

On the prudent assumption that Communist Russia may not accommodate our own disgracefully lagging program for preparedness, we should develop with utmost speed a force in being, as distinguished from paper plans, of such power as to deter sudden attack or promptly and decisively defeat it. This defense against sudden attack requires the quickest possible development of appropriate and completely adequate air power and the simultaneous readiness of coordinated air, land and sea forces, with all necessary installations, bases, supplies and munitions, including atomic energy weapons in abundance.[18]

A further indication of the GOP's attitude toward the war during the convention is to be found in the speeches made by leading party members or supporters. General MacArthur, while delivering the keynote address, used the opportunity to repeat his past criticisms of the Administration's handling of the war. He found particular fault with the government's disinclination to "win" the war, and its inclination to sit down and talk with the Communists.

> . . . it is fatal to enter any war without the will to win it. I criticize not the morality of the decision, but its irresponsibility and recklessness. We defeated the North Korean armies; but, when the Communist armies of China struck, our leaders lacked the courage to fight to a military decision, even though victory was then readily within our grasp. . . .

> And, after discarding victory as the military objective and thereby condemning our forces to a stalemated struggle of attrition and the Korean nation and people to progressive obliteration, we again yielded to Communist intrigue and entered into protracted armistice negotiations even though every lesson of experience had clearly shown such negotiations to be but the means whereby such an enemy gains time to reinforce his military capabilities.[19]

The delivery of the keynote address ended General MacArthur's participation in the 1952 campaign. Emmet John

---

[18] All quotes from the platform are to be found in *The New York Times,* July 11, 1952, p. 8. When the platform Committee first drafted the national defense plank, the key sentence on deterrent power read ". . . as distinguished from paper plans, of such *retaliatory striking power* as to deter sudden attack or promptly and decisively defeat it." Eisenhower and his advisors were successful in having the two words "retaliatory striking" removed from the final draft. It was believed that too great an emphasis on retaliation would lead both our allies and our potential enemies to think that we were not genuinely interested in the principles of collective security as a means of achieving peace in the world.

[19] *The New York Times,* July 8, 1952, p. 18.

Hughes, a member of the Eisenhower inner circle in 1952, relates the extent to which MacArthur was isolated from the campaign once the convention rejected his choice, Senator Taft.

> One of the most striking marks of the group around Dwight Eisenhower in the 1952 campaign was the absence of several who might have been expected to be present. Among those most conspicuously not present, in fact or in spirit, was General of the Army Douglas A. MacArthur. He was the military hero, if not the national hero, of Republican conservatives. Some decades before, Dwight Eisenhower had been a junior officer on his staff in the Philippines. Only weeks earlier, MacArthur had been the keynote speaker before the Republican convention that finally had nominated Eisenhower. For millions of orthodox Republicans, MacArthur was both the supreme symbol of, and the supreme authority on, the most sensitive issue of the political hour—the Korean War. Despite all this, *his counsel was never invited, his association never encouraged, his name never invoked, and his judgments never embraced.*[20]

The New York Times Index for 1952 supports this view that MacArthur was inactive during the campaign.

The day before he publicly voiced his support of Taft's nomination, former President Herbert Hoover lectured the convention on the failures of the present Administration. "General MacArthur well said that in war there is no substitute for victory. . . . But this Administration substituted appeasement on the Thirty-eighth Parallel just where we started from. Now after twelve months of negotiations on that appeasement question the Communists so far do not seem to want to be appeased. If in the meantime they have so increased their forces that the military initiative is now in their hands—the end is not yet."[21]

Other prenomination speeches were delivered by House

---

[20] Emmet John Hughes, *The Ordeal of Power* (New York, 1963), p. 36. Emphasis added.

[21] Herbert Hoover, "The Freedom of Men," *Vital Speeches*, July 15, 1952, p. 584.

Reprinted from *The Herblock Book* (Beacon Press, 1952)

Minority Leader Martin, Senator Joseph McCarthy, and former Ambassador to China, Patrick Hurley. Martin contended
that "with victory in its grasp, apparently (the Democrats)
decided the best way to win was to lose," while in a character-
istically hard-hitting assault on the Administration, McCarthy

declared that the major issue in the 1952 election was whether the United States should "continue to squander her blood, waste her resources and sacrifice her position of world leadership. . . . I promise you [with a G.O.P. victory] we won't be in any wars which we are afraid to win." The lack of cooperation from our allies in the United Nations effort in Korea was the main theme of Hurley's speech to the convention.[22]

Although no mention of Korea was made at the time of Eisenhower's formal nomination, when Dirksen placed Taft's name in nomination he included in his speech a scathing indictment of the Democratic party as the war party.

Once it was deemed the primary duty of government to keep the nation at peace. In the last twenty years those in power have given us the biggest, costliest, bloodiest war in the history of Christendom. They have given us more. They have given us an undeclared, unconstitutional one-man war in Korea, now in its third year. It has been an inferno for the holy blood of American youth. As one Korean G.I. put it, "We can't win, we can't loose, we can't quit." He might have added, "We can only die." [23]

The following day the delegates were polled. Six hundred and four votes were necessary to win the nomination, and on the first ballot Eisenhower led 595 to 500 (for Taft); before this tally could be announced, Minnesota switched 19 of its favorite-son votes to the General, thus swelling his total to 614. With victory now certain, over 200 delegates switched sides, giving Eisenhower a total of 845 when the revised results of the first ballot were announced. Of the remaining delegate votes, Taft received 280, Warren was third with 77, and MacArthur gleaned the final four.[24]

The General had once again conquered, despite his somewhat questionable disclaimers that he never really wanted the

[22] The Martin, McCarthy, and Hurley speeches were covered in *The New York Times*, July 10, 1952, pp. 14 and 21.

[23] *The New York Times*, July 11, 1952, p. 6.

[24] The most authoritative account of the convention is to be found in David Paul, *Presidential Nominating Policies in 1952* (Baltimore, 1954).

nomination. This attempt by Eisenhower to create the impression that he was a candidate yet somehow above politics was important in the creation of the image that his Presidency would be free of the deadening influences of the past. In the first volume of *The White House Years,* published in 1963, he once again contends that he became a candidate not by design but because of a great popular surge in his behalf. His own attitude toward the nomination, according to the book, was often one of apathy (a stance considerably at variance with the evidence when one recalls the fierce battle the Eisenhower camp waged in Chicago).

> Although my friends and I were confident, I was sure at that moment [when the delegates were being polled] that I would feel little disappointed if the balloting went against us. . . . As the voting went on we paid scant attention to the television set, which was filled with the dreary, time-consuming act of "polling the delegations." However, the principal events of the convention were so often reported and repeated over the television that, except by deliberately turning off the set, we could not have failed to keep abreast of the results.[25]

As a candidate for the Presidency, Eisenhower proved to be a clever politician; at very least he had the good sense to listen to shrewd professionals. The effectiveness of his drive toward victory increased steadily as November approached, and one of the major issues that he used to gain votes was the Korean War. At his first news conference (on June 5th) he had presented himself as an individual with no panaceas for ending the war; by the end of October Eisenhower was offered to the public as a man who had virtually ended one war and could surely terminate another.

While Eisenhower's opposition to the Administration's handling of the war was a relatively gradual process, party leaders (including the General) made it clear from the very beginning of the race that foreign policy would be the major issue in the battle with the Democrats. Nixon explained why:

---

[25] Eisenhower, p. 44.

"That is where the Administration had made its greatest failure. General Eisenhower can offer new leadership in foreign affairs, but Governor Stevenson must accept the Administration's foreign policy. The General has had no responsibility for the mistakes of the present Administration. He has criticized its Far Eastern policy, which the Governor will have to defend." [26]

While unwilling to disclose the party's strategy before the opening of the campaign on Labor Day, Nixon told a press conference in mid-August that the Administration would be criticized for its "no-victory" policy on the peninsula, though not for the actual intervention. The Vice-Presidential candidate also voiced his belief that the Democrats were vulnerable because they had not blockaded the China coast, "unleashed" Chiang Kai-shek, and bombed Chinese installations within Korea. Several days after the official opening of the campaign, the California Senator told a New England audience that foreign policy would be the major issue of the battle because it was the Administration's "Achilles heel." [27]

John Foster Dulles was another Republican leader who insisted that the party would emphasize the nation's diplomatic failures. After a meeting with Eisenhower and Nixon in early August, Dulles said that there was full agreement that foreign policy must be made "the major issue" of the election battle, and at an August 11th press conference Eisenhower supported Dulles' position that foreign policy would be the dominant factor in the race although he would not agree that he alone could stop the war.[28] Several days before the official opening of the contest, the Senate Republican Policy Committee published a campaign pamphlet entitled "Background Material on Major Campaign Issues in 1952." Foreign policy was

---

[26] *The New York Times,* July 27, 1952, p. 25.

[27] *The New York Times,* August 8, 1952, p. 10. For an account of the former Vice-President's press conference, see *The New York Times,* August 14, 1952, p. 15.

[28] "The Case for Ike," *Time,* August 18, 1952, p. 14, contains Dulles' views. For the Eisenhower press conference, see *The New York Times,* August 12, 1952, p. 1.

listed as the major issue, followed by corruption in government, Communism in government, high expenditures, and
civil rights.

Having decided to ignore Truman's preconvention plea to
leave the Korean War out of the race, the Republicans had to
determine how to best utilize the war. To some extent, responses to the war were developed as the battle progressed—
the most striking example of this was Eisenhower's announcement in late October that if victorious he would visit Korea.
Yet while it is true that the candidate's hostility toward the
Administration on the war issue grew as November approached, there were some attitudes that remained fairly constant. These included the contention that the Administration
had bungled the United States into a needless war; that once
the Communists had attacked, American intervention was
necessary; that isolationism was no longer a viable policy; and
that an all-out war over Korea must be avoided.

The charge that America was involved in a war on the
Korean peninsula because of the Administration's mismanage-
ment of our Far Eastern affairs was emphasized from July to
November. At a Republican campaign rally in Convention
Hall, Philadelphia, on September 4th, Eisenhower asked "Why
are we at war in Korea?"

> We are in that war because of (a) failure to observe some of
> the principles for preventing war which I shall outline tonight.
>
> We are in that war because this Administration grossly underes-
> timated the actual threat.
>
> We are in that war because this Administration allowed Amer-
> ica, in a time when strength was needed, to become weak.
> Consequently it felt compelled to take its force out of that
> region.
>
> We are in that war because, having helped set up the Korean
> republic, and knowing that strength was being massed against
> that republic north of its borders, there was a failure to build up
> adequate strength in Korea's own defense forces.

We are in that war because this Administration abandoned China to the Communists.

We are in that war because this Administration announced to all the world that it had written off most of the Far East as beyond our direct control.[29]

Two weeks before the election the General told a gathering in Detroit that the United States was militarily engaged on the peninsula of Korea because "free leadership failed to check and to turn back Communist ambition before it savagely attacked us. The Korean War—more perhaps than any other war in history—simply and swiftly followed the collapse of our political defenses. . . . We failed to read and to outwit the totalitarian mind."

In his first speech in favor of Eisenhower's election, Governor Dewey scored the Administration for removing American troops from Korea and compounding the blunder by announcing that the nation was outside of our defense perimeter. The party's foreign policy advisor, Dulles, told the New York Board of Trade that Truman and Acheson were guilty of "contributory negligence" in world affairs because they led the Russians to believe that we would not defend Korea. The future Secretary of State contended that had we made it clear to the world in advance that we intended to defend the Koreans against aggression, the Communists would not have attacked.[30]

Despite his belief that had the United States taken proper steps before 1950 there need not have been a Korean War, Eisenhower was careful to point out that once the aggression had been committed, Truman's decision to come to the aid of the Republic of Korea was correct. In Cincinnati—with Taft at his side—he said: "I believe that the decision to fight to hold Korea—like the decision to struggle so bravely to hold

---

[29] *The New York Times,* September 5, 1952, p. 20.

[30] The Eisenhower speech was covered in *The New York Times,* October 25, 1952, p. 8. Dewey's statement can be found in *The New York Times,* September 25, 1952, p. 1. and Dulles' in *The New York Times,* October 15, 1952, p. 20.

Berlin—was an inescapable decision." Eisenhower told a Virginia audience: "I believe, of course, that the Korean war was preventable, but I also believe that given the set of circumstances that came about in June of 1950 we had to re-enter that country."

To the end of the campaign he had not changed his mind on this point; in late October he said that United States intervention "was inescapable not only because this was the only way to defend the idea of collective freedom against savage aggression . . . [it] was inescapable because there was now in the plight into which we had stumbled no other way to save honor and self-respect." [31]

In his support for American involvement in the war, Eisenhower was running counter to the feelings of that segment of the party that no longer wished to associate itself with Truman's decision. Actually, by supporting intervention the candidate was reinforcing another of his major premises—that isolationism was a dead letter and must not be revived by the Republican party. He appealed to the memory of Senator Arthur Vandenberg in Flint, Michigan while calling for the rejection of isolationism:

> Enlightened self-interest demands that the free nations follow the way of collective security. The fervor of [Vandenberg's] faith was so contagious and his expression of it so eloquent that he ended once and for all the old American belief in isolationism.

> Differences still exist as to the best way to implement the concept of collective security. Those differences are at times important, but such differences are inevitable and healthy so long as the principle of isolationism has ceased to be a political force.[32]

The General repeated this theme many times in the ensuing weeks. In Newark he declared "I have given no encourage-

---

[31] For more complete coverage of these statements, see *The New York Times*, September 23, 1952, p. 16; *The New York Times*, September 27, 1952, p. 10; and *The New York Times*, October 25, 1952, p. 8.
[32] *The New York Times*, October 2, 1952, p. 20.

ment to the false notion that an isolated or isolationist America can continue to live either in peace or in security." In New York City he said: "Our highest purpose is to work with every resource at our command for real and lasting peace in this world. To this great job we must have allies. We cannot stand alone. Americans know that isolationism is dead. They know peace requires the combined strength, will and purpose of all the free nations." At Chicago: "I have long insisted—and I do now insist—that isolationism in America is dead as a political issue." [33]

It should be understood that if the Presidential nominee was supporting intervention and opposing isolationism, he was not in favor of a MacArthur-styled all-out war on the peninsula. At the San Francisco Cow Palace he insisted that the United States must guard against adopting "a stupidly aggressive attitude [in Korea] and so markedly increase the risk of global war. Modern war is not a conceivable choice in framing national policy. War would do unthinkable damage to every moral and material value we cherish." [34] Conversely, this rejection of a more aggressive military policy in Korea did not mean that Eisenhower was in any way sanctioning the Administration's peace efforts. While he did not speak on the subject of the peace negotiations until approximately the midpoint of the campaign, when he did he took the standard GOP view that the Democratic party's efforts were useless.

> In June of 1951, when we were driving back the Communist forces in Korea, the free world was electrified by what appeared to be a genuine offer by the Soviet to cooperate in reaching a peaceful solution in Korea. We and our Allies eagerly met them halfway. But as month after bloody month dragged by we came to realize that we had been swindled.

> Now, a year and three months later, we have learned a bitter lesson in "cold war" strategy. We know now how all this time

---

[33] Selections from these speeches reprinted in *The New York Times,* October 18, 1952, p. 8.; *New York Times,* October 30, 1952, p. 26; and *The New York Times,* November 1, 1952, p. 10.

[34] *The New York Times,* October 9, 1952, p. 24.

has been spent by the enemy. The Communist military position has been repaired. Beyond that it has probably been made half again as strong.

The Soviet trap was perfectly conceived, perfectly timed, perfectly sprung. For fifteen months now, free world diplomacy has been trying to climb the walls of a bear pit into which it fell.[35]

In all of this it would be a mistake to assume that the GOP or its standard-bearer had some coherent plan for ending the war. The platform is lacking in any concrete program for peace, and Eisenhower himself was unable to develop one. The only idea that even approached an alternative to the Administration's running of the war was the proposed strategy of substituting South Koreans for Americans on the front lines, a suggestion that was brought to light in Illinois on October 3rd.[36] Two days later Dulles explained in Rochester that such replacement of South Korean for American troops would destroy two of Russia's reasons for staying in the war. In the first place, Russia would be denied the advantage of tying up United States military might in a "remote peninsula." Secondly, the Russians would no longer be able to tell the Asians that the United States is waging a "race war, with white men killing yellow men by methods white people would not use against each other." In addition, the use of South Koreans on the front lines, Dulles held, would enable us to "show how Soviet Russia is recklessly sacrificing Asians to win Russia's old imperialist goals in Korea. We can show how Russia uses the war as an excuse to hold on to Manchuria instead of giving it back to China." [37]

As a guest of the "Man of the Week" television program, Governor Dewey supported the idea of sending South Koreans in significant numbers to the front lines. "There are 3,000,000 young Koreans who are ready, willing and able to defend Korea. We have been in this war almost two and a half

---

[35] *Ibid.*
[36] *The New York Times*, October 3, 1952, p. 16.
[37] *The New York Times*, October 5, 1952, p. 74.

years, and this Government hasn't enough Koreans trained to take over one-third of the front, and believe me if you get General Eisenhower as President I will make you this prophecy: the Koreans will be defending nine-tenths of that front within a year." [38] Senator Taft was another supporter of this concept, viewing it as a recognition by Eisenhower that "we cannot permanently maintain American troops on the continent of Asia." [39] It will be remembered that as Taft grew less and less sanguine about the possibility of achieving a full-scale victory in Korea, he increasingly asked for the alternative of a withdrawal of the troops, although in the main his sympathies rested with MacArthur's plan for victory.

Unable to develop a comprehensive program, the Republicans did the next best thing—they worked feverishly to create the impression that only the GOP and its leader could bring peace to the peninsula. The exact nature of this peace—aside from the assurance that it would be "honorable"—remained vague throughout the campaign. The great impact of the "I shall go to Korea" pledge of October 24th was an indication that many Americans had come to believe that only a Republican could end the war. In good part, no doubt, this was due to the frustration and discontent that resulted from the Truman Administration's attempt to wage, win and justify the war with concepts such as containment and limited war (which were neither well understood nor accepted). Protracted negotiations with an enemy who did not seem ready to end the war only added to the general climate of hopelessness. On August 11th, several weeks before the Labor Day opening of the contest, Eisenhower said in reference to the Korean War problem: "I am not going to be put in a position that I personally am a messiah, but I do think that Republicans generally can do a better job than the Democrats." [40] The demands of the campaign and/or the campaign managers,

---

[38] *The New York Times,* October 6, 1952, p. 12.
[39] *The New York Times,* October 4, 1952, p. 1.
[40] *The New York Times,* August 12, 1952, p. 1.

however, were such that by the time the race closed in Boston the messianic mantle was in place.

When House Minority Leader Joseph Martin and Senate Minority Leader Styles Bridges issued their joint report on the Eighty-second Congress, they charged that: "The Democratic Eighty-second Congress muddled to a dismal end . . . demonstrating conclusively that Democratic party leadership in Congress, as well as in the Executive Branch, cannot solve the critical issues of our times. [No solution was found for] peace except a stalemate war in Korea, a lagging defense program, and the grim reminder that our people will live under the shadow of war for years to come." [41] While these congressional leaders were telling the American people that the Democrats were unable to achieve peace, Dulles was picturing the General as the man who had won the crusade in Europe. He often reminded his audiences that the Democrats had squandered the "supreme security which General Eisenhower won in World War II," and ended his remarks by assuring his audience that "We can trust *the man who won the peace*, rather than the man who lost it." [42]

Governor Dewey was consciously seeking to create this very same impression when he told a Brooklyn Republican rally in mid-September that a victorious Eisenhower would provide the nation with its strongest guarantee against World War III. Crediting his party's candidate with winning the peace in Europe, Dewey declared that Stalin very much feared the prospect of Eisenhower as President of the United States because of his dominating influence over the whole free world. Several days later Dewey reminded his audience of the fact that eleven generals had become American Presidents without a major war occurring during the terms of these men —the lesson was obvious: generals hated war and knew how to avoid it. And at the close of the campaign the Governor

---

[41] *The New York Times,* August 17, 1952, p. 54.
[42] For example, see *The New York Times,* September 4, 1952, p. 20. Emphasis mine.

asked the rhetorical question "Who is Stalin most afraid of, Adlai Stevenson or Dwight Eisenhower?" [43]

While Eisenhower was careful before September to assure the public that he was in no way specially endowed to end the Korean War, he was soon creating the opposite impression. He began reasonably enough by criticizing the Democrats' efforts to achieve peace, but in October this tactic changed considerably, for the emphasis was now placed on the idea that the new administration would make the termination of war its first order of business. Hence at the San Francisco Cow Palace on the 8th he pledged: "full dedication to the job of finding an intelligent and honorable way to end the tragic toll of American casualties in Korea. No one can pledge you more. Nor can there be a more solemn pledge. For this war is reaching tonight into the homes of hundreds of thousands of American families. I do not believe that Korea must forever be a part of our American daily life." [44] In Texas he assured his audience that the Republicans alone were able to avert a threatened World War III.

> The first job of the new Administration will be to deal with this tragic conflict which reaches into every American home and threatens us with World War III.
>
> We cannot expect the same reckless drivers, who ignored the danger signs and ran us into the ditch, to get us out. We must get back on the road to a lasting peace behind a government of men equal to this mighty task.
>
> I pledge you my unceasing efforts to find the men and the means to build for peace. [45]

The climax of this particular appeal came in the course of a Detroit speech on October 24th, when Eisenhower pledged that if elected, he would go to Korea. The origin of this

---

[43] *The New York Times,* October 22, 1952, p. 14. For the Brooklyn speech, see *The New York Times,* September 25, 1952, p. 19.

[44] *The New York Times,* October 9, 1952, p. 24.

[45] *The New York Times,* October 15, 1952, p. 24.

campaign pledge is somewhat obscure, though it is clear that the decision to use it was made late in the race. Most commentators on the election credit Emmet John Hughes, a speech writer for Eisenhower during the 1952 campaign, with the idea. Hughes himself says in *The Ordeal of Power* that it was his idea,[46] and Sherman Adams supports him.[47] But in his memoirs Eisenhower is reluctant to name Hughes as the originator of the concept. He mentions Harry Kern, foreign affairs editor of *Newsweek* and Frank C. Hilton, director of the veterans division of the Republican national committee, as possible sources for the pledge. The general's conclusion is that "By late October, when I delivered the speech, it seems likely that this idea, possibly originating independently from several sources, had come into many minds." [48] Whatever the origin of the plan, it was a masterful stroke and extremely well timed. Eisenhower's military successes in Europe understandably encouraged the nation to believe that concrete results would emerge from this trip; it is hardly likely that a similar announcement by Stevenson or Truman would have created the same effect. Hence Eisenhower was building on his own military reputation and the carefully cultivated impression that only a Republican could end the war. He told the audience in Detroit that

> The first task of a new Administration will be to review and re-examine every course of action open to us . . . to bring the Korean war to an early and honorable end. . . .

> For this task a wholly new Administration is necessary. . . . The old Administration cannot be expected to repair what it failed to prevent.

> [The new Administration will] forego the divisions of politics and . . . concentrate on the job of ending the Korean war—until that job is honorably done.

---

[46] Emmet John Hughes, *The Ordeal of Power* (New York, 1963), pp. 32–34.

[47] Sherman Adams, *Firsthand Report* (New York, 1961), pp. 42–43.

[48] Eisenhower, p. 72.

That job requires a personal trip to Korea. . . . I shall make the trip. . . . I shall go to Korea.[49]

Obviously sensing the drama that the speech created, the candidate repeated it in Pittsburgh on October 27th and in Mineola on the following day; at the Chicago Stadium on the 31st he explained why he made the promise. "I am going for an obvious reason: to find out for myself what is being done there. I want to find out from those on the spot what more could be done to improve our situation and what could help bring that tragic war to an end at the earliest moment compatible with the honor of the United States." [50]

The GOP hammered away at its promise to concentrate on terminating the war, and at the end of October Eisenhower told a gathering in Pittsburgh that ". . . so long as a single American soldier faces enemy fire in Korea, the honorable ending of the Korean war and the securing of honorable peace in the world must be the first—the urgent and unshakable— purpose of a new administration." [51] At the Boston rally on November 3rd—election eve—he ended his contest with Stevenson by reciting his war experiences in an obvious attempt to create in the minds of his listeners the impression of a figure steeped in the knowledge of war, yet seeking peace.

I have learned that peace is the dearest treasure in the sight of free men. . . . I have learned this truth from . . . the sight of the scars of war upon men and upon cities and upon whole nations. I learned it from the charred bones that came out of the crematoriums of Dachau and Buchenwald.

I learned it from the faces of worn and weary French peasants. . . . I learned this truth from the horror of the life revealed to us by refugees fleeing enslaved nations of Eastern Europe. . . .

Because I have learned that peace is the dearest treasure of free men, I have dedicated myself to one supreme cause: to

[49] *The New York Times,* October 25, 1952, p. 8.
[50] *The New York Times,* November 1, 1952, p. 10.
[51] *The New York Times,* October 28, 1952, p. 20.

strive to keep war from ever again wounding the bodies and scarring the spirit of America's youth.

In pursuit of this cause I have dared to offer my services in the highest office of our nation.[52]

Interestingly, the last word of Eisenhower's last speech in the campaign was "peace."

While the General sought votes on the strength of his appeal as the candidate who was better able to end the war, he was careful to take a distinctly moderate position. He rejected isolationism—both Hoover's idea of "Fortress America" and Taft's concept of exclusive reliance upon a retaliatory air striking power while eschewing MacArthur's "there is no substitute for victory" approach. Equally important, while his party had been insisting that Korea must be unified if the peace was to be an honorable one, Eisenhower never once supported this view. On August 15th, Syngman Rhee spoke at his second inauguration as Korea's chief executive and told his nation that "the United Nations and our great and staunch friend, the United States of America, have declared that their aim is the same as ours—the restoration of all Korea as a free, independent, united and democratic nation." [53] The Republican candidate ignored the pitfall of unification and wisely avoided any reference to what the exact nature of this "honorable" settlement would be.

Insofar as solutions to our global problems were offered by the Republican party, they were limited to the rather general concept of liberation, a policy that was more centrally concerned with Eastern Europe than Asia. The platform specifically mentioned that the GOP would endorse this program, and during the campaign both Dulles and Eisenhower sought to keep liberation constantly before the public. In an address to the American Bar Association Foster Dulles expressed his hope "to set in motion the delicate, long range peaceful proc-

---

[52] *The New York Times,* November 4, 1952, p. 23.
[53] Syngman Rhee, "Korea Cannot Live Divided and Half Occupied," *Vital Speeches,* September 1, 1952, p. 703.

esses whereby the spiritual forces still latent within the captive world can be kept alive and coordinated and mobilized so as ultimately to assert themselves in ways which would peacefully divide from within the overextended monolithic imperialism of Soviet communism." [54]

In mid-October the future Secretary of State strongly suggested that liberation need not be limited to Eastern European countries; it had its application in our China policy as well.

> Why should we assume that China is dead and done for so far as we are concerned? Why should we assume that what Soviet communism could do in China, we cannot undo?

> It will, no doubt, take several years of resourceful and imaginative effort to undo the disaster. But the fact that it will take some time is not a reason for doing nothing, but a reason for getting started quickly. For our own safety, we need and must have a positive China policy. [55]

The substitution by the GOP of liberation for containment placed Eisenhower in a rather odd position, since he had been a major advocate and instrument of the containment policy in Europe. Nevertheless he became an enthusiastic supporter of Dulles' idea, declaring that this nation must "aid by every peaceful means, but only by peaceful means, the right to live in freedom. The containing of communism is largely physical and by itself an inadequate approach to our task. There is also the need to bring hope and every peaceful aid to the world's enslaved peoples. We shall never be truculent—but we shall never appease." In California he told his listeners that "We must . . . give to those already enslaved hope that will enable them to continue resisting the oppressor until his hold can be gradually weakened and loosened from within." [56]

In the preconvention period there was much talk of "deter-

---

[54] *The New York Times,* September 17, 1952, p. 1.
[55] *The New York Times,* October 11, 1952, p. 14.
[56] *The New York Times,* October 9, 1952, p. 24. For earlier statement of his policy see *The New York Times,* September 3, 1952, p. 12.

rent power," and this concept was written into the 1952 Republican platform after Eisenhower had watered down the wording of the national defense plank. But the idea of deterrent power apparently had little appeal to the Eisenhower strategists, for he never advocated this policy during the race. The closest he came to supporting this plank was to insist that the nation bolster its military preparedness; but as a comprehensive program for national defense it was not used in the campaign. Even Dulles, who had formulated the program several months earlier, rarely mentioned it in his speeches, although in Rochester in October he did say that "the prevention of such an attack as would start World War III depends on our possessing offensive striking power." [57] Such a sentence is not to be found in the speeches of the GOP standard-bearer, however.

Eisenhower himself was much more interested in promising that our defense expenditures need not be a crushing economic burden to the nation. Like Taft, Dulles, and a good many other Republican leaders, the general became a harsh critic of what he considered to be excessive military spending. Here again he used his military background to convince Americans that he had the experience to effectuate a change. For example, he told a gathering in Cincinnati that "The American people need a government that knows enough about arms and armies to work out the most defense at less cost and with the least delay." A month later he told a Paterson, N.J., audience that

We can't afford what we're spending and stay strong enough to lead the world toward peace. . . .

They believe that we can have and maintain military strength above our capacity to pay for it. . . .

Now whenever I say this . . . I am accused of saying America cannot afford to defend itself. I never said any such thing. I said that frugality, efficiency, information, knowledge properly used

---

[57] *The New York Times*, October 5, 1952, p. 74.

can bring us a defense organization that will be balanced with our capacity to pay and so will keep and make us strong.[58]

The candidate's major statement of his policy regarding national defense was issued in Baltimore on September 25th. In the course of this speech he warned that economic disaster would result from our huge military spending program.

> We must achieve both security and solvency. In fact, the foundation of military strength is economic strength. A bankrupt America is more the Soviet goal than an America conquered on the field of battle . . . our defense program need not and must not push us steadily toward economic collapse. . . . The cost of security today amounts to 75 percent of our enormous national budget. This means high taxes. Beyond this, the Administration finds in this fact its alibi for inflation and deficits and for the strain put on our whole economy.[59]

The party's foreign policy advisor, Dulles, was equally unhappy over the amount of our defense expenditure. During a speaking tour for Eisenhower he asked: "Are we planning to create a military establishment able, at any moment, to fight successfully by air, by sea and by land; in Asia, Africa and Europe; in the Artic and in the tropics? If so, we are bound to be economically ruined." [60]

Actually, the attack on the Administration's defense budget served two purposes. Defense costs were said to be excessive to the point of threatening to bankrupt the nation while at the same time it was charged that this ruinous outpouring of the nation's wealth was the root cause of the Democrats' much-publicized prosperity. In one of his major speeches on farm policy, the Presidential candidate told Kansas farmers that "as a foundation for the security of our agriculture and the nation, we must achieve a prosperity that is not based on the expenditures for war." A month later he declared that had it not been

---

[58] *The New York Times*, October 17, 1952, p. 18. For the Cincinnati speech, see *The New York Times*, September 23, 1952, p. 16.

[59] *The New York Times*, September 26, 1952, p. 12.

[60] *The New York Times*, October 5, 1952, p. 74.

for Korea the Fair Deal legislation might have placed the United States in serious economic straits.

> War, not the Fair Deal, brought about the end to unemployment. The legacy of war, not the Fair Deal, helped to sustain a high level of economic activity. Nearly one third of the high level production of the first five years after the war was due to making up the shortage created during the war. . . .

> Just as those war-bred shortages began to disappear, and the economy was beginning to weaken, along came Korea. Defense production again propped up the economy. If it had not been for the post-Korea rearmament program, Fair Deal policies might well have headed us right into the middle of a serious business recession.[61]

Dewey supported Eisenhower on this "war prosperity" issue, ridiculing the "you never had it so good" slogan of the opposition. "I say to you that when the domestic policies of a party have been a total failure for twenty years and the only way they can bring about full employment is by the dead and mangled bodies of young Americans, that party is a vulture and it should be cast into outer darkness." [62]

In the 1952 election, the existence of the Korean War gave strength to a number of other issues. Such questions as the high level of government spending, taxation, inflation, corruption and Communism in government would undoubtedly have been issues in 1952 without the war—but the war gave these national problems a greater sense of urgency because it caused the nation to become more anxious over threats to its very existence. Therefore one finds Eisenhower explaining in Worcester that "our campaign is a constructive, progressive crusade to liberate the American people from the shackles of expensive corruption and waste, from the straight-jacket of inflation and taxes, and from the terrifying shadow of war that a vacillating stop and go foreign policy has cast upon us." [63]

---

[61] *The New York Times,* October 3, 1952, p. 16. For the text of the Kansas speech, see *The New York Times,* September 7, 1952, p. 70.

[62] *The New York Times,* October 22, 1952, p. 14.

[63] *The New York Times,* October 21, 1952, p. 24.

Several days later he charged that "The inflation we suffer is not an accident; it is a policy." [64]

The existence of corrupt officials or (worse) those with Communist leanings or connections was also viewed as a threat to the national security. As Dewey said, "The only solution I know for the survival of this country is that we've got to get rid of the traitors and the incompetents and the crooks in Washington and get into the Government of this country the skill, the know-how and the vision to win the peace." [65] When a group of Republican governors began a series of radio addresses under the general title of "Choosing the Right President," the first speaker, Governor Val Peterson of Nebraska, issued a sharp indictment of Stevenson's alleged link with Alger Hiss and Acheson's foreign policy. "[Stevenson's service] with Alger Hiss and Dean Acheson began in the State Department on February 24, 1945. . . . I do sincerely believe that Adlai Stevenson's and Dean Acheson's policies mean more Koreas, more people blacked out behind the Iron Curtain and more dangers to America." [66] Richard Nixon did not go so far as to connect Stevenson with Hiss, but he did tell the nation in the course of his "Checkers" speech on September 23rd that the Democratic standard-bearer would do nothing to change the State Department.

> I say that those in the State Department that made the mistakes which caused that [Korean] war and which resulted in those losses should be kicked out of the State Department just as fast as we can get 'em out of there.

> And let me say that I know Mr. Stevenson won't do that because he defends the Truman policy and I know that Dwight Eisenhower will do that, and that he will give America the leadership that it needs. [63]

If Nixon was unwilling to link Stevenson and Hiss, McCarthy displayed no such reticence. Calling Adlai "Alger" twice during his nationwide speech on October 27th, the Senator attempted to associate Stevenson with either the American Communist party or with "left-wing" groups such as the Americans for Democratic Action. McCarthy also would have the country believe that the opposition candidate "and his whole camp, as well as every crook and Communist in Washington," greatly feared his plan to "scrub and flush and wash clean the foul mess of corruption and communism in Washington." [68]

While reading the campaign speeches and statements of Republican leaders on such topics as Communism, corruption, government spending, taxation, and inflation, one is struck by the frequency with which these leaders related these issues to the Korean War. Moreover, as the campaign progressed there was a remarkable increase in the stress placed on Korea. This fact is best evidenced in the campaign oratory of the party's spokesman, General Eisenhower, who shrewdly sought to monopolize on the desire of the American people for peace on the peninsula. As has been noted, the attitude of the Republicans toward the war at the time of the opening of the campaign was that American intervention was inevitable once the shooting war had begun on the peninsula. Of course the party also argued that there need not have been a Korean War if the Administration had not withdrawn American troops from Korea, if Acheson had not made his "perimeter speech," and if the United States had made it clear to the Communists that it would not tolerate a takeover of the Republic of Korea. This criticism, however, was relatively mild until Eisenhower delivered a major foreign policy address in Cincinnati on September 22nd. Charging that the shadow of war "haunts the hopes of all of us," the general drew a picture of a nation facing "plain peril." The root of the impending disaster was "the incompetence of political leaders which made military action necessary," the same political leaders who had condemned the American people to live "in a purgatory of improvisation." [69]

---

[68] *The New York Times,* October 28, 1952, p. 27.
[69] *The New York Times,* September 22, 1952, p. 16.

This change of tone was present throughout the month of October. On the 2nd he advocated a policy of replacing South Koreans for Americans on the front lines and a week later at the San Francisco Cow Palace he issued a slashing attack on the Panmunjom peace talks, labeling them a "swindle" and a "trap," and ridiculing the negotiations as fifteen months of sheer futility in which "free world diplomacy has been trying to climb the walls of a bear pit into which it fell." [70] By contrast, the General promised to make the ending of the Korean War the first order of business of the new administration. Finally, on the 24th of October came the "I shall go to Korea" speech. The pledge to visit the scene of the war was repeated several times between October 24th and November 4th, a clear indication of the party's recognition of the enormous confidence the American people had in this war hero. Eisenhower the man, rather than the Republican party, now bore the image of peacemaker.

❊   ❊   ❊

The American people went to the polls on November 4th and registered an impressive victory for General Eisenhower. The total popular vote was 61.5 million; Eisenhower won 33.8 million votes to Stevenson's 27.3 million. In terms of percentage, the General received almost 55 percent of the votes cast to his opponent's 44.3 percent. The electoral count was 442 to 89.

The Republicans, however, did not fare nearly so well in the congressional elections. In the Eighty-second Congress the Democrats had had a two-vote lead in the Senate; as a result of the 1952 election and Morse's becoming an "Independent," the Republicans held 48 seats in the new Congress, giving them a one-vote lead over the Democrats. In the House the GOP picked up 22 seats, thereby gaining a slim marginal lead, 221 to 213.

Less than two weeks after the election *U.S. News & World*

---

[70] *The New York Times,* October 9, 1952, p. 24.

Report published the results of an interview that they conducted among certain chief figures in the race. Taft alone did not believe that Korea was the deciding factor, citing instead the public's desire to "get rid of the New Deal—that is, the people were fundamentally against the whole spending-taxation philosophy." [71] Taft did, however, believe that this issue was "intensified tremendously" by corruption, Korea, and Communism. The man who defeated Taft for the nomination in 1948, Governor Dewey, believed that Korea was the major issue of the campaign. "I think that [the voters] understood the Administration had failed to realize the danger in Korea and had blundered us into a situation where a vacuum was created, and where, in effect, the Communists were invited in by the Administration." [72] House Leader Martin gave the same reason, stressing the effect of the President-elect's promise to go to Korea. "I think the people were very much dissatisfied with the Korean situation and didn't think there was any hope for them under the Democratic Administration, and when General Eisenhower said he would go over there and see what he could do to help things out, they rallied to his support." [73] Republican National Chairman Arthur E. Summerfield declared that the "Korean war, of course, was the first issue." [74] The Democrats apparently agreed with this analysis, for Wilson V. Wyatt, Stevenson's campaign manager, answered that ". . . there were several issues that were energizing forces, you might say. From the Republican side I think that the issue of Korea was perhaps dominant." [75] Truman's *Memoirs* charge that the Republicans won the election by "preying upon the false hopes of a nation in crisis." [76]

The danger exists in a study such as this of placing too much emphasis on the importance of Korea as an issue in the

---

[71] "What Happened in the Election," *U.S. News & World Report,* November 14, 1952, p. 66.

[72] *Ibid.,* p. 68.

[73] *Ibid.,* p. 72.

[74] *Ibid.,* p. 74.

[75] *Ibid.,* p. 69.

[76] Truman, *Memoirs,* II, p. 503.

1952 election. One must not forget that Eisenhower the man, the crusader in Europe, was a powerful force in the election. And one must not forget that this election was influenced by many things—corruption and Communism in government, McCarthyism, inflation, taxation, socialism, and Korea. This is not a history of the 1952 election—it is rather an attempt to discover the ways in which the party attempted to use the Korean War to gain control of the national government in 1952. When viewed from this angle, the party's shift from its June 1950 position becomes all the more remarkable. Whether or not one accepts the findings of the Survey Research Center that the Korean War was a minor issue once the voter retired to the privacy of the polling place,[77] it is nevertheless true that the Republican party itself relentlessly marketed the Korean War in an attempt to attract votes; the success of that appeal is a matter for a different kind of study.

---

[77] See above, p. 212.

Chapter 9

The Eisenhower Peace

On November 4, 1952 the American people gave General of the Army Dwight D. Eisenhower a mandate for change. Without specifying the details of his strategy, the campaigning General had carefully nurtured the impression in the minds of the electorate that only a Republican Administration and a Republican Congress could honorably end the Korean conflict. As President, Eisenhower achieved peace in Korea by treading a tortuous route between his desire to terminate rather than expand the war and his belief that unless the Communists were threatened with the use of force they would never agree to a settlement satisfactory to the United Nations Command. Acting upon this basic premise (and aided by such unforeseen events as the death of Stalin on March 5, 1953), the President confronted the Communist world with the threat of an atomic attack and the possibility of an invasion of the Chinese mainland. At the same time he demonstrated a willingness to work toward a negotiated peace, and thereby achieved his goal of an armistice.

There was one great irony in this victory for the Republican Administration: the armistice agreement was closely modeled after the aims that Truman had been seeking—and that so many Republicans had been attacking—since June of 1950. Furthermore, the GOP was by no means united behind the actions of the President. Powerful figures in the United States Senate—particularly Taft, Knowland, McCarthy, Langer, Jenner, and Malone—resented their party's signing a settlement which left the aggressors in possession of substantially the same area that they occupied before the summer of 1950. This conservative wing of the GOP was unable or unwilling to recognize that halting the Communists at the thirty-eighth parallel was in and of itself a signal victory; instead, they insisted that Korea must be unified, and they were willing to attack Communist China to achieve this end. Although pressured by this group, the Administration studiously avoided its counsel, threatening to use force *only to achieve its more limited goals of political and territorial sovereignty for the Republic of Korea and nonforcible repatriation of prisoners of war.*

Those of the President's party who were calling for stronger action in Korea had hoped for more. Jenner asserted in a Lincoln Day address in Idaho that the election of Eisenhower had given the country an opportunity to change the course of its response to the crisis in the Far East.

> It is in the field of foreign policy that Republicans waged their fiercest battle to give the American people the truth about the betrayal of China, the sellout in Korea, and the loss of our security in the Pacific, bought with so much blood and tears. There is no more honorable page in the history of the Congress of the United States than the fight by our Republican Senators and Representatives—with great help from a few Democrats— to stop the almost perfect Fair Deal-Communist conspiracy to let Asia fall without letting it look as if we pushed her.

> That question . . . is not settled. We have won the right to begin again. We cannot tell what difficulties we may meet in the future, but we have made a great beginning.[1]

But Eisenhower and Dulles (the Secretary of State designate as of November 21st) did not view the Korean War as a means of solving the problem of Communism in Asia. Their objectives were the settlement of the prisoners-of-war issue, and the acceptance of a militarily defensible line dividing North and South Korea. Problems of a less immediate nature, particularly the eventual political unification of Korea, were to be settled at the peace conference which was to follow the armistice. With agreement on the more immediate issues as-

---

[1] *Congressional Record,* February 27, 1953, p. A957.

sured by early July, the way was clear for the signing of the armistice on July 27th (Korean time). The Republic of Korea, however, refused to sign the truce, and so the document contained the signature of Mark W. Clark for the United Nations Command, Kim Il Sung for the People's Republic of Korea, and Peng Teh-huai for the Chinese People's Volunteers. It was also endorsed by the Senior United Nations Delegate, General Harrison, and the Senior Communist Delegate, General Nam Il.

* * *

As a result of the November elections the Republican party, for the first time since the Eightieth Congress, was in control of both houses of the legislature. The Republican margin was slim, however, for despite Eisenhower's dramatic victory, his party was unable to score comparable gains in the congressional races. Hence while the GOP was in control of both houses, it held a majority of only eight seats in the House of Representatives; the party's hold over the Senate was even more precarious, for the GOP held forty-eight seats, the Democrats occupied forty-seven, and Wayne Morse remained the sole Independent. Morse announced on November 29th that he would support his former Republican colleagues in the opening-day votes to decide the organization of the Senate— thus assuring the GOP that it would take control of that body. Not since the Hoover Administration had the Republicans been in control of both the executive and the legislature. The party leadership now became the congressional leadership: Representative Joseph Martin (Speaker of the House); Charles Halleck (House Floor Leader); Robert A. Taft (Senate Majority Leader); Styles Bridges (President Pro Tempore of the Senate); and Leverett Saltonstall (Majority Whip). Taft died on July 31, 1953, three days before the sine die adjournment of the first session of the Eighty-third Congress and during his illness Knowland, who was chairman of the

Republican Policy Committee, became Acting Majority Leader.

The Republican party's relationship to the Korean War changed dramatically as a result of the November elections, and although the GOP remained deeply divided in its quest for a solution to the crisis presented by the war, the party remained united in its determination to condemn Truman's handling of the situation. The former President and his Secretary of State, in the eyes of their political opponents, were guilty of gross misconduct in their method of dealing with the war. Lashing out at what he believed to be the Washington correspondents' prejudice in favor of the Democrats, Taft called for a complete investigation of the Truman Administration to prove to the American people the incompetence of that group in handling the Korean War. He cited as evidence of the mismanagement of the Democrats ". . . the lack of ammunition, the mishandling of prisoners, armistice negotiations which enabled the Communists to build up a tremendously strong force and remedy all their deficiencies, and the outrageous dismissal of MacArthur because he thought that the only purpose of war was victory." [2] Styles Bridges told an April meeting of the Women's Division of the Republican National Committee that the new Administration should be applauded for replacing the "desolate Truman-Acheson policy in Korea with a policy which has a definite goal, and which will enable the United States to finish its job and discharge its obligations to its allies." He also cited as the most significant accomplishment of the first ninety days of the Eisenhower era the regaining by the United States of the offensive against the Communists: "No longer do we wait to see what the Communists are going to do before we initiate a program of action." [3]

As in earlier phases of the Republican attack on the Truman Administration, the desire for an outright military victory against the Communists lurked beneath the surface of the

[2] *The New York Times,* April 7, 1953, p. 21.
[3] *Congressional Record,* April 24, 1953, p. A2151.

GOP's response to the Korean War. This was particularly true of those who believed, as MacArthur did, that victory was the sole legitimate goal of warfare. At a West Point Founder's Day dinner on March 15th the General once again insisted that the concept of limited war be repudiated.

> Oblivious to lessons of military, history and the American tradition, a new concept has arisen from outside our ranks which tends to disavow victory as a combat objective and to advocate in its stead a new kind of tactic on which to base the battle.

> The result can be nothing but failure, nothing to repay the terrible human sacrifice of war. We of the military shall always do what we are told to do. But if this nation is to survive, we must trust the soldiers once our statesmen fail to preserve the peace.[4]

Taft continued to support the General, condemning the former administration for its "outrageous" refusal to adopt MacArthur's view of the war, and he was warmly supported by Jenner, who was of the opinion that if we did not get our way at Panmunjom we should "resume full-scale war, but that war will be carried on with no holds barred." [5] Even after the armistice was signed, Pennsylvania's Senator Martin voiced his regret at an American Legion meeting that the United States had not followed MacArthur's advice. "Even though we have reached a cease-fire agreement with the enemy the uncertainty of the world situation makes our defense plans the most difficult in our history. The terrible losses we have sustained in the Korean stalemate and the situation in which we find ourselves today, point with tragic emphasis to the truth spoken by a great American soldier, when he said: "In war there is no substitute for victory." [6]

Throughout the course of the peace negotiations the Eisenhower-Dulles strategy ran counter to this demand by conservative Republicans to fight a full-scale war to achieve our

---

[4] *The New York Times,* March 15, 1953, p. 3.
[5] *Congressional Record,* May 26, 1953, p. 5557.
[6] *Congressional Record,* August 3, 1953, p. A5010.

ultimate goals in Korea and the Far East. In a nationwide broadcast a week after the President's inauguration, Dulles made it clear that the Administration's goal was the peaceful solution to our Asian problems.

> We will not try to meet the Soviet strategy of encirclement by ourselves starting a war. Take that for certain. A few people here and there in private life have suggested that war with Soviet Russia was inevitable, and that we'd better have it soon rather than later because they said time is running against us. President Eisenhower is absolutely opposed to any such policy and so, of course, am I and all of my associates in the State Department and the Foreign Service. We shall never choose a war as the instrument of our policy.[7]

Throughout the January to July period leading figures in the executive branch stressed this same theme, which was best expressed by the President in his April 16th speech to the American Society of Newspaper Editors. After calling for the "immediate cessation of hostilities and the prompt initiation of political discussions leading to the holding of free elections in a united Korea," Eisenhower called for all peaceful nations to dedicate themselves to a new kind of war. "This would be a declared, total war, not upon any human enemy, but upon the brute forces of poverty and need. The peace we seek, founded upon a decent trust and cooperative effort among nations, can be fortified—not by weapons of war—but by wheat, by cotton, by milk and by wool; by meat, timber and rice."[8]

The lines were thus drawn within the Republican party. It must be remembered, however, that many congressional Republicans (particularly those from the East, along with the chairman of the Senate Foreign Relations Committee, Wiley) were strongly backing the Eisenhower-Dulles position. But there was a powerful group composed of Taft, Knowland, McCarthy, Flanders, Malone, Jenner, Langer, and Bricker (to mention only the most prominent) who were keenly disap-

---

[7] *Congressional Record,* January 30, 1953, p. 677.
[8] *The New York Times,* April 17, 1953, p. 4.

pointed in the Administration's decision to seek limited goals in the war.

The first important step taken by Eisenhower in relation to the Korean War was to redeem his election pledge to go to Korea. A news blackout protected the President's mission, and so it was not until he left Seoul on December 5th that the country knew of his trip, which began on the morning of November 29th. Eisenhower was accompanied to Korea by his designated Secretary of Defense, Charles E. Wilson; the Chairman of the Joint Chiefs of Staff, General Omar N. Bradley; Admiral Arthur Radford; and others, including six members of the press. The trip is significant because Eisenhower returned with a clear course of action: to seek an honorable peace on the peninsula and to threaten the Communists with an expanded war if our basic demands for such a settlement were not met. His decision to seek a negotiated peace was readily apparent, for nine days after his return he told a New York City audience: "I return . . . with renewed confidence that a satisfactory solution in Korea can be speeded. I know that it will demand common sense and care, much foresight and much patience. But no more in Korea than anywhere else in the world is honorable peace beyond the power of free men to achieve when they pursue it intelligently and energetically.[9]

Mark Clark reports in his book *From the Danube to the Yalu* that it was evident from his meetings with Eisenhower in Korea that the President-elect's object was an honorable peace, not military victory.

> I had received no instructions from Washington on what Ike wanted to discuss, but I had prepared a list of subjects I knew would be of interest to him. These included a detailed estimate of the forces and plans required to obtain a military victory in Korea should the new administration decide to take such a course.
>
> To me the most significant thing about the visit of the President-elect was that I never had the opportunity to present this

---

[9] *The New York Times*, December 15, 1952, p. 6.

estimate for his consideration. The question of how much it would take to win the war was never raised. It soon became apparent, in our many conversations, that he would seek an honorable truce.[10]

A close observer of Eisenhower's first administration, Robert J. Donovan, has written that "The trip was a very significant one in some respects. The view Eisenhower got of the dour life of the American combat soldiers and the dissipation of American resources in a remote, indecisive struggle intensified his determination to obtain a settlement one way or another."[11] At the same time, Eisenhower hinted that the application of increased force to achieve a settlement was under active consideration. The most telling indication of this resolve to take stronger military action if a negotiated settlement proved impossible is contained in Eisenhower's speech at LaGuardia Airport in New York City when he returned on December 14th.

> This journey marks not the end but the beginning of a new effort to conclude honorably this phase of the global struggle.
>
> This is not the moment to state more than resolve. For we face an enemy whom we cannot hope to impress by words, however eloquent, but only by deeds—*executed under circumstances of our own choosing.* . . . I believe that the architects of aggression can be made to realize that it would be fateful folly to ignite other conflagrations like the Korean conflict elsewhere in the world.[12]

This decision to threaten the use of force must not be confused with the action urged upon the Administration by the more militant members of the party. They wished to forceably unite North and South Korea while the Administration was willing to settle for the division of the country so long as the hostilities were ended and the repatriation question

---

[10] Clark, p. 233.
[11] Robert J. Donovan, *Eisenhower: The Inside Story* (New York, 1956), p. 17.
[12] *The New York Times*, December 15, 1952, p. 6.

settled. Yet there were times when the two views tended to dovetail, as in the case of MacArthur's suggestion, while addressing the National Association of Manufacturers on December 5th, that ". . . there is a clear and definite solution to the Korean conflict . . . without an unduly heavy price in friendly casualties or any increased danger of provoking universal conflict." [13] He went on to state that if Eisenhower asked to see the plan he would show it to the President-elect, but only to him. Esienhower, obviously interested, dramatically sent a message to MacArthur from the ship *Helena* (the scene of his meeting with Dulles after his return from Korea) and told the general: "I appreciate your announced readiness to discuss these matters with me, and assure you I am looking forward to informal meetings in which my associates and I may obtain the full benefit of your thinking and experience." The reply was equally enthusiastic: "I am grateful for your interest in my views concerning solution of problems involved in the Korean war and the Far East. This is especially so because, despite my ultimate personal and professional connection and well-known concern therewith, this is the first time that the slightest official interest in my counsel has been evidenced since my return." [14]

Arrangements were made for MacArthur to meet with Eisenhower and Dulles on the 17th of December; to ensure that there would be no misunderstanding of his position, MacArthur prepared a memorandum on the 14th for presentation to the President-elect and the Secretary of State designate. This memorandum included the following points:

> (a) Call a two-party conference between the President of the United States and Premier Stalin to be held at a mutually agreed upon neutral point. . . .
> (b) That such a conference explore the world situation as a corollary to ending the Korean War;
> (c) That we insist that Germany and Korea be permitted to

---

[13] Discussed in *The New York Times,* December 29, 1952, p. 1.
[14] MacArthur, *Reminiscences,* pp. 408–09.

unite under forms of government to be popularly determined upon;

(d) That thereafter we propose that the neutrality of Germany, Austria, Japan and Korea be guaranteed by the United States and the Soviet with all other nations invited to join as co-guarantors;

(e) That we agree to the principle that in Europe all foreign troops should be removed from Germany and Austria, and in Asia from Japan and Korea;

(f) That we urge that the United States and the Soviet undertake to endeavor to have incorporated in their respective constitutions a provision outlawing war as an instrument of national policy, with all other nations invited to adopt similar moral limitations;

(g) That at such conference, the Soviet be informed that should an agreement not be reached, it would be our intention to clear North Korea of enemy forces. (*This could be accomplished through the atomic bombing of enemy military concentrations and installations in North Korea and the sowing of fields of suitable radio-active materials, the by-product of atomic manufacture,* to close the major lines of enemy supply and communication leading south from the Yalu, with simultaneous amphibious landings on both coasts of North Korea);

(h) That the Soviet should be further informed that, in such an eventuality, it would become necessary to neutralize Red China's capability to wage modern war.[15]

In the concluding paragraph of his memorandum, MacArthur wrote that "The Soviet is not blind to the dangers which actually confront it in the present situation, and it might well settle the Korean War on equitable terms such as those herein outlined, just as soon as it realizes we have the will and the means to bring the present issues to a prompt and definite determination."[16]

There can be little doubt that MacArthur actually transmitted this plan to Eisenhower, for Sherman Adams writes in his *Firsthand Report* that in the summer of 1960 he asked Eisen-

---

[15] *Ibid.,* p. 411. Emphasis added.
[16] *Ibid.,* p. 412.

hower about the nature of MacArthur's plan to end the war and was told of the suggestion to use the atomic bomb. "The solution," Adams relates, "was a precisely stated intention to drop an atomic bomb after full notification to the North Koreans of our purpose. MacArthur was sure that there was not the remotest chance we would actually have to carry out our threat; the Communists would simply throw up their hands and the war would be over." [17] Then too, on April 19, 1953, MacArthur assured Senator Byrd that such a warning "provides the leverage to induce the Soviet to bring the Korean struggle to an end without further bloodshed." [18] As will be seen, when such a threat was transmitted to the Communists in May of 1953 it became a powerful factor in the settlement of the Korean War.

The trip to Korea and the expressed willingness to consider MacArthur's plan both occurred while Eisenhower was still President elect. On January 20th the General became President and devoted nearly his entire inaugural address to foreign affairs and world peace. Without rendering in detail his future policy toward Korea, Eisenhower clearly voiced his intention of negotiating peace from a position of strength. "Realizing that common sense and common decency alike dictate the futility of appeasement, we shall never try to placate an aggressor by the false and wicked bargain of trading honor for security. Americans, indeed, all free men, remember that in the final choice a soldier's pack is not so heavy a burden as a prisoner's chains . . . in our quest for an honorable peace, we shall neither compromise, nor tire, nor ever cease." [19]

If the inaugural address was characterized by a lack of specifics, such was not the case with Eisenhower's first State of the Union address on February 2nd. It was in this message

---

[17] Adams, p. 48.

[18] For an account of the message to Byrd, see *The New York Times*, April 25, 1953, p. 2.

[19] Dwight D. Eisenhower, *The Public Papers of the Presidents of the United States: 1953* (Washington, 1960), pp. 1–8.

that the President announced his decision that the Seventh Fleet shall no longer "protect" Communist China from attack from Formosa.

> In June 1950, following the aggressive attack on the Republic of Korea, the United States Seventh Fleet was instructed both to prevent attack upon Formosa and also to ensure that Formosa should not be used as a base of operations against the Chinese Communist mainland.
>
> This has meant, in effect, that the United States Navy was required to serve as a defensive arm of Communist China. Regardless of the situation of 1950, since the date of that order the Chinese Communists have invaded Korea to attack the United Nations forces there . . . there is no longer any logic or sense in a condition that required the United States Navy to assume defensive responsibilities on behalf of the Chinese Communists, thus permitting those Communists with greater impunity to kill our soldiers and those of our United Nations allies in Korea.
>
> I am, therefore, issuing instructions that the Seventh Fleet no longer be employed to shield Communist China. Permit me to make [this] crystal clear. This order implies no aggressive intent on our part. But we certainly have no obligation to protect a nation fighting us in Korea.[20]

The obvious implication behind this announcement, despite Eisenhower's disavowal of aggressive intent, was that the new Administration, scarcely two weeks old, would not shrink from threatening the Communists with an extension of the war if they did not cooperate. The "unleashing" of Chiang Kai-shek was at this point clearly a symbolic gesture, but it left the door open for possible United States military aid to Formosa should there be a decision to attack the mainland. The President's party was clearly delighted with this action. After listening to the speech Knowland told his colleagues

> Such neutralizing action [by Truman] in relation to Formosa lost its validity when the Communist forces in China joined the

---

[20] *Ibid.*, pp. 12–34.

forces in North Korea in the attack upon the Republic of Korea
and upon the United Nations forces then in Korea . . . the
action at that point was tantamount to the use of the United
States Navy to defend a part of Communist China at a time
when Communist China was attempting to destroy our own
forces and was inflicting heavy casualties upon our forces in
Korea.[21]

Wiley assured the Senate that the decision of the President
was so important because now "we shall not make it possible
for the Communists to center their energies and their attacks
upon our troops in Korea." He also stressed the fact that the
deneutralization order would open the way for Nationalist
Chinese bombing of 2,000 miles of railroad running from
Manchuria to Canton, the South China Sea, and French Indo
China.[22] At a Lincoln Day dinner in New York City, Governor
Thomas Dewey voiced strong approval of the President's action. "We intend no longer to let Communists murder American boys while we protect the aggressor's flank. We intend no
longer to see nation after nation fall and content ourselves
with diplomatic protests."[23]

As was to be expected, one of the warmest supporters of the
deneutralization order was General MacArthur, who stated
that the "sanctuary immunity" granted to Red China because
of Truman's instructions to the Seventh Fleet "unquestionably
predominately influenced Red China to enter the Korean conflict after the North Korean armies had been destroyed." Mac-
Arthur went on to explain that "in the absence of assurance
that his bases of attack and lines of supplies to his rear would
be safe, no military commander lacking both naval force and
air cover would have committed large forces across the Yalu
River."[24]

The days immediately following the deneutralization order

---

[21] *Congressional Record*, February 2, 1953, p. 736.
[22] *The New York Times*, February 5, 1953, p. 1. Also see *Congressional Record*, February 6, 1953, p. 917.
[23] *The New York Times*, February 13, 1953, p. 4.
[24] Quoted in *Congressional Record*, February 13, 1953, p. 1060.

might be viewed as a "honeymoon" period for Eisenhower and his Republican critics. Many of the party's most influential members were soon calling on the Administration to take stronger action: they sought a stronger blockade against Communist China; the adoption of the doctrine of "hot pursuit"; closer cooperation from our allies; and a guarantee that Communist China would not be admitted to the United Nations in return for cooperating at Panmunjom.

On the question of the blockade, Knowland declared early in February that he was in favor of Admiral Arthur W. Radford's plan to blockade Communist China even if we failed to secure the cooperation of the Allies in this endeavor.[25] Senator Taft, on a February 8th broadcast of "Youth Wants to Know," reasoned that since the United States was already "at full war" with Communist China the bombing of Manchurian supply bases or the blockading of the China coast would not extend the war. "A war's a war—it could be no worse than now. . . . People seem to be asleep to the fact that we are at war with Red China now."[26] While Taft did believe that it would be better if we could establish such a blockade with the cooperation of our allies, he did not rule out the possibility of acting alone.

Dulles patiently explained on several occasions that while the possibility of a naval blockade was under active consideration, "we have been making [very strong efforts] to get all of our allies to cut off their commercial intercourse with the enemy, certainly to the extent that it is of military value, contraband of war. In a speech to the American Society of Newspaper Editors on April 18th the Secretary of State once again emphasized the Administration's efforts to get *voluntary* compliance with its attempt to halt the flow of strategic goods.[27] Clearly, this policy fell short of the demands of those who sought an all-out blockade.

---

[25] *The New York Times,* February 8, 1953, p. 4.
[26] *The New York Times,* February 9, 1953, p. 1.
[27] *Congressional Record,* April 20, 1953, p. A1986. For Dulles' earlier statement, see *The New York Times,* February 19, 1953, p. 3.

Throughout this period those Republicans who had taken a "hard line" toward the fighting of the war continually complained that the United States had in the past foolishly eschewed the doctrine of "hot pursuit" into Manchuria. Since the new Administration was following the very same policy, the implication was that now that the Republicans were in control Manchuria should no longer occupy the position of a privileged sanctuary. Senators Styles Bridges and William Knowland charged that such a strategy had been approved by not only "every responsible commander in Korea" but by President Truman himself. Yet when the Department of State discovered, after some "informal soundings," that "two or three" of our allies did not approve of the action the plan was dropped.[28]

The disinclination of the Allies to follow the doctrine of "hot pursuit" was only one of the things that kept alive the Republicans' resentment toward our United Nations partners. Malone continued to lash out at every opportunity against the trading policies of Marshall Plan nations, asserting that the only effective weapon to use against those who insisted upon trading with Iron Curtain countries was to cut off their aid. Ideologically in accord with Malone, Langer asserted on the Senate floor that it was not circumstances that caused us to give up our goal of halting aggression to the Yalu but rather the pressure that was brought to bear by "our associates of the United Nations [who] threw their weight around on behalf of their own pitiful little egoisms." McCarthy declared that when considering England's trade with Red China, "we should perhaps keep in mind the American boys and the few British boys too, who had their hands wired behind their backs and their faces shot off with machine guns . . . supplied by those flag vessels of our allies." [29]

---

[28] *Congressional Record*, February 6, 1953, p. 918. Also see *Congressional Record*, March 11, 1953, p. A1229; *Congressional Record*, June 30, 1953, p. 7667 and *Congressional Record*, May 26, 1953, p. 5555.

[29] *Congressional Record*, May 14, 1953, p. 4911. For Malone's statement, see *Congressional Record*, April 14, 1953, pp. 3069–70. Langer is represented in *Congressional Record*, June 30, 1953, p. 7667.

But it was Attlee's speech of May 13th to the Parliament that caused anti-British sentiments to reach new heights. Attlee, leader of the Labor Opposition, complained that it was far too risky to allow the United States to negotiate alone at Panmunjom on behalf of the United Nations: "there are elements in the United States that do not want a settlement. . . . There are people who want an all-out war with China and against communism in general and there is a strong influence of the Chiang Kai-shek lobby." [30] With these doubts in mind, Attlee suggested to Prime Minister Churchill that England and other United Nations members send advisers to the Korean peace conference in an attempt to strengthen the hand of the American Administration. The speech greatly agitated that segment of the GOP that was under attack by Attlee. Knowland interpreted the speech as meaning that "if we do not accept their advice, and if the Chinese Communists persist in the war, we must be prepared to go it alone." His response was a stinging attack on the policies followed by the English in relation to the Korean War. "So be it. It is unfortunate that they did not take that position in June of 1950, if their intent was to give half-hearted support to the resistence of his first overt act of aggression, and to spending the remainder of the time in placing such restrictions upon our Armed Forces that we would be denied the opportunity for achieving the victory, which alone would have assured a united Korea . . . and which would have been a deterrent to further aggression in the world." [31]

The GOP's attitude toward the Allies and the United Nations was further complicated by the fact that many party members viewed the world body as totally ineffective in dealing with the Korean War. Knowland's attitude toward the U.N. was characterized by the belief that working in concert with other nations was harmful to our own security. He asked his colleagues: "were our hands not tied by the neutralists in the United Nations, some acting by fear and some by design?

---

[30] *The New York Times,* May 13, 1953, p. 6.
[31] *Congressional Record,* May 13, 1953, p. 4861.

. . . Are we to be immobilized until we can be struck a mortal blow?" [32] A major battle developed within the Republican ranks when Majority Leader Taft prepared a speech on this subject for delivery before the National Conference of Christians and Jews in Cincinnati on May 26th. By this time the Ohio Senator was too ill to appear in person, and so his speech was read for him by his son, Robert Jr. The Senator argued that the proposed truce was utterly unsatisfactory, in good part because it had been necessary for us to conciliate U.N. members. Underlying this major premise was Taft's belief that no hope existed of achieving a meaningful settlement, and so the entire attempt should be abandoned.

> I believe we might as well forget the United Nations as far as the Korean war is concerned. I think we should do our best now to negotiate this truce, and if we fail, then let England and our other allies know that we are withdrawing from all further peace negotiations in Korea.

> Even the best truce under present conditions will be extremely unsatisfactory. It will divide Korea along an unnatural line and create an unstable condition likely to bring war again at any moment. It will release a million Chinese soldiers, who no doubt will promptly be moved down to Southern China for use against Chiang Kai-shek or against the French in Indo-China.

> It seems to me that from the beginning we should have insisted on a general peace negotiation with China, including a unification of Korea under free Koreans, and a pledge against further expansion in Southeast Asia. If we once make this present truce, no matter what we put in the agreement about further negotiations for [a] unified Korea it is not more likely to occur than a united Germany.

> I believe we might as well abandon any idea of working with the United Nations in the East and reserve to ourselves a completely free hand. [33]

---

[32] *Congressional Record,* March 16, 1953, p. 1973.
[33] White, *The Taft Story,* pp. 134–135. Also see *The New York Times,* May 27, 1953, p. 6.

Eisenhower, of course, had been and remained a staunch supporter of the United Nations, and Taft in effect had forced the President's hand on the issue of cooperating with our allies to achieve a peace settlement. After hesitating two days Eisenhower decided to reject Taft's concept of acting unilaterally in Korea.

> If you are going to go it alone one place, you of course have to go it alone everywhere. If you are going to try to develop a coalition of understanding based upon decency, on ideas of justice, common concepts of government, established by the will of free men, then you have got to make compromises. . . .

> No single free nation can live alone in the world. We have to have friends. Those friends have got to be tied to you, in some form or another. We have to have that unity in basic purposes that comes from a recognition of common interests.[34]

Another avowed backer of the U.N. was Senator Wiley; placing himself in basic disagreement with three powerful GOP senators—Taft, Knowland, and McCarthy—the chairman of the Foreign Relations Committee told a Memorial Day audience at Arlington National Cemetery that "We did not 'go it alone' in the Nineteen Forties. We are not going to go it alone in the Nineteen Fifties. Unity among our allies is essential. It must be a living unity, not just a token of lip service. No nation in the twentieth century can live unto itself alone, and no nation can be strong unto itself alone." [35] Massachusetts' Saltonstall also supported the President's camp, and he assured a Memorial Day gathering in his native state that ". . . we cannot go it alone. . . . We have only six percent of the world's inhabitants and lack many raw materials necessary to the healthy working of our economy in time of peace as in time of emergency . . . we must not for a single second forget that we need them and that they need us." [36]

---

[34] *The New York Times*, May 29, 1953, p. 4.
[35] *The New York Times*, May 31, 1953, p. 1.
[36] *Ibid.*, p. 3.

The debate over the necessity for and the effectiveness of the United Nations in the Korean War pales as a cause of interparty friction when compared with the overriding issue of the unification of Korea. It will be remembered that before the November election party members from the Mid- and Far West had been insisting that Truman's failure to press the fight on the peninsula to unite North and South constituted a repudiation of the initial aims of the United Nations. These Republicans had failed to see that a differentiation had to be made between the political and military goals of the United Nations—politically the aim was unification; militarily the aim was the restoration of the territorial integrity of the Republic of Korea. Truman's decision to cross the thirty-eight parallel in October of 1950 actually ran counter to the U.N.'s aims in the summer of 1950. The July 27th resolution of the Security Council stated that United Nations members shall "furnish such assistance to the Republic of Korea as may be necessary to repel the armed attack and to *restore* the international peace and security in the area." [37]

During the Presidential race just ended, Eisenhower was extremely careful not to commit himself to the side of those Republicans insisting upon the unification of Korea as the military goal of the war. This is important because the armistice Eisenhower supported in July was based upon the theory that we had achieved our objective in repelling the aggressor from the Republic of Korea. To those who believed that the initial goal was unification, the terms of the proposed truce were by no means satisfactory. The major spokesmen for this view were Knowland and Flanders. The Vermont Senator voiced his disenchantment with the new Administration when he mourned the fact that "Somewhere along the line the same influence which guided the Truman-Acheson administration got hold of our new administration. It was with sickness of heart that we heard anew the proud boast that we had successfully resisted aggression as if the loss of hundreds of

---

[37] For a more complete discussion of this aspect of Republican thought in the earlier phases of the war, see Chapter 5.

thousands of lives and billions of dollars had been well spent in bringing us back to the starting ground of June 25, 1950." [38] It was, perhaps, a foregone conclusion that both Jenner and Langer would accept a similar view. [39] Taft was another powerful backer of the anti-Administration position, for he contended that the proposed settlement would create an unnatural line and an unstable condition which would eventually lead to the resumption of war. [40]

In the face of powerful Republican critics calling for the unification of Korea as the military goal of the United Nations, the Administration clung to its conviction that it would fight for unification only at a political conference after the armistice was signed. As the possibility of this kind of armistice increased, Rhee's hostility to the terms of the proposed settlement grew. Recognizing this, the President sought to mollify the South Korean leader by writing to him and outlining his reasons for not supporting the forcible unification of North and South Korea.

> The enemy has proposed an armistice which involves a clear abandonment of the fruits of aggression. The armistice would leave the Republic of Korea in undisputed possession of substantially the territory which the Republic administered prior to the aggression, indeed this territory will be somewhat enlarged.
>
> The proposed armistice, true to the principles of political asylum, assures that the thousands of North Koreans and Communist Chinese prisoners in our hands, who have seen liberty and who wish to share it, will have the opportunity to do so and will not be forcibly sent back into Communist areas. . . .
>
> It is my profound conviction that under these circumstances acceptance of the armistice is required of the United Nations

---

[38] *Congressional Record*, July 1, 1953, p. 7765. For a sample of Knowland's view, see *Congressional Record*, May 13, 1953, p. 4861; *Congressional Record*, June 13, 1953, p. A3448; and *The New York Times*, July 6, 1953, p. 1.

[39] See *Congressional Record*, May 26, 1953, p. 5555 and *Congressional Record*, June 30, 1953, p. 7667.

[40] *The New York Times*, May 27, 1953, p. 6.

and the Republic of Korea. We would not be justified in prolonging the war with all the misery that it involves in the hope of achieving, by force, the unification of Korea. . . .

We remain determined to play our part in achieving the political union of all countries so divided. But we do not intend to employ war as an instrument to accomplish the worldwide political settlements to which we are dedicated and which we believe to be just.[41]

Two days later Ambassador to the United Nations Lodge made it clear that he did not believe that unity was the object of the war. "I don't think we ever have committed ourselves to kill our young men in order to unify Korea. I don't think there is such a commitment. I think if we get an armistice where we are it will constitute a repulsion of the aggression that took place. Whether that's a victory or not is a matter of how you define words. But I don't think we're committed at all to fight a bloody war to unify Korea." [42]

Many Republican congressional leaders supported this view, particularly Wiley and Smith (N.J.). The latter told the Senate that "I am one of those who is deeply sympathetic with Dr. Rhee's aspirations to unite and free his country and I feel a real inspiration as I review his noble life of patriotic duty to a great cause. But it is my considered judgment that the fighting must cease and that we must seek our objectives through peaceful means." [43]

In *Mandate for Change* Eisenhower has reasserted his belief that the proper course of action in the settlement of the Korean War was the acceptance of unification as our political, not military, goal.

The United States entered the Korean War to carry out a "police action," with no objective more ambitious than the expulsion of Communist forces from the Republic of Korea. . . . Since the beginning of the war, no statement of American or

---

[41] *Congressional Record,* June 8, 1953, p. 6161.
[42] *The New York Times,* June 9, 1953, p. 4.
[43] *Congressional Record,* June 25, 1953, p. 7285.

United Nations military objectives went further than to express the determination to reestablish the northern frontier of the Republic. . . . Ambassador Warren Austin in the United Nations Security Council said that the *United States government's action was solely for the purpose of restoring the Republic of Korea to its status prior to the invasion.*[44]

While the party remained deeply divided on the issue of unification, Eisenhower's position on the prisoners-of-war issue was widely accepted. Throughout the early months of his Presidency Eisenhower had made it absolutely clear that there were "certain principles inherent in the United Nations Command position which are basic and not subject to change. No prisoners will be repatriated by force. No prisoners will be coerced or intimidated in any way. And there must be a definite limit to the period of their captivity. The procedures in handling the prisoners must reflect these principles." [45] The Russians, for their part, had their own ideas on this question and two weeks after Eisenhower's political sweep Andrei Vyshinsky, Russia's chief delegate to the United Nations, voiced his country's disapproval of an Indian compromise resolution on the question of the repatriation of prisoners. This plan (which the United States found satisfactory) stated that force would not be employed against prisoners of war to prevent or effect their return to their homelands. The Indian proposal also called for the creation of a repatriation commission (made up of representatives from neutral nations) to expedite the return of prisoners of war. Should there by any nonrepatriated prisoners ninety days after the signing of an armistice, their status was to be determined by a postwar political conference that was to be called into being under the terms of the armistice agreement. Those who refused to return to their homes would become wards of the United Nations. By a vote of 54–5 the General Assembly approved this plan on December 3rd, and on December 14th Chou En-lai de-

---

[44] Eisenhower, pp. 172–74. Emphasis his.
[45] *The New York Times,* May 27, 1953, p. 3.

nounced the Indian proposal as illegal and void; North Korea rejected it three days later.

A way around this impasse was offered by General Mark Clark, Commander-in-Chief of the United Nations forces, when, on February 22nd, he sent a letter to Kim Il Sung (the North Korean leader) and Peng Teh-huai (commander of the Chinese People's Volunteers) suggesting that a plan be worked out for the exchange of sick and wounded prisoners. On March 28th—three weeks after Stalin's death—the Communists replied that they would agree to such an exchange and hoped that it would lead to a meaningful settlement of the entire prisoners-of-war question. More important, in the course of agreeing to a liaison meeting to discuss these matters, the Communists sent Clark the text of a statement issued by Chou En-lai after his return from Stalin's funeral. The text was endorsed by Kim Il Sung and stated that the two Communist governments "propose that both parties to the negotiations should undertake to repatriate immediately after the cessation of hostilities all those prisoners of war in their custody who insist upon repatriation and to hand over the remaining prisoners of war to a neutral state so as to ensure a just solution to the question of their repatriation." [46] This in effect broke the deadlock over item four of the agenda. As a result of liaison meetings beginning April 6th, 6,670 Communist and 684 United Nations prisoners were soon exchanged.

Thus the willingness of the Chinese Communists to continue the talks despite Rhee's action (rather than Rhee's promise of cooperation) actually made possible the final settlement. In his study of the Panmunjom talks William Vatcher offers several reasons for the change in attitude by the Chinese Communists: the fear that the Administration would allow the forces of Chiang Kai-shek to fight in Korea; the inability of the Communists to obtain further propaganda from the conference because the world press had tired of this tactic; the economic strain of the Korean War on the Chinese economy;

---

[46] Quoted in William Vatcher, *Panmunjom* (New York, 1958), pp. 181–82.

the fear that China's increased prestige might be lost in an expanded war; and the death of Stalin.[47] It is particularly important to note here that the new Russian government endorsed Chou's statement of March 28th, for Foreign Minister Molotov wrote to the United Nations Command: "I am authorized to state that the Soviet Government expresses its full solidarity with this noble act. . . . There can be no doubt that the peoples of the whole world, desiring to put an end to the war in Korea . . . will welcome this proposal with warm sympathy and offer it full support." [48]

The new Russian government's cooperation unfortunately did not solve all of the issues involved in the thorny prisoners-of-war question; throughout April and the early part of May the disposition of nonrepatriated prisoners remained a stumbling block at Panmunjom. The United Nations was against the Communist plan of sending nonrepatriated prisoners to another country, and the Communists did not want to grant them Korean civilian status. Hoping to avoid another stalemate, the Administration met with its allies and presented Clark with a series of final proposals on May 23rd. These instructions stated that all prisoners were to be transferred to the Neutral Nations Repatriation Commission (Czechoslovakia, Poland, Sweden, Switzerland and India) which would guarantee that those prisoners who wished to return home could do so. A 90- or 120-day period was allocated for the purpose of "explaining" to prisoners the advantages of returning home, and those still not repatriated would either become civilians or be referred to the General Assembly. As commander of the United Nations forces, Clark was further instructed to break off the talks (rather than recess them) and "carry on the war in new ways never yet tried in Korea" if this plan was rejected.[49]

Despite the impact and influence of the death of Stalin on the eventual outcome of the Korean War, the single most

---

[47] *Ibid.*, pp. 177–78.
[48] Quoted in *ibid.*, p. 182.
[49] Clark, p. 257.

important element influencing the termination of the war was this decision by the Eisenhower Administration to threaten the Communists with the use of atomic weapons if the negotiations were not brought to a successful conclusion. The apparent unwillingness of the Communists in the spring and early summer of 1953 to risk an expanded war made the settlement possible. In the first volume of his memoirs Eisenhower outlines his strategy in warning the Communists that he would expand the war beyond the Korean borders and employ atomic weapons at the same time. It will be noted that the former President believes that this warning brought about an improvement in the armistice talks.

> . . . to keep the attack from becoming overly costly, it was clear that we would have to use atomic weapons. This necessity was suggested to me by General MacArthur while I, as President-elect, was still living in New York . . . such weapons would obviously be effective for strategic targets in North Korea, Manchuria, and on the Chinese coast. . . .
>
> The lack of progress in the long-stalemated talks . . . demanded, in my opinion, definite measures on our part to put an end to those intolerable conditions. One possibility was to let the Communist authorities understand that, in the absence of satisfactory progress, we intended to move decisively without inhibition in our use of weapons, and would no longer be responsible for confining hostilities to the Korean peninsula. . . . In India and in the Formosa Straits area, and at the truce negotiations at Panmunjom, we dropped the word, discreetly, of our intention. We felt quite sure it would reach Soviet and Chinese Communist ears.
>
> Soon the prospects for armistice negotiations seemed to improve.[50]

Several other principals in the Korean War support this view of the former President. At the Geneva conference on Korea in April of 1954 Dulles said that the truce came "only after the Communists realized that, unless there was a quick

---

[50] Eisenhower, pp. 180–81.

armistice, the battle areas would be enlarged so as to endanger the sources of aggression in Manchuria. Then and only then did the Communist rulers judge that it would be expedient to sign the armistice." [51] In the now-famous "brinkmanship" article in *Life* Dulles told of the effect of his and Eisenhower's use of the threat of force.

> You have to take chances for peace, just as you must take chances in war. Some say that we were brought to the verge of war. Of course we were. . . . The ability to get to the verge without getting into the war is a necessary art. If you cannot master it, you inevitably get into war. If you are scared to go to the brink, you are lost. We've had to look it square in the face—on the question of enlarging the Korean war, on the question of getting into the Indochina war, on the question of Formosa. We walked to the brink and we looked it in the face. We took strong action. [52]

Assistant to the President Sherman Adams has written that "Although not as blunt and specific as MacArthur has suggested, it was indeed the threat of atomic attack that eventually did bring the Korean War to an end on July 26, 1953." [53] Adams relates that in the spring of 1953 the Administration ordered atomic missiles installed on Okinawa and that in May Dulles told Nehru in India that if a truce could not be arranged the United States "could not be held responsible for failing to use atomic weapons."

> This message was planted deliberately in India so that it would get to the Chinese Communists, as it did. Long afterward, talking one day with Eisenhower about the events that led up finally to the truce in Korea, I asked him what it was that brought the Communists into line. "Danger of an atomic war," he said without hesitation. "We told them we could not hold it to a limited war any longer if the Communists welched on a

---

[51] Quoted in Rees, p. 418.

[52] James Shepley, "How Dulles Averted War," *Life*, January 16, 1956, p. 78.

[53] Adams, p. 48.

treaty of truce. They didn't want a full-scale war or an atomic attack. That kept them under some control." [54]

In addition, there can be little doubt that the Administration transmitted to the United Nations Command its intention of using atomic weapons, for General Mark Clark writes that in May, for the first time, "I was granted authority from Washington to *terminate,* not recess, the Panmunjom truce talks if the Reds refused our final order . . . then I was to prosecute the war along lines we had not yet taken to make the Communists wish they had accepted our terms." This new concept very much appealed to the commanding general, who has written that these orders "sounded more like the American way of doing business." [55]

Admiral G. Turner Joy, the United Nations chief negotiator at Panmunjom until he was succeeded by Major General William K. Harrison, Jr. in May of 1952, is convinced that the threat of an expanded war in which atomic weapons would be employed explains the Communists' willingness to agree with the United Nations position on repatriation.

> What influenced them most, I feel certain, were ominous sounds of impending *expanded* warfare. . . . During the spring of 1953, the United States began running out of patience. Serious consideration was being given to extending United Nations Command military operations into Red China. The threat of atomic bombs was posed. . . . Thus at the last, the one negotiating factor that Communists respect above all else was beginning to appear: naked massive power and the willingness to use that power when necessary. . . . In understandable prudence, they took the only step open to them to remove the growing threat of a holocaust in Red China.[56]

In May the United States informed Nehru of its intention to expand the war if the Communists continued their delaying

---

[54] *Ibid.,* pp. 48–49 and 102. Also see Donovan, pp. 116–18.

[55] Clark, p. 257. Emphasis his.

[56] C. Turner Joy, *How Communists Negotiate* (New York, 1955), pp. 161–62. Emphasis his.

tactics at Panmunjom; yet two months elapsed before the official signing of the armistice. The reasons for the delay cover the full spectrum of the important to the insignificant, from Rhee's release of anti-Communist prisoners of war to the demand of the Communists that they be allowed to hang Picasso's "peace doves" at the entrance of the building where the armistice was to be signed. The behind-the-scenes maneuverings of the governments of the United States, Russia, and Red China had left Syngman Rhee waiting in the wings, a role intensely resented by the aging patriot-president. He therefore resolutely refused to cooperate with any agreement which left his country divided or which acquiesced to the occupation of a portion of Korea by Communist troops. So hostile was he to the proposed truce that he threatened to release all nonrepatriated prisoners of war in South Korean hands and to withdraw his troops from the United Nations Command. To make the proposed armistice more palatable to the Korean leader, Mark Clark was authorized to offer him the following: a pledge by the sixteen nations of the United Nations Command that they would again aid South Korea should that country be attacked, and that such defense need not necessarily be confined to Korea; United States aid in building up the Republic's army, navy, and air force; and a billion dollars in economic aid for the rehabiliation of the country.

None of this satisfied Rhee, and on June 18th he ordered the release of 25,000 anti-Communist prisoners of war. Shocked by this action, Dulles met with Eisenhower and then issued a statement declaring Rhee's action to be in direct violation of the authority of the United Nations Command. Assistant Secretary of State Walter Robertson was immediately sent to Seoul, and he was able to pacify Rhee to the extent that the Korean leader agreed not to take any further overt action to torpedo the armistice talks; to abide by the terms of the armistice; and to withdraw his demand that all Chinese soldiers be removed from Korean soil. In return, the United States renewed its pledge to formulate a sixteen-nation agreement to aid South Korea in the event of attack; aid in the buildup of the Korean army, navy, and air force; and extend a billion dollars in aid to help rehabilitate the country.

Finally, at 10:00 a.m. on July 27th (Korean time) the Senior United Nations Command Delegate, General William K. Harrison, Jr., and the Senior Communist Delegate, General Nam Il, signed eighteen copies of the armistice agreement without saying a word to one another. Shortly after hearing of the official signing of the truce, Eisenhower addressed a nation-wide radio and television audience. Importantly, he warned the country that the armistice did not mean that the Communist menace could now be ignored.

Tonight we greet with prayers of thanksgiving the official news that an armistice was signed almost an hour ago in Korea. It will quickly bring to an end the fighting between the United Nations forces and the Communist armies. . . .

In this struggle we have seen the United Nations meet the challenge of aggression, not with pathetic words of protest, but with deeds of decisive purpose. . . .

There is, in this moment of sober satisfaction, one thought that must discipline our emotions and steady our resolutions. It is this: we have won an armistice on a single battleground, not peace in the world.

We may not now relax our guard nor cease our quest. Throughout the coming months, during the period of prisoner screening and exchange, and during the possibly longer period of the political conference which looks toward the unification of Korea, we and our United Nation allies must be vigilant against the possibility of untoward developments.[57]

News of the signing did not heal the fundamental division in the Republican party concerning the conduct of the war. While many Democrats and pro-Eisenhower Republicans approved of the terms offered to the Communists, conservative members of the President's party contended that the 1952 platform had called for stronger action against the Commu-

---

[57] *The New York Times,* July 27, 1953, p. 4.

nists. In a speech in Pennsylvania on August 1st, Martin expressed his support of MacArthur's plan for victory, insisting that "you cannot go into a military campaign with any hope of success without victory as its objective." [58] Jenner told his fellow senators two days later that "we must give notice now to the other nations in the conference [the political conference to follow the armistice], and in the United Nations that the cease-fire agreement was the end of an era, the last tribute to appeasement. We are done with the illusions of the forties." [59] Although Taft died two days after the agreement had been reached, it had been plain for some time that he was opposed to its contents. It was Taft's belief that a victory had not been won against aggression because the truce would leave the Far East in "an unstable condition likely to bring war again at any moment." [60]

This group of conservatives also disagreed with the President and the Secretary of State on the question of the effectiveness of the role that the United Nations played in the challenge of the Korean War. In his official announcement to the Senate of the signing of the armistic agreement, Knowland declared "While we should appreciate the token contribution of 35,000 men from 17 of the 60 members of the United Nations, neither we nor they should misrepresent to the American people or to the free world that this example represents effective collective security in action. It does not." [61] Even Alexander Wiley, who had been a strong supporter of the Administration's efforts to conclude the war, spoke very warily of the agreement.

It is a step. We hope it will be a step in the right direction. We hope it will eventuate in an armistice period during which men can work out a peace not only with the present participants but with the real villains [the Chinese Communist regime and the Kremlin]. . . .

---

[58] *Congressional Record,* August 3, 1953, p. A5010.
[59] *Ibid.,* p. 11000.
[60] *The New York Times,* May 27, 1953, p. 6.
[61] *Congressional Record,* July 27, 1953, p. 9853.

The people who handled [the truce] faced the facts and the realities. Having come to the conclusion they did, it is not for me to censure or even to judge.

It must be assumed that those who negotiated the truce felt there was some hope that the real parties in interest might be brought into peace arrangements. . . .

At least we have stopped the killing of Americans.[62]

This reluctance on the part of many in Eisenhower's own party to endorse the newly won peace was shared by General MacArthur, who was decidedly hostile to the entire settlement. In January of 1955 the General was in Los Angeles to deliver a speech at the dedication of a monument erected in his honor in MacArthur Park. He used the occasion to blast the Eisenhower peace:

Although it [patriotism] has been from the beginning the main bulwark of our national strength and integrity, seductive murmurs are arising that it is now outmoded by some more comprehensive and all-embracing philosophy; that we are provincial and immature or reactionary and stupid when we idealize our own nation; that there is a higher destiny for us under another and more general flag; that no longer when we send our sons and daughters to the battlefield should we see them through all the way to victory; that we can call upon them to fight and even to die in some half-hearted and indecisive effort; that we can plunge them recklessly into war and then suddenly decide that it is a wrong war, or in a wrong place, or even that we can call it not a war at all but by some more euphonious or gentler name; that we can treat them as expendables although they are our own flesh and blood; and even in times of peace, for some romantic reason, they must share—not as a gesture of generosity but as a bounden duty—their natural blessings and goods, built from nothing to a height never before reached by man, with others because, whether through neglect or not, they have not fared so well; that we, the most powerful nation in the world,

---

[62] *The New York Times,* July 28, 1953, p. 8.

have suddenly become dependent upon others for our security and even our welfare.[63]

During an address to the Los Angeles County Council of the American Legion that same month, MacArthur again voiced his disenchantment with the President's settlement of the Far Eastern crisis.

Strategically, the problem there [the Far East] has developed along classical lines—the familiar case of a concentrated enemy in a central position deployed against scattered allies. Red China, inherently weak in industrial output for modern war but strong in manpower, engaged on three fronts—Korea, Indo-China and in a civil war with Nationalist China. Fighting on all three simultaneously meant defeat, but individually the chances were excellent. The hope for victory depended on getting a cease fire on some fronts so that the full potential of its limited military might could be thrown against the remaining one or ones. This is what has happened and is happening. First was the cessation of the civil war action by the isolation in the Formosa area which practically immobilized National China, one of the allies. Red China then concentrated against Korea and Indo-China. But even the double front was too much for its strained resources. So a cease-fire was obtained in Korea. This immobilized the so-called United Nations Forces and the South Koreans and left Red China free to concentrate on the third front—Indo-China and the French. Successful there, the Reds now turn back to the old first front located in Formosa. As Napoleon Bonaparte once said: "Give me allies as an enemy so that I can defeat them one by one."[64]

It should be remembered that MacArthur and those Republicans cited above were suspicious of the armistice agreement because the GOP had agreed to a settlement that reflected the basic aims of the recently discredited Truman Administration. Eisenhower did not seek to unify the country by force, and he

---

[63] Douglas MacArthur, *A Soldier Speaks: Public Papers and Speeches of General of the Army Douglas MacArthur* (New York, Frederick A. Praeger, Inc., 1965), p. 306. Reprinted by permission. Also see MacArthur, *Reminiscences,* p. 414.

[64] *Ibid.,* pp. 319–20.

did not use the Korean War to settle the other pressing problems in the Far East. The philosophy behind his strategy in the Korean War was very closely allied to that of containment. Had Truman attempted to sign such an armistice he would have been denounced by both the GOP and the general public. Yet while Eisenhower suffered the attacks of certain members of his party who had hoped for stronger action in the Far East, he won the sincere gratitude of the American people for ending the war. Perhaps the best explanation for this phenomenon is contained in a column written by Walter Lippmann during the 1956 Republican convention. At this time the GOP was applauding Eisenhower's role in the settlement as his greatest accomplishment; Lippmann was interested in discovering why the General was able to sign such a truce and Truman was not.

> The answer to this question . . . is that President Eisenhower signed an armistice which accepted the partition of Korea and peace without victory because, being himself the victorious commander in World War II and a Republican, he could not be attacked as an appeaser. President Truman and Secretary Acheson, on the other hand, never seemed able to afford to make peace on the only terms the Chinese would agree to, on the terms, that is to say, which President Eisenhower did agree to. The Democrats were too vulnerable to attack from the political followers of General MacArthur and of the then powerful Senator McCarthy, and indeed to attack from the whole right wing of the Republican party.[65]

Today, fifteen years after the signing of the armistice ending the Korean War, the embattled peninsula remains divided. By July 30, 1953, both sides had withdrawn their troops to positions agreed upon at either side of the demilitarized zone, and these positions are still occupied by Communist and anti-Communist forces. A month later the General Assembly of the United Nations passed a resolution stating that the objectives of the United Nations remain the achievement of a

---

[65] Walter Lippmann, "Eisenhower and Korea," *Herald Tribune*, August 24, 1956, p. 12.

unified, independent, and democratic Korea by peaceful means. In October of 1953 United States Ambassador Arthur Dean met with representatives from North Korea and Communist China to discuss the details of the political conference called for under the terms of the armistice settlement, but the Communists soon accused the United States of conspiring with Rhee to release 25,000 nonrepatriated prisoners of war, and Dean suspended the talks; they remained suspended until April of 1954 when the Big Four agreed to hold a Geneva conference on Korea. The two sides met from April 26th to June 15th, but could not agree on the question of how to achieve a unified Korea. The Allies insisted that elections be supervised by the United Nations, while the Communists would agree only to a joint commission consisting of equal representatives of North and South Korea. On this issue the conference at Geneva deadlocked. In 1958 the North Korean and Communist Chinese governments sent notes to the countries who had constituted the United Nations Command, claiming that Chinese troops had been withdrawn from the peninsula and insisting that the United Nations withdraw from Korea as well. Further consideration of the unification of the country depended upon such withdrawal.

Thus Rhee did not achieve his goal of a unified Korea—either by military or by political means. Aside from massive American economic and military aid, he had to be content with the "Declaration of Sixteen," signed in Washington on July 27, 1953 by those nations who had fought under the United Nations Command in Korea. These nations agreed to support the armistice and work for a united Korea. Despite the promise of this declaration, a divided Korea and an unstable condition in the Far East were accepted by a Republican President as realities of the postwar world.

* * *

Much of what has been presented in this study of the Republican party's response to the Korean War rests upon the value judgment that it is the duty of an opposition party to present alternative policy proposals. This is as true in the area of foreign affairs as it is in the realm of domestic policy. Many, of course, would sharply disagree with this analysis. Value judgments are by their very nature highly subjective and do not lend themselves to standard "proofs." Some years ago the Committee on Political Parties of the American Political Science Association issued a highly controversial report advocating greater party centralization and a greater expression of the fundamental differences between the parties. Included in this report—although admittedly not part of the report's central theme—was the following passage dealing with the responsibility of an opposition party to present alternative proposals. "The argument for a stronger party system cannot be divorced from measures designed to make the parties more fully accountable to the public. The fundamental requirement of such accountability is a two-party system in which the opposition party acts as the critic of the party in power, developing, defining and presenting the policy alternatives which are necessary for a true choice in reaching public decisions." [66] This study adheres to that view.

It would be a mistake, however, to overlook the difficulties confronting an opposition party in fulfilling this duty. More specifically, it would be unfortunate to overlook the dissension that often divides such a party within its own ranks. And too, one must not fail to recognize the difficulties involved in determining who speaks for the opposition party. In Chapter 1 of this study Stephen K. Bailey was quoted as follows:

> If the in-party has problems in creating a clear party image, the task is many times more difficult for the out-party. No real answer has yet been found to the question of who speaks for the party when it does not control the White House, or when no presidential campaign is in progress. Over the years, some of the major contenders for the job of out-party spokesman have been

---

[66] "Toward a More Responsible Two-Party System," A Report of the Committee on Political Parties, *The American Political Science Review*, Supplement, XLIV, No. 3 (September, 1950), p. 18.

congressional leaders, national committee chairman, national committee executive committees, ex-Presidents, defeated presidential candidates, *ad hoc* groups established by the national committees, congressional policy committees, congressional campaign committees, and most recently, a permanent advisory council to a national committee. . . .[67]

Despite these obvious difficulties, a value judgment can be made concerning the Republican party's response to the Korean War, for the party was neither consistent nor sincere in its development of an alternative to the policies formulated by Truman and the Democratic party. The major spokesmen for the GOP first supported American intervention, then retreated from the implications of that support; they steadfastly called for the American withdrawal from the Korean War, and then passionately associated themselves with the "no substitute for victory" philosophy of General MacArthur. Finally, this same party nominated for the Presidency a military hero whose platform lacked any concrete program for peace even as it disavowed both unification and an all-out military victory. Hence the conclusion that when the nature of a party's dissent indicates that its members are motivated more by political expediency than by a desire to present a consistent and viable alternative to Administration policies, censure is in order.

---

[67] Stephen K. Bailey, *The Condition of Our National Political Parties* (The Fund for the Republic, 1959), p. 9.

Appendix

This Appendix deals with the voting pattern of Republican senators in critical roll-call votes taken during the Korean War.

It contains both a breakdown of the vote in terms of the five sections of the United States, along with specific information on how each Republican senator voted.

It attempts to highlight the sectional cleavage within the party.

A. Vote to make General Marshall an exception to the law stating that only a civilian could become Secretary of Defense (see pp. 64–65 of text).

	TOTAL	Eastern	Midwest	South	Mountain	Pacific
YEAS						
R	10	4	4	–	–	2
D	37	6	7	17	6	1
NAYS						
R	20	1	12	–	5	2
D	1	–	–	–	1	–
NOT VOTING						
R	12	8	4	–	–	–
D	16	3	1	7	4	1

A. How the Republican senators voted

SENATOR	STATE	AREA
YEAS:		
Cordon	Oregon	Pacific
Darby	Kansas	Midwest

SENATOR	STATE	AREA
Gurney	South Dakota	Midwest
Ives	New York	Eastern
Lodge	Massachusetts	Eastern
Morse	Oregon	Pacific
Saltonstall	Massachusetts	Eastern
Smith	Maine	Eastern
Thye	Minnesota	Midwest
Wiley	Wisconsin	Midwest

NAYS:

Butler	Nebraska	Midwest
Cain	Washington	Pacific
Donnell	Missouri	Midwest
Dworshak	Idaho	Mountain
Ecton	Montana	Mountain
Ferguson	Michigan	Midwest
Hendrickson	New Jersey	Eastern
Hickenlooper	Iowa	Midwest
Jenner	Indiana	Midwest
Kem	Missouri	Midwest
Knowland	California	Pacific
Langer	North Dakota	Midwest
Malone	Nevada	Mountain
Millikin	Colorado	Mountain
Mundt	South Dakota	Midwest
Schoeppel	Kansas	Midwest
Taft	Ohio	Midwest
Watkins	Utah	Mountain
Wherry	Nebraska	Midwest
Young	North Dakota	Midwest

NOT VOTING:

Aiken	Vermont	Eastern
Brewster	Maine	Eastern
Bricker	Ohio	Midwest
Bridges	New Hampshire	Eastern
Capehart	Indiana	Midwest
Flanders	Vermont	Eastern

SENATOR	STATE	AREA
McCarthy	Wisconsin	Midwest
Martin	Pennsylvania	Eastern
Smith	New Jersey	Eastern
Tobey	New Hampshire	Eastern
Vandenberg	Michigan	Midwest
Williams	Delaware	Eastern

B. Formal approval of General Marshall as Secretary of Defense (see pp. 64–65 of text).

	TOTAL	Eastern	Midwest	South	Mountain	Pacific
YEAS						
R	15	6	7	–	1	1
D	42	7	7	19	8	1
NAYS						
R	11	–	5	–	4	2
D	0	–	–	–	–	–
NOT VOTING						
R	16	7	8	–	–	1
D	12	2	1	5	3	1

B. How the Republican senators voted

SENATOR	STATE	AREA
YEAS:		
Darby	Kansas	Midwest
Donnell	Missouri	Midwest
Dworshak	Idaho	Mountain
Gurney	South Dakota	Midwest
Hendrickson	New Jersey	Eastern
Ives	New York	Eastern
Morse	Oregon	Pacific
Mundt	South Dakota	Midwest
Saltonstall	Massachusetts	Eastern
Schoeppel	Kansas	Midwest
Smith	Maine	Eastern
Thye	Minnesota	Midwest

SENATOR	STATE	AREA
Tobey	New Hampshire	Eastern
Wiley	Wisconsin	Midwest
Williams	Delaware	Eastern

NAYS:

Butler	Nebraska	Midwest
Cain	Washington	Pacific
Ecton	Montana	Mountain
Jenner	Indiana	Midwest
Knowland	California	Pacific
Langer	North Dakota	Midwest
Malone	Nevada	Mountain
Millikin	Colorado	Mountain
Watkins	Utah	Mountain
Wherry	Nebraska	Midwest
Young	North Dakota	Midwest

NOT VOTING:

Aiken	Vermont	Eastern
Brewster	Maine	Eastern
Bricker	Ohio	Midwest
Bridges	New Hampshire	Eastern
Capehart	Indiana	Midwest
Cordon	Oregon	Pacific
Ferguson	Michigan	Midwest
Flanders	Vermont	Eastern
Hickenlooper	Iowa	Midwest
Kem	Missouri	Midwest
Lodge	Massachusetts	Eastern
McCarthy	Wisconsin	Midwest
Martin	Pennsylvania	Eastern
Smith	New Jersey	Eastern
Taft	Ohio	Midwest
Vandenberg	Michigan	Midwest

C. Kem Amendment to the General Appropriations Act, calling for a half-a-billion dollar reduction in aid to Western Europe (see pp. 68–69 of text).

	TOTAL	Eastern	Midwest	South	Mountain	Pacific
YEAS						
R	10	2	6	–	2	–
D	2	1	–	1	–	–
NAYS						
R	20	9	7	–	1	3
D	39	6	5	19	8	1
NOT VOTING						
R	12	2	7	–	2	1
D	13	2	3	4	3	1

C. How the Republican senators voted

SENATOR	STATE	AREA
YEAS:		
Butler	Nebraska	Midwest
Capehart	Indiana	Midwest
Dworshak	Idaho	Mountain
Kem	Missouri	Midwest
Langer	North Dakota	Midwest
Malone	Nevada	Mountain
Martin	Pennsylvania	Eastern
Mundt	South Dakota	Midwest
Wherry	Nebraska	Midwest
Williams	Delaware	Eastern
NAYS:		
Brewster	Maine	Eastern
Bricker	Ohio	Midwest
Bridges	New Hampshire	Eastern
Cordon	Oregon	Pacific
Ferguson	Michigan	Midwest
Flanders	Vermont	Eastern
Gurney	South Dakota	Midwest
Hendrickson	New Jersey	Eastern
Hickenlooper	Iowa	Midwest
Ives	New York	Eastern
Knowland	California	Pacific
Lodge	Massachusetts	Eastern

SENATOR	STATE	AREA
Morse	Oregon	Pacific
Saltonstall	Massachusetts	Eastern
Smith	New Jersey	Eastern
Smith	Maine	Eastern
Taft	Ohio	Midwest
Thye	Minnesota	Midwest
Watkins	Utah	Mountain
Young	North Dakota	Midwest

NOT VOTING:

Aiken	Vermont	Eastern
Cain	Washington	Pacific
Darby	Kansas	Midwest
Donnell	Missouri	Midwest
Ecton	Montana	Mountain
Jenner	Indiana	Midwest
McCarthy	Wisconsin	Midwest
Millikin	Colorado	Mountain
Schoeppel	Kansas	Midwest
Tobey	New Hampshire	Eastern
Vandenberg	Michigan	Midwest
Wiley	Wisconsin	Midwest

D. Byrd-Bridges Amendment to the General Appropriations Act, calling for a 10 percent reduction in allocations to the Executive Department (see pp. 68–69 of text).

	TOTAL	Eastern	Midwest	South	Mountain	Pacific
YEAS						
R	36	12	16	–	5	3
D	19	4	3	9	2	1
NAYS						
R	2	–	2	–	–	–
D	29	4	4	13	8	–
NOT VOTING						
R	4	1	2	–	–	1
D	6	1	1	2	1	1

D. How the Republican senators voted

SENATOR	STATE	AREA
YEAS:		
Aiken	Vermont	Eastern
Brewster	Maine	Eastern
Bricker	Ohio	Midwest
Bridges	New Hampshire	Eastern
Butler	Nebraska	Midwest
Capehart	Indiana	Midwest
Cordon	Oregon	Pacific
Darby	Kansas	Midwest
Donnell	Missouri	Midwest
Dworshak	Idaho	Mountain
Ecton	Montana	Mountain
Ferguson	Michigan	Midwest
Flanders	Vermont	Eastern
Gurney	South Dakota	Midwest
Hendrickson	New Jersey	Eastern
Hickenlooper	Iowa	Midwest
Ives	New York	Eastern
Kem	Missouri	Midwest
Knowland	California	Pacific
Lodge	Massachusetts	Eastern
McCarthy	Wisconsin	Midwest
Malone	Nevada	Mountain
Martin	Pennsylvania	Eastern
Millikin	Colorado	Mountain
Morse	Oregon	Pacific
Mundt	South Dakota	Midwest
Saltonstall	Massachusetts	Eastern
Schoeppel	Kansas	Midwest
Smith	New Jersey	Eastern
Smith	Maine	Eastern
Taft	Ohio	Midwest
Thye	Minnesota	Midwest
Watkins	Utah	Mountain
Wherry	Nebraska	Midwest
Wiley	Wisconsin	Midwest
Williams	Delaware	Eastern

SENATOR

NAYS:	STATE	AREA
Langer	North Dakota	Midwest
Young	North Dakota	Midwest

NOT VOTING:		
Cain	Washington	Pacific
Jenner	Indiana	Midwest
Tobey	New Hampshire	Eastern
Vandenberg	Michigan	Midwest

E. Capehart Amendment to the Defense Production Act, which attempted to strike out Title IV (price control). See p. 69 of text.

	TOTAL	Eastern	Midwest	South	Mountain	Pacific
YEAS						
R	6	1	4	–	1	–
D	0	–	–	–	–	–
NAYS						
R	27	9	13	–	3	2
D	48	9	7	21	10	1
NOT VOTING						
R	9	3	3	–	1	2
D	6	–	1	3	1	1

E. How the Republican senators voted

SENATOR	STATE	AREA
YEAS:		
Bricker	Ohio	Midwest
Capehart	Indiana	Midwest
Ecton	Montana	Mountain
Kem	Missouri	Midwest
Taft	Ohio	Midwest
Williams	Delaware	Eastern

SENATOR

NAYS:	STATE	AREA
Aiken	Vermont	Eastern
Brewster	Maine	Eastern
Butler	Nebraska	Midwest
Darby	Kansas	Midwest
Donnell	Missouri	Midwest
Dworshak	Idaho	Mountain
Ferguson	Michigan	Midwest
Hendrickson	New Jersey	Eastern
Hickenlooper	Iowa	Midwest
Ives	New York	Eastern
Knowland	California	Pacific
Langer	North Dakota	Midwest
Lodge	Massachusetts	Eastern
McCarthy	Wisconsin	Midwest
Martin	Pennsylvania	Eastern
Millikin	Colorado	Mountain
Morse	Oregon	Pacific
Mundt	South Dakota	Midwest
Saltonstall	Massachusetts	Eastern
Schoeppel	Kansas	Midwest
Smith	New Jersey	Eastern
Smith	Maine	Eastern
Thye	Minnesota	Midwest
Watkins	Utah	Mountain
Wherry	Nebraska	Midwest
Wiley	Wisconsin	Midwest
Young	North Dakota	Midwest

NOT VOTING:		
Bridges	New Hampshire	Eastern
Cain	Washington	Pacific
Cordon	Oregon	Pacific
Flanders	Vermont	Eastern
Gurney	South Dakota	Midwest
Jenner	Indiana	Midwest
Malone	Nevada	Mountain
Tobey	New Hampshire	Eastern
Vandenberg	Michigan	Midwest

F. Taft Amendment to Defense Production Act, which attempted to eliminate Title V (wage control). See p. 69 of text.

	TOTAL	Eastern	Midwest	South	Mountain	Pacific
YEAS						
R	28	6	16	–	5	1
D	1	–	–	1	–	–
NAYS						
R	10	6	2	–	–	2
D	47	9	7	21	9	1
NOT VOTING						
R	4	1	2	–	–	1
D	6	–	1	2	2	1

F. How the Republican senators voted

SENATOR	STATE	AREA
YEAS:		
Brewster	Maine	Eastern
Bricker	Ohio	Midwest
Bridges	New Hampshire	Eastern
Butler	Nebraska	Midwest
Capehart	Indiana	Midwest
Cordon	Oregon	Pacific
Darby	Kansas	Midwest
Donnell	Missouri	Midwest
Dworshak	Idaho	Mountain
Ecton	Montana	Mountain
Ferguson	Michigan	Midwest
Hickenlooper	Iowa	Midwest
Jenner	Indiana	Midwest
Kem	Missouri	Midwest
McCarthy	Wisconsin	Midwest
Malone	Nevada	Mountain
Martin	Pennsylvania	Eastern
Millikin	Colorado	Mountain
Mundt	South Dakota	Midwest
Saltonstall	Massachusetts	Eastern

SENATOR	STATE	AREA
Schoeppel	Kansas	Midwest
Smith	New Jersey	Eastern
Taft	Ohio	Midwest
Thye	Minnesota	Midwest
Watkins	Utah	Mountain
Wherry	Nebraska	Midwest
Wiley	Wisconsin	Midwest
Williams	Delaware	Eastern

NAYS:

Aiken	Vermont	Eastern
Hendrickson	New Jersey	Eastern
Ives	New York	Eastern
Knowland	California	Pacific
Langer	North Dakota	Midwest
Lodge	Massachusetts	Eastern
Morse	Oregon	Pacific
Smith	Maine	Eastern
Tobey	New Hampshire	Eastern
Young	North Dakota	Midwest

NOT VOTING:

Cain	Washington	Pacific
Flanders	Vermont	Eastern
Gurney	South Dakota	Midwest
Vandenberg	Michigan	Midwest

G. Defense Production Act: Final Vote (see p. 70 of text).

	TOTAL	Eastern	Midwest	South	Mountain	Pacific
YEAS						
R	36	11	19	–	3	3
D	49	9	7	22	10	1
NAYS						
R	3	1	–	–	2	–
D	0	–	–	–	–	–

	TOTAL	Eastern	Midwest	South	Mountain	Pacific
NOT VOTING						
R	3	1	1	–	–	1
D	5	–	1	2	1	1

G. How the Republican senators voted

SENATOR	STATE	AREA
YEAS:		
Aiken	Vermont	Eastern
Brewster	Maine	Eastern
Bricker	Ohio	Midwest
Bridges	New Hampshire	Eastern
Butler	Nebraska	Midwest
Capehart	Indiana	Midwest
Cordon	Oregon	Pacific
Darby	Kansas	Midwest
Donnell	Missouri	Midwest
Dworshak	Idaho	Mountain
Ferguson	Michigan	Midwest
Gurney	South Dakota	Midwest
Hendrickson	New Jersey	Eastern
Hickenlooper	Iowa	Midwest
Ives	New York	Eastern
Jenner	Indiana	Midwest
Kem	Missouri	Midwest
Knowland	California	Pacific
Langer	North Dakota	Midwest
Lodge	Massachusetts	Eastern
McCarthy	Wisconsin	Midwest
Martin	Pennsylvania	East
Millikin	Colorado	Mountain
Morse	Oregon	Pacific
Mundt	South Dakota	Midwest
Saltonstall	Massachusetts	Eastern
Schoeppel	Kansas	Midwest
Smith	New Jersey	Eastern
Smith	Maine	Eastern
Taft	Ohio	Midwest
Thye	Minnesota	Midwest

SENATOR	STATE	AREA
Tobey	New Hampshire	Eastern
Watkins	Utah	Mountain
Wherry	Nebraska	Midwest
Wiley	Wisconsin	Midwest
Young	North Dakota	Midwest

NAYS:

Ecton	Montana	Mountain
Malone	Nevada	Mountain
Williams	Delaware	Eastern

NOT VOTING:

Cain	Washington	Pacific
Flanders	Vermont	Eastern
Vandenberg	Michigan	Midwest

H. McClellan Amendment to the Wherry Resolution on the troops-to-Europe issue (see pp. 136–137 of text).

	TOTAL	Eastern	Midwest	South	Mountain	Pacific
YEAS						
R	38	7	19	–	7	5
D	11	2	–	7	2	–
NAYS						
R	8	8	–	–	–	–
D	35	5	8	16	6	–
NOT VOTING						
R	1	–	1	–	–	–
D	3	–	–	1	1	1

H. How the Republican senators voted

SENATOR	STATE	AREA
YEAS:		
Bennett	Utah	Mountain
Brewster	Maine	Eastern
Bricker	Ohio	Midwest
Bridges	New Hampshire	Eastern

SENATOR	STATE	AREA
Butler	Maryland	Eastern
Butler	Nebraska	Midwest
Cain	Washington	Pacific
Capehart	Indiana	Midwest
Carlson	Kansas	Midwest
Case	South Dakota	Midwest
Cordon	Oregon	Pacific
Dirksen	Illinois	Midwest
Dworshak	Idaho	Mountain
Ecton	Montana	Mountain
Ferguson	Michigan	Midwest
Hendrickson	New Jersey	Eastern
Hickenlooper	Iowa	Midwest
Jenner	Indiana	Midwest
Kem	Missouri	Midwest
Knowland	California	Pacific
Langer	North Dakota	Midwest
McCarthy	Wisconsin	Midwest
Malone	Nevada	Mountain
Martin	Pennsylvania	Eastern
Millikin	Colorado	Mountain
Morse	Oregon	Pacific
Mundt	South Dakota	Midwest
Nixon	California	Pacific
Schoeppel	Kansas	Midwest
Smith	Maine	Eastern
Taft	Ohio	Midwest
Thye	Minnesota	Midwest
Watkins	Utah	Mountain
Welker	Idaho	Mountain
Wherry	Nebraska	Midwest
Wiley	Wisconsin	Midwest
Williams	Delaware	Eastern
Young	North Dakota	Midwest

NAYS:

Aiken	Vermont	Eastern
Duff	Pennsylvania	Eastern

SENATOR	STATE	AREA
Flanders	Vermont	Eastern
Ives	New York	Eastern
Lodge	Massachusetts	Eastern
Saltonstall	Massachusetts	Eastern
Smith	New Jersey	Eastern
Tobey	New Hampshire	Eastern

NOT VOTING:

Vandenberg	Michigan	Midwest

I. Senate Resolution Number 99 (Wherry Resolution). See pp. 136–137 of text.

	TOTAL	Eastern	Midwest	South	Mountain	Pacific
YEAS						
R	27	14	8	–	2	3
D	42	7	7	20	8	–
NAYS						
R	19	1	11	–	5	2
D	2	–	–	2	–	–
NOT VOTING						
R	1	–	1	–	–	–
D	5	–	1	2	1	1

I. How the Republican senators voted

SENATOR	STATE	AREA
YEAS:		
Aiken	Vermont	Eastern
Brewster	Maine	Eastern
Bridges	New Hampshire	Eastern
Butler	Maryland	Eastern
Capehart	Indiana	Midwest
Carlson	Kansas	Midwest
Duff	Pennsylvania	Eastern
Flanders	Vermont	Eastern
Hendrickson	New Jersey	Eastern

SENATOR	STATE	AREA
Hickenlooper	Iowa	Midwest
Ives	New York	Eastern
Knowland	California	Pacific
Lodge	Massachusetts	Eastern
McCarthy	Wisconsin	Midwest
Martin	Pennsylvania	Eastern
Millikin	Colorado	Mountain
Morse	Oregon	Pacific
Nixon	California	Pacific
Saltonstall	Massachusetts	Eastern
Smith	New Jersey	Eastern
Smith	Maine	Eastern
Taft	Ohio	Midwest
Thye	Minnesota	Midwest
Tobey	New Hampshire	Eastern
Watkins	Utah	Mountain
Wiley	Wisconsin	Midwest
Young	North Dakota	Midwest

NAYS:

Bennett	Utah	Mountain
Bricker	Ohio	Midwest
Butler	Nebraska	Midwest
Cain	Washington	Pacific
Case	South Dakota	Midwest
Cordon	Oregon	Pacific
Dirksen	Illinois	Midwest
Dworshak	Idaho	Mountain
Ecton	Montana	Mountain
Ferguson	Michigan	Midwest
Jenner	Indiana	Midwest
Kem	Missouri	Midwest
Langer	North Dakota	Midwest
Malone	Nevada	Mountain
Mundt	South Dakota	Midwest
Schoeppel	Kansas	Midwest
Welker	Idaho	Mountain
Wherry	Nebraska	Midwest
Williams	Delaware	Eastern

SENATOR *NOT VOTING:*	STATE	AREA
Vandenberg	Michigan	Midwest

J. Wherry motion calling for open sessions during the MacArthur Hearings (see p. 158 of text).

	TOTAL	Eastern	Midwest	South	Mountain	Pacific
YEAS						
R	36	12	15	–	4	5
D	1	–	–	–	1	–
NAYS						
R	0	–	–	–	–	–
D	41	5	8	22	6	–
NOT VOTING						
R	10	3	4	–	3	–
D	8	2	1	2	2	1

J. How the Republican senators voted

SENATOR *YEAS:*	STATE	AREA
Bennett	Utah	Mountain
Brewster	Maine	Eastern
Bricker	Ohio	Midwest
Bridges	New Hampshire	Eastern
Butler	Nebraska	Midwest
Butler	Maryland	Eastern
Cain	Washington	Pacific
Carlson	Kansas	Midwest
Case	South Dakota	Midwest
Cordon	Oregon	Pacific
Dirksen	Illinois	Midwest
Dworshak	Idaho	Mountain
Ecton	Montana	Mountain
Ferguson	Michigan	Midwest
Flanders	Vermont	Eastern
Hendrickson	New Jersey	Eastern
Hickenlooper	Iowa	Midwest

SENATOR	STATE	AREA
Ives	New York	Eastern
Kem	Missouri	Midwest
Knowland	California	Pacific
Langer	North Dakota	Midwest
Lodge	Massachusetts	Eastern
McCarthy	Wisconsin	Midwest
Martin	Pennsylvania	Eastern
Millikin	Colorado	Mountain
Morse	Oregon	Pacific
Mundt	South Dakota	Midwest
Nixon	California	Pacific
Saltonstall	Massachusetts	Eastern
Schoeppel	Kansas	Midwest
Smith	New Jersey	Eastern
Tobey	New Hampshire	Eastern
Wherry	Nebraska	Midwest
Wiley	Wisconsin	Midwest
Williams	Delaware	Eastern
Young	North Dakota	Midwest

NAYS:
———

NOT VOTING:

Aiken	Vermont	Eastern
Capehart	Indiana	Midwest
Duff	Pennsylvania	Eastern
Jenner	Indiana	Midwest
Malone	Nevada	Mountain
Smith	Maine	Eastern
Taft	Ohio	Midwest
Thye	Minnesota	Midwest
Watkins	Utah	Mountain
Welker	Idaho	Mountain

K. Battle Act (see pp. 187–188 of text).

	TOTAL	Eastern	Midwest	South	Mountain	Pacific
YEAS						
R	18	7	6	–	1	4
D	37	6	7	17	6	1

	TOTAL	Eastern	Midwest	South	Mountain	Pacific
NAYS						
R	16	3	9	–	4	–
D	0	–	–	–	–	–
NOT VOTING						
R	12	5	4	--	2	1
D	13	1	2	7	3	–

K. How the Republican senators voted

SENATOR	STATE	AREA
YEAS:		
Aiken	Vermont	Eastern
Case	South Dakota	Midwest
Cordon	Oregon	Pacific
Duff	Pennsylvania	Eastern
Hendrickson	New Jersey	Eastern
Hickenlooper	Iowa	Midwest
Ives	New York	Eastern
Knowland	California	Pacific
Langer	North Dakota	Midwest
Martin	Pennsylvania	Eastern
Millikin	Colorado	Mountain
Morse	Oregon	Pacific
Nixon	California	Pacific
Saltonstall	Massachusetts	Eastern
Smith	New Jersey	Eastern
Thye	Minnesota	Midwest
Wiley	Wisconsin	Midwest
Young	North Dakota	Midwest
NAYS:		
Bricker	Ohio	Midwest
Bridges	New Hampshire	Eastern
Butler	Nebraska	Midwest
Butler	Maryland	Eastern
Capehart	Indiana	Midwest
Dirksen	Illinois	Midwest
Dworshak	Idaho	Mountain

SENATOR	STATE	AREA
Ecton	Montana	Mountain
Kem	Missouri	Midwest
Mundt	South Dakota	Midwest
Schoeppel	Kansas	Midwest
Taft	Ohio	Midwest
Watkins	Utah	Mountain
Welker	Idaho	Mountain
Wherry	Nebraska	Midwest
Williams	Delaware	Eastern

NOT VOTING:

Bennett	Utah	Mountain
Brewster	Maine	Eastern
Cain	Washington	Pacific
Carlson	Kansas	Midwest
Ferguson	Michigan	Midwest
Flanders	Vermont	Eastern
Jenner	Indiana	Midwest
Lodge	Massachusetts	Eastern
Malone	Nevada	Mountain
McCarthy	Wisconsin	Midwest
Smith	Maine	Eastern
Tobey	New Hampshire	Eastern

Bibliography

MATERIAL REGULARLY CONSULTED

Congressional Record, 1950–1953.

United States Congress. *Military Situation in the Far East.* Hearings before the Joint Senate Committee on Armed Services and Foreign Relations, 82nd Congress, 1st Session, Washington, 1951.

The *New York Times,* 1950–1953.

Truman, Harry S. *Public Papers of the Presidents of the United States, 1950–1953.* Washington, 1965.

Eisenhower, Dwight D. *Public Papers of the Presidents of the United States, 1953.* Washington, 1965.

The Papers of Senator H. Alexander Smith. Princeton University Library.

BOOKS

Adams, Sherman. *Firsthand Report.* New York, 1961.

Adler, Selig. *The Isolationist Impulse.* New York, 1957.

Bailey, Stephen K. *The Condition of Our National Political Parties.* The Fund for the Republic, 1959.

Bartlett, Ruhl J. *The Record of American Diplomacy.* New York, 1964.

Binkley, Wilfred E. *American Political Parties: Their Natural History.* New York, 1962.

Burns, James MacGregor. *The Deadlock of Democracy: Four Party Politics in America,* rev. ed. Englewood Cliffs, 1963.

Campbell, Angus, *et al. The Voter Decides.* Evanston, 1954.

Chamberlain, William H. *America's Second Crusade.* Chicago, 1950.

Clark, Mark W. *From the Danube to the Yalu.* New York, 1954.

Donovan, Robert J. *Eisenhower: The Inside Story.* New York, 1956.

David, Paul. *Presidential Nominating Policies in 1952*. Baltimore, 1954.

Eisenhower, Dwight D. *The White House Years, Vol. I.: Mandate for Change*. Garden City, 1963.

Fulbright, J. William. *The Arrogance of Power*. New York, 1966.

Goldman, Eric. *The Crucial Decade—and After*. New York, 1960.

Graebner, Norman A. *The New Isolationism*. New York, 1956.

Harris, Louis. *Is There a Republican Majority?* New York, 1954.

Hess, Stephen, and Broder, David S. *The Republican Establishment*. New York, 1967.

Higgins, Trumbull. *Korea and the Fall of MacArthur*. New York, 1960.

Hughes, Emmet John. *The Ordeal of Power*. New York, 1963.

Joy, C. Turner. *How Communists Negotiate*. New York, 1955.

Kennan, George F. *American Diplomacy, 1900–1950*. Chicago, 1951.

Kissinger, Henry A. *Nuclear Weapons and Foreign Policy*. New York, 1957.

Leckie, Robert. *Conflict: The History of the Korean War, 1950*. New York, 1952.

———— *The March to Glory*. Cleveland, 1960.

Lubell, Samuel. *Revolt of the Moderates*. New York, 1956.

MacArthur, Douglas. *Reminiscences*. New York, 1964.

———— *A Soldier Speaks: Public Papers and Speeches of General of the Army Douglas MacArthur*. New York, 1965.

McPhee, William N. and Glaser, William A., eds. *Public Opinion and Congressional Elections*. New York, 1962.

Morgenstern, George E. *Pearl Harbor: The Story of the Secret War*. New York, 1947.

Neustadt, Richard E. *Presidential Power: The Politics of Leadership*. New York, 1960.

Osgood, Robert E. *Limited War*. Chicago, 1957.

Paige, Gleen D. *The Korean Decision*. New York, 1968.

Panikkar, K. M. *In Two Chinas*. London, 1955.

Rees, David. *Korea: The Limited War*. New York, 1964.

Rovere, Richard H. *The Eisenhower Years*. New York, 1956.

———— and Schlesinger, Arthur M., Jr. *The MacArthur Controversy and American Foreign Policy*. New York, 1965.

Spanier, John. *The Truman-MacArthur Controversy and the Korean War*. Cambridge, 1959.

Taft, Robert A. *A Foreign Policy for Americans.* Garden City, 1951.

Tansill, Charles C. *Back Door to War.* Chicago, 1952.

Truman, Harry S. *Memoirs, Vol. II: Years of Trial and Hope.* Garden City, 1956.

Vandenberg, Arthur H., Jr., ed. *The Private Papers of Senator Vandenberg.* Boston, 1952.

Vatcher, William. *Panmunjom.* New York, 1958.

Westerfield, H. Bradford. *Foreign Policy and Party Politics: Pearl Harbor to Korea.* New Haven, 1955.

White, William S. *Citadel: The Story of the United States Senate.* New York, 1956.

———— *The Taft Story.* New York, 1954.

Whiting, Allen S. *China Crosses the Yalu.* New York, 1960.

Whitney, Courtney. *MacArthur: His Rendezvous with History.* New York, 1956.

Willoughby, Charles A. *MacArthur, 1941–1951.* New York, 1954.

ARTICLES

The American Political Science Association, "Toward a More Responsible Two-Party System," A Report of the Committee on Political Parties, *The American Political Science Review,* Supplement, XLIV, No. 3. September, 1950.

Bridges, Styles. "The United Nations and Red China," *The Department of State Bulletin,* October 16, 1950.

Burns, James MacGregor, "White House vs. Congress," *The Atlantic,* Vol. 205. March, 1960.

Dulles, John Foster. "Can We Stop Russian Imperialism?," *United States Department of State Bulletin,* December 10, 1951.

———— "Far Eastern Problems: Defense Through Deterrent Power," *Vital Speeches,* June 1, 1951.

———— "A Policy of Boldness," *Life,* May 19, 1952.

Eisenhower, Dwight D. "Korea," *Vital Speeches,* February 15, 1951.

Heckscher, August. "The Republican Record," *Foreign Policy Bulletin,* October 1, 1952.

Hoover, Herbert. "The Freedom of Men," *Vital Speeches,* July 15, 1952.

———— "Western Hemisphere Gibraltar," *Vital Speeches,* January 1, 1951.

Hoover, Herbert. "Where We Are Now," *Vital Speeches*, November 1, 1950.

Judd, Walter H. "The Mistakes That Led to Korea," *Reader's Digest*, November, 1950.

Lippmann, Walter. "Eisenhower and Korea," *Herald Tribune*, August 24, 1956.

Rhee, Syngman. "Korea Cannot Live Divided and Half Occupied," *Vital Speeches*, September 1, 1952.

Shepley, James. "How Dulles Averted War," *Life*, January 16, 1956.

Taft, Robert A. "And If We Are Elected to Office," *Colliers*, November 4, 1950.

——— "The Dangerous Decline of Political Morality," *Reader's Digest*, November, 1950.

——— "Faults of the Present Administration," *Vital Speeches*, March 15, 1952.

Tyler, Gus. "The Mid-Term Paradox," *The New Republic*, November 7, 1950.

UNSIGNED ARTICLES

"The Case for Ike," *Time*, August 18, 1952.

"Connelly," *U.S. News & World Report*, May 5, 1950.

"The G.O.P. and Korea," *The Nation*, September 2, 1950.

"G.O.P. and McCarthyism," *The New Republic*, October 30, 1950.

"Has G.O.P. Played Rough Enough to Win an Election," *Saturday Evening Post*, November 4, 1950.

"MacArthur," *U.S. News & World Report*, September 1, 1950.

"Taft," *U.S. News & World Report*, June 13, 1952.

"What Happened in the Election," *U.S. News & World Report*, November 14, 1952.

"Why I Won—Why I Lost," *U.S. News & World Report*, November 17, 1950.

INDEX